FREUD'S BRAIN

FREUD'S BRAIN

Neuropsychodynamic Foundations of Psychoanalysis

LAURENCE MILLER, Ph.D.

THE GUILFORD PRESS
New York   *London*

© 1991 The Guilford Press
A Division of Guilford Publications, Inc.
72 Spring Street, New York, NY 10012

Last digit is print number: 9   8   7   6   5   4   3   2   1

Library of Congress Cataloging-in-Publication Data

Miller, Laurence, 1951–
    Freud's brain: neuropsychodynamic foundations of psychoanalysis / Laurence Miller.
       p.   cm.
    Includes bibliographical references and index.
    ISBN 0-89862-762-1
    1. Psychoanalysis. 2. Hysteria—Physiological aspects.
3. Dreams—Physiological aspects. 4. Parapraxis—Physiological aspects. 5. Neuropsychology. 6. Freud, Sigmund, 1857–1939.
I. Title.
    [DNLM: 1. Behavior—physiology. 2. Brain—physiopathology.
3. Dreams—psychology. 4. Freudian Theory. 5. Hysteria. WM 460
M648f]
RC506.M523 1991
612.8—dc20
DNLM/DLC
for Library of Congress   91-16480
                                               CIP

*For Harry and Sophie,
and their generations.*

Preface

If psychoanalysis is going to endure, even flourish, some of its fundamental tenets are going to have to change. Freud's original theory of the instincts has all but been discarded, or so reworked and transformed as to bear little relationship to the original formulations. The importance of sexuality has remained firm, although sexuality now tends to be conceptualized in more social–adaptive, object relations, or phylogenetic–sociobiological terms. The unconscious and the ego have proven to be resilient concepts of psychological functioning, although not necessarily in the original Freudian topographic sense. Psychoanalytic psychotherapy and its offshoots still find vital application to some kinds of clinical situations but not to others; for the sake of scientific rigor and clinical credibility, we had better learn to tell the difference.

It would be tragic indeed if the baby of psychodynamic personality theory were to be prematurely chucked out with the bathwater of traditional Freudian metapsychology. Revision, rather than elision, may restore psychoanalysis to what I believe will ultimately be remembered as its most significant contribution: a grand clinical–epistemological theory of mental life that can account for many—but not all—important human phenomena.

Recently, many scholars have looked to the brain for answers. The present volume takes as its subject the three fundamental pillars of data and theory on which Freud's psychoanalysis was originally built: hysteria, dreams, and parapraxes, or "Freudian slips." All three grew out of Freud's early experience in the clinical neurology of thought and behavior, what we today call *neuropsychology*.

This book is an attempt to bring the modern-day findings and concepts of neuropsychology to bear on these three fundamental Freudian pillars. My intent is neither to "defend" nor "debunk" psychoanalytic theory; Freud's contribution to the science of the mind stands on its own merits.

Rather, by returning to the neuropsychological roots of psychoanalysis, we can gain a fresh perspective on its relevance to our present-day theories and clinical practices.

Let me here acknowledge the roles of several people in bringing this book to light. Jon Winson of Rockefeller University provided part of the original impetus for my interest in mind–brain issues through his earlier works and by his encouragement of my own endeavors at several points along the way. Martin Schulman and Shirley Panken, editors at *The Psychoanalytic Review*, supported the development of many of this book's ideas, which appeared in that journal over the years in the form of my papers and reviews. Marty also introduced me to Seymour Weingarten, Editor in Chief of The Guilford Press, who helped guide the preparation of the final manuscript. Thanks again to agent John Ware for his continuing efforts in securing apposite outlets for my works, and special gratitude once more goes to my family, Joan and Halle, for their understanding support of my single-minded preoccupation while completing projects of this type.

My years of teaching neuropsychology at Seton Hall University encouraged me to look closely at the relevance of brain–behavioral concepts to the real world of practical clinical realities. This perspective was shaped in part by the questions and challenges of a bright and motivated group of graduate students, many of whom took the initiative in assimilating the neuropsychological concepts of the classroom with their own clinical skills in productive and creative ways.

A note on brain matters: although I have tried throughout this book to be as clear as possible, one occupational hazard of spanning such traditionally disparate clinical and academic domains as neuropsychology and psychoanalysis is that some parts of the discussion may occasionally prove thick going for readers not familiar with one or the other area. No special knowledge of nervous system structure and function is a prerequisite for understanding this book, and I have made every effort to explain and demystify relevant brain concepts throughout the text. Rather than pad these pages with potentially confusing neuroanatomical drawings, I have chosen to rely on verbal description with regard to brain systems and functions. Should visual supplementation be desired—that is, should the reader feel drawn to find out what such structures as the limbic system, locus coeruleus, basal ganglia, and cortical homunculus actually *look like*—it is with my blessing that I refer him/her to any of the standard works in this field that may be found in most libraries.

In a previous work (Miller, 1990) I tried to forge an integrative synthesis between the brain–behavioral sciences and certain aspects of psychodynamic personality theory in a kind of "neuropsychology meets ego psychology." The present book goes back a little further and deeper to consider the neuropsychodynamic foundations of the original sources of the Freudian model of the mind, the three main domains that Freud himself felt most required explication in order to fully develop a comprehensive theory of mental life, and to establish what we might call in this case a sort of "neuropsychology meets metapsychology."

In these endeavors, what are being offered are beginnings, not ends; first steps, not last words. Let us hope to understand, and understand that our hopes may have real, practical, and healing consequences.

Acknowledgments

The author gratefully acknowledges permission to reprint excerpts from the following publications:

Breuer, J., & Freud, S. *Studies on Hysteria*. Reprinted by permission of Basic Books, Inc., a division of HarperCollins Publishers.

Damasio, A. R., Graff-Radford, N. R., & Damasio, H. Transient partial amnesia. *Archives of Neurology*, 1983, 40, 656–657. Copyright 1983 by the American Medical Association.

Epstein, A. W. Body image alterations during seizures and dreams of epileptics. *Archives of Neurology*, 1967, 16, 613–619. Copyright 1967 by the American Medical Association.

Fleishman, J. A., Segall, J. D., & Judge, F. P. Isolated transient alexia: A migrainous accompaniment. *Archives of Neurology*, 1983, 40, 115–116. Copyright 1983 by the American Medical Association.

Freud, S. *On Aphasia: A Critical Study*. Reprinted by permission of International Universities Press, Inc.

Freud, S. *The Interpretation of Dreams*. Translated from the German and edited by James Strachey. Published in the United States by Basic Books, Inc., 1956 by arrangement with George Allen & Unwin Ltd. and The Hogarth Press Ltd. Reprinted by permission of Basic Books, Inc., a division of HarperCollins Publishers.

Freud, S. Some points for a comparative study of organic and hysterical motor paralyses (Vol. 1), The unconscious (Vol. 12), *Standard Edition of the Complete Psychological Works of Sigmund Freud*. Translated and edited by James Strachey. Reprinted by permission of Basic Books, Inc., a division of HarperCollins Publishers; Sigmund Freud Copyrights; the Institute of Psycho-Analysis; and The Hogarth Press Ltd.

Freud, S. *The Psychopathology of Everyday Life*. Translated from the German by Alan Tyson. Edited by James Strachey. Reprinted by permission of W. W. Norton & Co., Inc. Editorial matter copyright 1965, 1960 by James Strachey. Translation copyright 1970 by Alan Tyson.

Freud, S. *The Ego and the Id*. Translated by Joan Riviere. Revised and edited by James Strachey. Reprinted by permission of W. W. Norton & Co., Inc. Copyright 1960 by James Strachey.

Joseph, R. The neuropsychology of development: Hemispheric laterality, limbic language and the origin of thought. *Journal of Clinical Psychology*, 1982, 38, 4–33. Reprinted by permission of the author and Clinical Psychology Publishing Co., Inc.

Kubie, L. S. Some implications for psychoanalysis of modern concepts of the organization of the brain. *Psychoanalytic Quarterly*, 1953, 22, 21–52. Reprinted by permission of The Psychoanalytic Quarterly.

Ostow, M. A psychoanalytic contribution to the study of brain function: I. The frontal lobes. *Psychoanalytic Quarterly*, 1954, 23, 317–338. Reprinted by permission of The Psychoanalytic Quarterly.

Ostow, M. A psychoanalytic contribution to the study of brain function: II. The temporal lobes. III. Synthesis. *Psychoanalytic Quarterly*, 1955, 24, 383–423. Reprinted by permission of The Psychoanalytic Quarterly.

Contents

PART IV. FREUDIAN SLIPS

PART V. INTEGRATION

PART ONE

Introduction

I am at the moment tempted by the desire to solve the riddle of the structure of the brain; I think brain anatomy is the only legitimate rival you have or ever will have.
—SIGMUND FREUD,
letter to Martha Bernays, May 1885

CHAPTER 1

Freud's Life, Freud's Work, Freud's Brain

Sigmund Freud did not discover the unconscious. He was not the first to analyze dreams or to speculate on the psychodynamic significance of slips of the tongue. The sexual theory of the neuroses did not originate with him, and he was not the first to use the term "ego." The one term he *did* coin—"agnosia"—is today most clearly associated with neurology, not psychology or psychiatry (the term "parapraxis" may have originated with Freud, but this is controversial).

Freud's contribution lay not primarily in the invention or discovery of paradigmatically novel concepts or findings. Rather, he was able to pull together the relevant threads and swatches of scientific, philosophical, and cultural material from his contemporary zeitgeist and weave them into his own original grand synthesis: the quiltwork mantle that we know today as psychoanalysis.

The story of Freud's life—and that of his patients, his contemporaries, and the psychoanalytic movement as a whole—has been, and continues to be, a source of inexhaustible fascination for a veritable army of able chroniclers. So in this introduction, as throughout this book, I will make no pretense at a comprehensive accounting of Freud's life and work; this is, after all, not primarily a work of psychohistory but more a historically tinged reconceptualization of some fundamental Freudian concepts. I urge the reader to sample the varied smorgasbord of historical offerings available within the archives of Freud scholarship.

Here it is necessary to provide a bit of historical context for the discussion that follows in the main body of the text if only to point out that, unlike the impression one gets from many historical accounts, Freud's early involvement in neurology was not simply a passing fancy, something

3

to fiddle with until psychoanalysis came along. Rather, the study of the brain was Freud's intense passion for at least the first decade of his scientific career. He reveled in clinical neurology: he thoroughly mastered its principles and techniques, he flaunted his prowess in it, he took on his mentors and colleagues in it, he made seminal contributions to it, and, as this book will show, he never really left it—and neither should we. The following biographical account is adapted from a number of sources (Amacher, 1965; Bernfeld, 1944; Ellenberger, 1970; Fancher, 1973; Freud, 1925; Holt, 1965, 1989; Jones, 1953; Sulloway, 1979; Triarhou & del Cerro, 1985).

Sigmund Freud was born on May 6, 1856, in Freiberg, Moravia, then a part of the greater Austro-Hungarian Empire but now in Czechoslovakia. Freud's mother, Amalia, was the second wife of the considerably older Jakob Freud and had Sigmund when she was twenty-one and her husband forty-one. Freud grew up in a household surrounded by family members of widely divergent ages—half siblings older than his mother, full siblings younger than himself, a comparatively young mother, and an older, patriarchal father. When Sigmund was four, the family moved to Vienna, where Freud was to remain until the last year of his life.

Most historical accounts make a point of Freud's precocious intellectual bent, which was apparent from an early age. Seeming to recognize that their child was destined for a life of the mind, the Freuds indulged young Sigmund's bookish proclivities by providing him with a special room of the house where he could absorb himself uninterruptedly in his studies and by setting up a private expense account at a local bookstore, which their son avidly took advantage of.

As a youth, Freud's intellectual tastes ran to history, languages, literature, and philosophy, and at that period in his life he seemed drawn to a career in law or politics, professions he felt would provide an avenue for making his own distinct mark upon the world. Reportedly, it was at a reading of Goethe's poem "On Nature" that Freud had the epiphany that abruptly swerved his interests in the direction of the natural sciences. It is at this point that he entered the medical school of the University of Vienna in 1873, at the age of seventeen.

Despite his apparent scholarly gifts, Freud was hardly the model student. Many of his grades were less than outstanding, and he took years longer than the average student to pass his qualifying exams. This, however, seemed to be the result of the same intellectual omnivorousness that characterized his early self-directed studies: instead of taking the straight and narrow track to matriculation, Freud's academic pursuits included side excursions into various elective courses and research projects.

Perhaps the single strongest influence during this time was Ernst Brücke, one of the leading exponents of the growing "new physiology," a school of thought—a movement, really—that adopted a strictly scientific-determinist orientation called *mechanism*, in reaction to the *vitalism* of many earlier physiologists who had claimed that life should be regarded as a qualitatively different state of matter. According to the mechanists, living things, like all matter, could be reduced to their elemental components and were therefore subject to the laws of nature and amenable to precise scientific study. In Brücke's lab Freud discovered the world of the brain and, guided by his mentor's keen interest in neuronal mechanisms and the neurophysiology of behavior, made several important discoveries in his own right.

When Freud finally did graduate, financial and possibly anti-Semitic prejudicial considerations put a damper on his desire to pursue a career of pure academic research, and he halfheartedly entered a training program for private practice physicians at the Vienna General Hospital. While there, however, he came under the spell of Theodor Meynert, the director of the hospital's psychiatric clinic and one of the leading brain anatomists and pathologists of his day. Although several historians have described Meynert as an archmechanist, it is probably closer to the truth to call him—to use the parlance of modern neuropsychology—a "localizationist."

This was the era when neurophysiologists had begun mapping out the sensory and motor areas of animals' brains by electrical stimulation experiments and when clinical neurologists were attempting to construct even more complex maps of higher human faculties by studying structure–function correlations in individuals with focal brain damage. With Wernicke, Meynert is most closely associated with the idea that specific loci in the brain represent specific psychological functions, a position Freud would later skewer in his *On Aphasia* monograph.

Freud's stint at the Vienna General Hospital was important for another reason. It was while there that he honed his skill in the *anatomicoclinical method*, the verification of localized neuroanatomical diagnoses of clinical neurological syndromes by careful postmortem study of the brains of the deceased patients. Freud quickly became renowned for his knowledge of clinical neurology and neuroanatomy, and his lectures on these subjects eventually attracted students from abroad. Indeed, Freud (1925) himself made no bones about his proficiency in this area:

> In the course of the following years, while I continued to work as a junior physician, I published a number of clinical observations upon organic diseases of the nervous system. I gradually became familiar with the ground; I was able to localize the site of a lesion in the medulla oblongata so accurately that the pathological anatomist had no further information to add; I was the first person in Vienna to send a case for autopsy with a diagnosis of polyneuritis acuta. The fame of my diagnoses and their post-mortem confirmation brought me an influx

of American physicians, to whom I lectured upon the patients in my department in a sort of pidgin-English. (p. 19)

By 1885 Freud's reputation in clinical neurology enabled him to win a highly coveted grant from the Vienna General Hospital to go and study with Charcot in France; there he learned much about hysteria and hypnosis. He also visited Liébeault in Nancy in 1889 and may have met Janet during this visit. On his return to Vienna, after a tour of duty as an army physician, where his service was apparently well regarded, Freud married Martha Bernays, began his private practice, and became the director of a neurology department at a small children's hospital, where he lost no time in becoming the resident expert in childhood cerebral palsy and publishing an important tract in that field.

In the interim he had been taken under the wing of an older physician, Josef Breuer, whose research on the brain mechanisms of balance and on the neurophysiology of respiration is still cited in textbooks today and who was later to collaborate with Freud in the *Studies on Hysteria*. Another early confidant was Wilhelm Fliess, whose somewhat bizarre ideas on sexuality and the "nasal reflex neurosis" did not prevent Freud from using him as a productive sounding board during the time when many of the most important ideas in psychoanalysis were being conceived and developed (see Sulloway, 1979, for an in-depth, if controversial, treatment of the Freud–Fliess relationship).

In the period from 1895 to 1900 Freud's efforts were mainly devoted to developing a theory of the neuroses and the method of psychoanalytic therapy to treat them. Noting that many of his patients reported dreams during their analyses, Freud, with characteristic thoroughness, began the earnest study of this nocturnal mental activity, which till then was largely regarded as the province of philosophers, poets, and spiritualists. In 1900 he published *The Interpretation of Dreams*, regarded by most Freud scholars—not to mention Freud himself—as his masterpiece.

First, hysteria and the neuroses, then dreams; the stage was set for elaborating a fully comprehensive theory of mental life, but something was missing. In 1901 the third leg of the grand theory of psychoanalysis was completed when Freud included the realm of normal waking experience—the theory of the parapraxis, or "Freudian slip," as it came to be called—in his psychodynamic model. The psychopathology of the neurology and psychiatry clinic was now extended to "the psychopathology of everyday life." Throughout their changes and revisions, their emendations and transformations, the clinical and metapsychological foundations of psychoanalysis have rested on these three pillars of Freudian data and theory: hysteria, dreams, and parapraxes.

And the legacy of Freud the neurologist—the *neuropsychologist*—breathed lustily into his psychoanalytic theory throughout its continued development. To date, authors of virtually all accounts of Freud and the brain have felt compelled to pay homage to the famous *Project for a Scientific Psychology* (Freud, 1895), an originally discarded but posthumously published tract outlining a cell-to-cell neurophysiology of mental life, intended by Freud only as a sort of thinking-out-loud exercise in correspondence with his friend Fliess. Nevertheless, it was seized upon with a shrill hurrah when it was unearthed in the 1950s because it seemed so much like a vindication of the "scientific" aspects of psychoanalysis, which by that time was coming under serious attack from other branches of psychology and psychiatry, that is, from behaviorism on one side and biopsychiatry on the other. Yet almost completely ignored have been Freud's prepsychoanalytic writings in clinical neurology, which, more than anything else, point to the origin of psychoanalysis in the kind of neuropsychological model we could embrace comfortably today.

A note on terminology: the term *neuropsychodynamic* is used to describe this book's approach to elaborating a model of brain and psyche. My coinage of this term has been determined not merely by authorial neologistic license but more by its literal appropriateness: "neuro" because we are, after all, dealing with the brain; "psycho" because our primary interest is in how the brain mediates the workings of the mind and behavior; and "dynamic" because we recognize the fluid, ever-changing, and interactive nature of brain functioning while eschewing a static, localizationist approach—as did Freud. And to fully conceptualize the neuropsychodynamic model, we need to examine the data from brain-injured, psychopathological, and normal states of mind—again, as did Freud.

Freud is said to have abandoned neuroscience because it could not accommodate the scope of his psychodynamic model. But as this book will show, clinical neuropsychology may be veritably indispensable for elaborating the truly integrative neuropsychodynamic theory that was then, and continues to be, the model of Freud's brain.

PART TWO

Hysteria

The expectation of eternal fame was so beautiful, as was that of certain wealth, complete independence, travels, and lifting the children above the severe worries that robbed me of my youth. Everything depended upon whether or not hysteria would come out right.

—SIGMUND FREUD,
letter to Wilhelm Fliess, September 1897

CHAPTER 2

"Studies on Hysteria": The Cases

As a *clinical* discipline, psychoanalysis began with hysteria. This section of the book first reviews the case material that led Freud to his fundamental insights about this condition and its sufferers, next compares the symptomatology of these cases with some of the phenomena recorded in the archives of modern neurology and neuropsychology, and then integrates Freud's theoretical formulations with modern neuroscientific data to elaborate a comprehensive neuropsychodynamic model of hysteria and the hysterical personality.

Since the general life histories of Breuer and Freud's famous cases—especially Anna O—have been well described elsewhere, this chapter focuses primarily on the *symptoms* of hysteria as described by Breuer and Freud rather than attempting to relate in detail the *stories* behind the cases. For good general accounts of the historical background of some of these colorful patients, the reader is referred to Ellenberger (1970, 1972) and Fancher (1973).

Breuer's Case: Anna O

Even though Anna O was not actually a patient of Freud himself and details of her therapy were related to Freud over a decade after Breuer treated her, this case has by now become the quintessentially "Freudian" account of hysteria. This is largely due to the richness of the clinical material it contains, to the fact that it appears first in the case history section of *Studies on Hysteria*, to the preoccupation with this case by later writers up to the present time, and to the general consensus among Freud scholars that, historically, it was one of the key clinical influences that led Freud to a psychodynamic conceptualization of the neuroses. As we

11

will see, however, the other cases described in *Studies on Hysteria* are, from a neuropsychodynamic point of view, just as compelling.

At the time of her falling ill, Fräulein Anna O was twenty-one years old; Breuer makes a point of her exceptional knowledge, wit, educational refinement, intellectual doggedness, and strength of will. Apparently, this was to emphasize the contrast between Anna and many of the hysterics seen in the French clinic of Charcot, who tended to be poor, unschooled peasants and commoners. Inasmuch as some of Anna's distant relatives had suffered psychoses of an unclear nature, Breuer regarded her as having a "moderately severe neuropathic heredity" (Breuer & Freud, 1895, p. 21). Her parents, however, were normal in every respect, and Anna herself had apparently shown no overt signs of disturbance prior to the development of the illness that brought her to Breuer's attention.

Her difficulties began in July 1880 when her father took to his bed with a protracted, and ultimately fatal, illness. Anna, who was particularly attached to her father, willingly assumed the arduous task of sick-nursing. She remained continually vigilant at his bedside, slavishly attended to his every need and eventually, inevitably, exhausted herself in these duties to the point of her own physical and mental deterioration. By December 1880 Anna was in such poor shape that Breuer, who was at that time the family physician, was called in to treat her.

The specific symptom that precipitated the summoning of Breuer was Anna's severe and persistent cough, but the doctor soon realized that there was more going on than he first suspected. Breuer recounts the panoply of symptoms displayed by Anna over the course of her illness, which included at first a left-sided occipital headache and a convergent squint with diplopia that was made worse by excitement. Anna also complained that the walls of the room seemed to be falling over, a perception that Breuer attributed to a disorder of the obliquus muscle, one of the extraocular muscles that move the eye. Her eyes periodically deviated to the right, so that when her hand reached out for something it always went to the right of the object. Macropsia, an illusion in which objects appear to be abnormally large, was also present.

There was a selective paralysis of the muscles in the front of the neck, so that Anna could only move her head by pressing it backwards with her hands between her raised shoulders and moving her whole back. Also present was an anesthesia and contracture of the right arm, which soon spread to the right leg, which in turn became fully extended, moved toward the midline and rotated inwards. This symptom later appeared in the left leg and from there spread to the left arm, with only the fingers of that extremity retaining some power of voluntary movement. The contracture appeared to be most severe in the upper arms whereas the shoulders were less affected.

During this time Anna displayed two quite different states of consciousness, which alternated frequently and abruptly and which became more differentiated in the course of the illness. In the first of these states she was melancholy and anxious but recognized her surroundings and appeared relatively intact. The other state, which Breuer referred to by the French term *absence*, was a different matter: Anna was plagued by hallucinations and was, to use her own term, "naughty," shouting abusively at people and pelting them with cushions, ripping up her sheets and tearing the buttons off her clothes—so far as her various motor impairments would allow. During these frenetic states if anyone left or entered the room or a piece of furniture or fixture shifted position, Anna would complain of having "lost" some time and would remark upon the gap in her train of conscious thoughts. Attempts at reassurance by well-meaning bedside attendants were met with a further fusillade of pillows, accompanied by raging accusations directed at people allegedly trying to deceive and persecute her.

Breuer also describes extremely rapid swings of mood and general mental state, leading at one moment to an ebullient, high-spirited Anna and in the next instant to a stubborn, oppositional Anna, now gripped by frightening visions of her hair and ribbons transmogrified into hideous black snakes. Through much of this, she seemed to retain some perspective on the unreality of these symptoms, regarding them as alien to her true nature, symptoms that psychologists today would call "ego-dystonic." During periods of relative lucidity, Anna would complain of a profound "darkness" in her head, of not being able to think, of becoming blind and deaf, and, most notably, of having two selves, a real one and an evil one that forced her to behave badly.

Along with Anna's contractures, Breuer describes several disorders of speech. At first, Anna seemed to have had difficulty finding the right words for what she wanted to say, and this problem gradually worsened. During her "absence" states, she would often stop in the middle of a sentence, repeat her last words, and, after a short pause, go on talking. Progressively, she lost almost total command of grammar and syntax in her native German. Instead, she developed the curious practice of painstakingly stringing words and sentences together out of four or five different languages. The result was a virtually complete loss of normally intelligible speech. When writing (contractures permitting), she used the same polyglot jargon. For two weeks she became completely mute, unable to articulate so much as a syllable in spite of what looked like frantic efforts to speak.

It was at this point that Breuer gained his first insight into the psychogenic etiology of Anna's afflictions. Breuer knew that Anna was quite upset over something, but she had stoically determined not to speak of it. Breuer was able to discern what was bothering her and persuaded her to tell him about it, whereupon the speechless condition resolved, accompanied by the return of normal movement to Anna's left arm and leg. But in place of muteness, a different kind of linguistic perturbation appeared. Anna now spoke only in English—apparently, however, without knowing that she was doing so. Nevertheless, she could still understand people who spoke to her in her native German. In moments of extreme anxiety she would revert to near-total speechlessness or else employ her curious polyglot communication. At those times when she seemed at her best, French and Italian became the languages of choice, with concomitant amnesia for her English-speaking episodes.

Presently, a violent outburst of excitement took place, followed by a profound stupor that lasted about two days and from which Anna emerged in a greatly changed state. At first she was far quieter, and her feelings of anxiety were greatly diminished. The anesthesia and contracture of her right arm and leg persisted, but in less severe form. A peculiar visual disturbance ensued: when viewing a bunch of flowers, Anna could make out only one flower at a time, as opposed to perceiving them all simultaneously as a bouquet. Associated with this was an inability to recognize people's faces in the ordinary manner of just looking at them. Instead, she had to do laborious "recognizing work," which involved singling out a salient characteristic of that person's face and then reasoning back to the person involved—for example, "this person's nose is such-and-such, so he must be so-and-so."

Anna described the people she saw around her as "wax figures," disconnected from her own reality. In fact, the presence of some of her close relatives came to be more and more distressing to her. If someone whom she ordinarily liked entered the room, Anna would recognize him and would become generally aware of things in her environment for a time; soon, however, she would sink back into her own broodings and the visitor was blotted out. Breuer notes, perhaps with some pride, that he was the only person whom Anna always recognized when he came in. As long as he continued to talk to her, Anna remained in contact with her surroundings and seemed animated and lively, except, of course, when this happy state was interrupted by one of her hallucinatory absences. Meanwhile, she had begun writing again but this time with her left hand, which was less stiff than the right, and now using Roman printed letters; she spent some time copying the alphabet in this manner from her edition of Shakespeare. Overall, however, she seemed to be getting better.

Then her father died. Anna plunged into a state of despondency and apathy, and many of the previous symptoms returned, including her absences. The latter, however, were beginning to show some peculiar characteristics. For example, there developed a regular diurnal pattern to Anna's alternating states of consciousness. In the afternoon she began to slip into a somnolent twilight state; this progressed after sunset to a deeper trance-like condition that she herself referred to as "clouds."

Breuer then discovered that if during this cloud state Anna was able to recount the hallucinations she had experienced during the course of the day, she would awake from the cloud state later that evening in a clearheaded, calm, and cheerful frame of mind. She would then draw or write quite rationally and normally until about four in the morning, when she went to bed. The next day, this whole sequence would be repeated. Breuer remarked on the contrast between these two Annas: by day, the wild-eyed, Bedlamesque mental patient, tormented by hallucinations, shouting and flinging objects; by night, the lucid, rational, bourgeois Victorian young lady, quietly pursuing the genteel life of the mind.

But, Breuer noted, the mere passage of hours was not in itself sufficient to maintain this diurnal cycle of alternating obtundation and lucidity. It was necessary that Anna have the opportunity to express herself during her cloud state; otherwise, the next day she was as irritable and disagreeable as ever. And if yet a second consecutive evening was permitted to go by without this conversational release, the following morning produced an Anna whom Breuer could only describe as "positively nasty."

Breuer surmised that these early evening sessions, which Anna herself came to call her "talking cure"—and later, more whimsically, "chimney-sweeping"—were necessary for clearing out the pathological products of Anna's mind. The hypnoidal "cloud" state facilitated this process, presumably by letting down the guard of normal consciousness. Deprived of this outlet, Breuer reasoned, the noxious psychological burden festered within Anna's psyche and was responsible for the bizarre daytime symptoms and horrid behaviors.

At this point, the very character of Anna's alternating daily mental cycle had begun to change and to assume a fairly regular configuration. During the first stage of this cycle she was oriented to the correct date and year whereas in the second stage, the absence, or cloud state, she appeared to be living in the previous winter and had forgotten all subsequent events—except, however, that her beloved father had died. Moreover, there was a definite orderliness to this time displacement: she lived through the previous winter day by day. This temporal pattern of the clinical picture was to prove of great importance in Anna's subsequent treatment by Breuer.

The first clue to an effective therapy for Anna's affliction came when she abruptly developed hydrophobia, an aversion to drinking fluids, which lasted for six weeks. Each attempt to swallow any liquid was met by a wave of uncontrollable revulsion, and Anna was compelled, despite a parching thirst, to get her fluid intake entirely from fruits. During one of the trance-like confessional reveries of the cloud sessions, Anna began describing to Breuer an incident, forgotten to normal waking consciousness, in which she was disgusted and repelled by the sight of a dog drinking water from a woman's glass. This, apparently, was the first time she had revealed the incident and, more importantly, expressed its full emotional impact. Upon emerging from the cloud state, Anna immediately asked for a glass of water and drained it. The hydrophobia never appeared again.

Breuer surmised that there must be a connection between certain hysterical symptoms and certain forgotten memories—*hidden* memories, it seemed—which were typically those of a loathsome or otherwise disturbing nature. Accordingly, the revelation of such a memory during spontaneously generated altered states of consciousness—Anna's "clouds," for example—seemed to release or unbind the hysterical symptom associated with the memory, freeing the patient from its grasp. This was especially true if the memory was reexperienced in all of its original emotional intensity. If these twilight states of consciousness were so conducive to the expression of hidden memories, reasoned Breuer, why wait for them to come around on their own? Why not seize the therapeutic initiative and deliberately induce such states as a more systematic form of "chimney-sweeping"?

Thus, Breuer's treatment of Anna O began in earnest as he started using hypnosis to help Anna relive various forgotten unpleasant events. With results surpassing his expectations, Breuer discovered that virtually every hysterical symptom could be traced back to some traumatic event that was completely isolated from waking consciousness. If he could induce Anna to recall those experiences, along with the associated feelings, the symptoms astonishingly evaporated. But it had to be done in a certain way: for each symptom, all the occasions on which it had first appeared had to be described, in exact reverse chronological order.

So, for example, the origin of Anna's squint and other visual disturbances was traced back to a time when she was sitting by her father's sickbed, distraught over his condition but not wanting to alarm or disturb him by any overt maudlin display. When her father asked her the time, she had to bring her watch close to her face and squint through welled-up tears to read the dial—hence the squint symptom.

Similar mechanisms seemed to account for the other main symptoms of Anna's illness. For example, on another occasion at her father's bedside, her arm had been resting on the headboard for a long time when, in her exhausted state, she was abruptly startled by what she thought was a black snake darting out of the wall. Recoiling, she discovered to her horror that her arm had fallen asleep from the pressure of the headboard and could not be moved easily or quickly. She tried to scream for help, but panic strangled her voice. Now terror-stricken, she could remember only the words of an English prayer she had once learned, and she repeated them over and over. This whole episode, too, had been banished from conscious memory, but when it was recalled under Breuer's hypnosis, Anna let loose all the fear and despair of the original incident.

In this manner, Anna's paralytic contractures and anesthesias, various disorders of vision and hearing, eye deviations, neuralgias, tremors, speech disorders, reading disability, and death's head hallucinations were gradually "talked away." Breuer dubbed this technique the *cathartic method* (after the Greek *katharos*, "to purify by purging") and found it effective for the elimination of all but a handful of symptoms, which seemed to have developed during the period when Anna was confined to bed. These more stubborn symptoms included the extension of the paralytic contractures to the left side of Anna's body, and Breuer was ready to admit that their resistance to the cathartic method may well have been because they in fact had no immediate psychical cause.

The treatment of Anna O's hysteria seems to have been regarded by Breuer as tantamount to her moral salvation. He took pains to point out that had not the products of Anna's "bad self" been diligently and continuously disposed of through the cathartic method, "we should have been faced by an hysteric of the malicious type—refractory, lazy, disagreeable and ill-natured; but as it was, after the removal of those stimuli, her true character, which was the opposite of all these, always appeared at once" (Breuer & Freud, 1895, p. 46).

Breuer then made an intriguing observation, one that speaks to the whole relationship of hysteria to volition. He noted that even in the throes of Anna's worst hallucinations and atrocious behavioral states, a "clear-sighted and calm observer," as she herself put it, often sat in a corner of her mind and looked on with some objective detachment at all the mad business, a function of what psychologists today might call an "observing ego." During a temporary abatement of the most florid of the hysterical phenomena, while she was passing through a bout of depression, Anna remarked upon the idea that perhaps she had not been ill at all and that the whole childish affair had in fact been a simulation. And among hysterics, Breuer observed, Anna O was not alone in this.

> When a disorder of this kind has cleared up and the two states of consciousness have once more become merged into one, the patients, looking back to the past, see themselves as the single undivided personality which was aware of all the nonsense; they think they could have prevented it if they had wanted to, and thus they feel as though they had done all the mischief deliberately. (Breuer & Freud, 1895, p. 46)

We will return repeatedly to this issue of neuropsychology, psychodynamics, and volition, particularly as it applies to hysteria and parapraxes. But first we continue with the original clinical descriptions.

Freud's Cases

Although not usually considered in modern accounts of the history of psychoanalysis and hysteria (Anna O steals the spotlight), Freud's own cases in the *Studies* are nevertheless important for elucidating the relationship between hysteria and brain states. Again, the present account glosses over the story lines in these cases in favor of a description of the key clinical symptoms.

The first of Freud's cases is Frau Emmy von N, whose problems included convulsive, tic-like movements of her face and neck muscles and whose speech was frequently interrupted by a curious "clacking" vocalization. She also stammered, which Freud regarded as another species of tic, a symptom that had first appeared five years earlier when she was sitting by the bedside of her very ill younger daughter, endeavoring to keep "absolutely quiet."

Frau Emmy also suffered from short bouts of "neck cramps," which Freud attributed to a variant of migraine. This was apparently evidenced by the fact that Frau Emmy's neck cramps, like some other forms of migraine attacks, were accompanied by a delirious state. In addition, she complained of cold and pain sensations running from her lower back down her left leg; in his account of this case Freud criticized the many physicians of his day who were too quick to dismiss such symptoms as psychogenic. Had they only taken the effort to palpate the affected muscles, Freud asserted, they would have discovered the nodules indicative of the true organic, neuralgic nature of these myopathies. At least in his early days, it seems, Freud was hardly the radical psychodynamic determinist that many of his biographers and followers have painted him.

But for the kinds of symptoms that really do represent manifestations of actual psychogenically based hysteria, Freud introduced the term *conversion* to signify the transformation of psychical excitation into chronic somatic manifestations, a mechanism he believed to be important in the genesis of true hysteria. However, Frau Emmy showed very little of this conversion; her psychological disturbances remained, for the most part, in the psychical domain, much as in the case of the other neuroses, for example, phobias and obsessions.

In wrestling with this dilemma—what we might today call the "mind–body problem"—Freud arrived at the following theoretical compromise: Frau Emmy was undoubtedly a personality with a "severe neuropathic heredity," which at this stage of his thinking Freud regarded as a necessary, or at least facilitative, constitutional substrate for the development of full-blown hysteria. However, such a predisposition had to be activated for the syndrome to appear, and it is in this activating function that psychological factors played their role in determining the precise manifestation of Frau Emmy's hysterical symptoms.

The second patient in this series is Lucy R, referred to Freud by a colleague whom history has revealed to be Wilhelm Fliess, an ear, nose, and throat specialist with some unique ideas about nasal sex, whose surgical treatment of Lucy almost resulted in her hemorrhaging to death (see Ellenberger, 1970, and Sulloway, 1979, for a fuller account of the Freud–Fliess relationship). Fliess had been treating Lucy for recurrent suppurative rhinitis secondary to local infection of the ethmoid bone in the nose. Freud was called in when, in spite of being apparently cured of any organic illness, Lucy persisted in complaining of a complete loss of her sense of smell. Upon examination, Lucy's nose was found to have normal sensation of touch but was entirely devoid of olfactory sensitivity—she had lost her sense of smell. Paradoxically, however, this defect did not prevent her from being continuously tormented by the presence of one or two noxious subjective olfactory sensations. In addition, she appeared depressed and fatigued and complained of heaviness in her head, diminished appetite, and "loss of efficiency."

This case impressed Freud because, here too, no strong constitutional hysterical or other "neuropathic" predisposition appeared to set the stage for the development of Lucy's symptoms. Although he seems to have been reluctant to abandon entirely the concept of predisposing factors, Freud deemed Lucy's hysteria an "acquired" one. This then paved the way for the further exposition of a more general theory of such acquired hysterias.

If there is one thing essential for hysteria to develop, asserted Freud, it is that a psychologically disruptive incompatibility should develop between the ego and some idea presented to it. The hysterical method of defense involves the isolation of the disturbing feeling and the conversion of the psychical energy produced by the disruption into a "somatic innervation," or bodily symptom, in this case Lucy's anosmia, or loss of smell sensation. This separation and isolation serves the function of repressing the incompatible idea from the ego's consciousness. But even as Freud the physician-scientist was conceptualizing his conversion model in such seemingly psychodeterministic terminology, Freud the philosopher-moralist could not help observing that

> the mechanism which produces hysteria represents on the one hand an act of moral cowardice and on the other a defensive measure which is at the disposal of the ego. Often enough we have to admit that fending off increasing excitations by the generations of hysteria is, in the circumstances, the most expedient thing to do; more frequently,

of course, we shall conclude that a greater amount of moral courage would have been of advantage to the person concerned. (Breuer & Freud, 1895, p. 123)

Here, as in Breuer's comments on Anna O, the question arises as to the possible role of some volitional element in the hysterical process, a kind of self-serving willfulness that plays such devilishly obnoxious games with mind–body relationships.

The striking feature about Freud's next case, Elizabeth von R, was the presence of a bland unconcern for impairment, termed by the French *la belle indifférence*, that seemed to characterize the clinical picture of hysterical conversion in many cases. Elizabeth's disorder had developed gradually during the previous two years and varied greatly in intensity. She walked with the upper part of her body bent foward but without using any kind of support like a crutch or a cane, and her gait disturbance corresponded to no recognized organic clinical disorder. However, she complained of great pain in ambulating and was quickly overcome by fatigue both in walking and standing, requiring her to stop and rest at frequent intervals. These breaks would afford some relief but did not eliminate the pains entirely.

Freud pointed out that Elizabeth's pains, like many hysterical symptoms, were of "an indefinite character," something in the nature of a "painful fatigue." The pains seemed to radiate outward from a fairly large but ill-defined area of the anterior surface of the right thigh. In this area the skin and muscles were particularly sensitive to pressure and pinching, although pricking with a needle was met with unconcern. This dysesthesia could be observed more or less over the whole of both legs. Since general motor power of the legs was intact and reflexes were essentially normal, Freud felt that there were no grounds for suspecting the presence of any serious organic illness.

Nevertheless, Freud could not overlook the similarities between Elizabeth's affliction and some of the more common etiologies of pain syndromes known at the time. In particular, he singled out "common chronic muscular rheumatism," which involved a rheumatic infiltration of the muscles and produced a diffuse sensitivity to pressure in those areas. This diagnosis was confirmed by the presence of numerous hard fibers in the muscle substance, which were the sites of greatest sensitivity. But psychological factors were not so easily abandoned. Instead, Freud reasoned, the neurotic-hysterical process took advantage of an otherwise nonserious organic syndrome and, investing it with repressed psychical energy, greatly exaggerated its importance.

Thus, theorized Freud, Elizabeth's chronic pain syndrome was not *created* by the neurosis but "merely used, increased and maintained by it"

(Breuer & Freud, 1895, p. 174), a process Freud had identified in other patients with hysterical chronic pain syndromes. These always had at their core a genuine organically based pain. In fact, Freud observed, it was the commonest and most widespread of human pains that seemed to be most often chosen as the kernel of a full-blown hysterical efflorescence. These included the periosteal and neuralgic pains accompanying dental disease, the many kinds of everyday headaches, and the "rheumatic muscular pains" whose contributory role Freud felt so often went unrecognized in cases of hysterical pain syndromes.

Still, for Freud, the key fascination of hysteria remained in the domain of the psychical:

> I have not always been a psychotherapist. Like other neuropathologists, I was trained to employ local diagnoses and electro-prognosis, and it still strikes me myself as strange that the case histories I write should read like short stories and that, as one might say, they lack the serious stamp of science. I must console myself with the reflection that the nature of the subject is evidently responsible for this, rather than any preference of my own. The fact is that local diagnosis and electrical reactions lead nowhere in the study of hysteria, whereas a detailed description of mental processes such as we are accustomed to find in the works of imaginative writers enables me, with the use of a few psychological formulas, to obtain at least some kind of insight into the course of that affection. Case histories of this kind are intended to be judged like psychiatric ones; they have, however, one advantage over the latter, namely an intimate connection between the story of the patient's sufferings and the symptoms of his illness—a connection for which we still search in vain in the biographies of other psychoses. (Breuer & Freud, 1895, pp. 160–161)

But it was in his description of the case of Frau Cäcilie M that Freud made clear the nature of the symbolic relationship between hysterical symptoms and the underlying psychodynamics that shape and motivate them. This case perhaps also comes closest to what is both clinically and colloquially meant when someone is described as having "hysterical" symptoms. Indeed, Freud commented that he "had not found such an extensive use of symbolization in any other patient" (Breuer & Freud, 1895, p. 180).

Interestingly, Frau Cäcilie was a woman of great artistic gifts and was the author of a number of "poems of great perfection." Such "poetry," apparently, was expressed as well in her hysterical symptomatology. For example, lancinating pains in the chest occurred whenever Frau Cäcilie experienced something whose psychological impact was like "a stab in the heart." Hysterical pain related to thinking—"something's come into my head"—was described as being like nails driven into the skull; these pains always cleared up as soon as the problems surrounding them were resolved. After an insult, the thought "I shall have to swallow this" was accompanied by a strange sensation in the throat, which Freud, in a footnote, likened to one of the auras of epilepsy. Frau Cäcilie seemed to have had a whole catalog of these ideational/symbolic symptom combinations running in parallel with one another. Sometimes, explained Freud, the sensation would call up the idea to explain it, while at other times the idea seemed to create the sensation by means of symbolization; on still other occasions the temporal sequence of the symbol–symptom association was unclear.

> It is my opinion, however, that when a hysteric creates a somatic expression for an emotionally-colored idea by symbolization, this depends less than one would imagine on personal or voluntary factors. In taking a verbal expression literally and in feeling the "stab in the heart" or the "slap in the face" after some slighting remark as a real event, the hysteric is not taking liberties with words, but is simply reviving once more the sensations to which the verbal expression owes its justification. (Breuer & Freud, 1895, pp. 180–181)

Freud next invokes Charles Darwin to explain the relationship between hysterical symptoms and symbolization. In this evolutionary conception, hysterical symptoms may be seen as a phylogenetically primitive nonverbal analogue to more recently evolved verbal symbolization.

> All these sensations and innervations belong to the field of "the Expression of the Emotions" which, as Darwin (1872) has taught us, consists of actions which originally had a meaning and served a purpose. These now for the most part have become so much weakened that the expression of them in words seems only to be a figurative picture of them, whereas in all probability the description was once meant literally; and hysteria is right in restoring the original meaning of the words in depicting its unusually strong innervations. Indeed, it is perhaps wrong to say that hysteria creates these sensations by symbolization. It may be that it does not take linguistic usage as its model at all, but that both hysteria and linguistic usage alike draw their material from a common source. (Breuer & Freud, 1895, p. 181)

Here, then, is one of the first Freudian articulations of the unity of psychic life, as expressed in the form of hysterical symptoms. In this view, hysteria best exemplifies what psychologists would today call a "body language," and the expression of this language in the phylogenetically higher form of actual human speech is what enables the repressed material to escape symbolic somatic entombment, thus freeing the person from the symptom's grasp.

More generally, what shall we make of these cases? The very bizarreness of the phenomena reported by Breuer and Freud has been taken by many to imply that they must exist outside the range of normal psychic life on the one hand and of typical organic brain impairment on the other. However, if it could be shown that organic processes may produce "hysterical-like" effects, this might from one direction bring their basic nature back into the realm of the normal neuropsychodynamics of the human brain-mind.

CHAPTER 3

Brain Syndromes and the Phenomenology of Hysteria

If anything about hysteria has not changed, it is the confusion and disagreement that clinicians and researchers have always had, and continue to have, about its essential nature. If the patients really "can" move, talk, and so forth, then why "don't" they?

Hysteria, Then and Now

Early in this century the famed neurologist Henry Head (1922) defined hysterical paralysis by the fact that it was usually possible to demonstrate motor signs of good functioning in a supposedly paralyzed part. More recently, Slater (1965) has pointed out that the signs of hysteria are actually signs not of disease but of health: the "speechless" patient can phonate to some degree, the "anesthetic" patient can detect certain sensations, the "amnesic" patient can selectively remember, and so on.

In practice, many clinicians seem to agree with Ziegler and colleagues (1963) that a diagnosis of conversion hysteria ordinarily requires, first, that through appropriate medical evaluation no adequate pathophysiological explanation for the symptom can be found and, second, that there is some evidence of emotional disturbance that is being "masked" by the patient's preoccupation with his or her symptom.

Patients with hysteria tend to be highly suggestible; indeed, with appropriate and subtle suggestion the symptom may be transferred from one body area to another, transformed into a different symptom, or even entirely eliminated for variable periods of time (Ludwig, 1980). Conversion hysteria involving the "classic" paralyses or anesthesias is not presently a

24

common disorder in routine peacetime clinical practice but occurs much more frequently in military psychiatry, especially in times of war (Merskey & Buhrich, 1975).

These "classic," and often dramatic, cases also tend to come from socioculturally backward areas, where there is greater cultural acceptance of the symptoms. Such individuals tend to simulate organic disease processes as they conceive of them, and the nature of such simulations typically betrays their lack of medical sophistication. At the other extreme, more medically knowledgeable patients, such as those who work in health care settings, can often replicate even complex disease entities with great precision. Ziegler and colleagues (1960) report the case of a nurse who accurately simulated recurrent episodes of multiple sclerosis, and one neurologist's secretary so perfectly feigned symptoms of a third ventricular cyst that the diagnosis was only disconfirmed by ventriculography.

Although it may vary in the sophistication of its expression, the general tendency to develop hysterical symptoms is apparently no respecter of socioeconomic class, occurring approximately equally in lower- and middle-class patients (Woodruff et al., 1971). Modern opinions differ with regard to the gender ratios of hysterics, with some authorities reaffirming the traditional view of overwhelming female predominance (Woodruff et al., 1971) and others reporting up to a forty percent male prevalence (Ziegler et al., 1960).

More important than which sex contributes more subjects to the hysteric subject pool may be the question of how the two sexes each express their respective forms of conversion symptomatology. According to Ziegler and colleagues (1963), women are likely to utilize conversion reactions as a lifelong behavior pattern and to a more extreme degree than men, who, in ordinary civilian circumstances, are more likely to have a single, time-limited conversion symptom associated with an episode of severe emotional stress. When conversion reactions of long duration and involving multiple symptoms do occur in men, they are usually in the context of escape from aversive circumstances (prison, the military) or revolve around litigation and compensation issues, although in most other respects, the manifestations are the same for both sexes (Woodruff et al., 1971; Ziegler et al., 1960, 1963). With regard to symptom type, Whitlock (1967) found that female hysterics seem to develop states of dysphonia and/or mutism more commonly than males, who, for their part, show a higher incidence of dissociative reactions manifested by fugues and amnesias.

Hysteria runs in families. First degree female relatives of women with hysteria are ten times more likely to develop the syndrome than women in the general population (Woodruff et al., 1971). Ziegler and colleagues (1960) found that one group of patients with conversion reactions were youngest children more frequently than by chance; however, another large group of patients had been the oldest of their sex and often had been singled out by the opposite-sex parent as a particular favorite. A substantial number of patients in this series were adolescents who had problems in role shifting and of identification with conflicting groups, resulting in interpersonal difficulties that involved sexual and dependency issues.

Conversion symptoms may also be found in psychopathological conditions other than hysteria, for example, in schizophrenia, alcoholism, and psychopathy (antisocial personality); however, in these cases the conversion symptoms are more apt to be monosymptomatic (Ludwig, 1980; Woodruff et al., 1971; Ziegler et al., 1960, 1963). Ziegler and colleagues (1963) report that many of their patients judged to be using conversion symptoms to fend off psychotic processes in fact became overtly psychotic when the symptoms were removed by hypnotic suggestion.

With these basic points in mind, we can now begin to examine the neuropsychological phenomena that may shed light on the manifestations and mechanisms of hysteria. As we will see, virtually every hysterical symptom reported by Breuer and Freud has an analogue in some known form of altered neurocognitive functioning. But, as will be argued in a subsequent chapter—indeed, throughout this book—these observations should *not* be taken to mean that hysterical symptoms are always caused by organic brain disease or injury. Rather, our neuropsychodynamic model asserts that the psychical impetus provided by the person's personality takes advantage of brain dynamics that are usually only seen in their boldest form in structural organic disorders of the brain but that may occur more transiently, more subtly, and in more complexly organized ways, interwoven with ordinary aspects of behavior, when expressed in the form of "functional," or "hysterical," symptoms.

Not to jump ahead, however, we first consider the phenomenology of hysteria, then deal with mechanism and theory. In going through the neuropsychological cases presented in this chapter, the reader is urged to note the parallels between the symptoms reported here and those chronicled by Breuer and Freud in their own cases, as described in the last chapter. After that, we will be in a much better position to consider *why* these similarities should exist.

Disorders of Sensation and Perception

In 1909 Balint described a new neurologic syndrome under the name "psychic paralysis of gaze." Since then, *Balint's syndrome*, as it came to be called, has been reported only rarely in its full-blown form. It is associated with extensive bilateral lesions of the parietal lobe, although often some involvement of the temporal and occipital areas is present as well (Balint, 1909; Gloning et al., 1968; Bender et al., 1971), and the most severe cases may include frontal lobe involvement (Hecaen & de Ajuriaguerra, 1954; Hecaen et al., 1950). The main features of the syndrome consist of a clinical triad: (1) psychic paralysis of gaze, or visual fixation; (2) simultagnosia; and (3) optic ataxia.

Psychic paralysis of gaze is apparent when the patient is unable to voluntarily move the eyes from the point of fixation to a point in the peripheral visual field: that is, the eyes seem "glued" to what the patient is currently looking at. When fixed upon some object, the eyes will follow it, but when not so riveted, they wander. Extraocular muscle function is intact. *Simultagnosia* is the inability to see more than one object at a time from the entire visual environment; only the most prominent stimuli reach consciousness. For example, a small object presented too closely to be seen as a whole is ignored, but a larger object viewed from a sufficient distance to be appreciated in its entirety is easily recognized (Hecaen & de Ajuriaguerra, 1954). *Optic ataxia* is the inability to perform coordinated movements of the extremities using visual cues as a guide. Patients with optic ataxia do poorly on tests of visual search (e.g., reaching for objects). However, automatic functions such as walking or eating may be performed normally.

Juergens and colleagues (1986) describe the case of a sixty-four-year-old man who had been in generally good health until he suffered two left hemisphere strokes, producing mild right-sided weakness and mild aphasia. Surgery to remove the stenotic lesions of the carotid artery that were causing the problem was unsuccessful, and eleven days postoperatively the patient complained of a "swimming sensation" in his eyes and asked to see a psychiatrist for his depression. The next morning he complained of "blindness" in that he could not see "anything smaller than a hand in front of my nose" (p. 597). Except for the vision problem, the neurologic findings were unchanged. An apparent paradox was that he could see features on a nurse's face across the room but stated that he could not see the examiner's hand when it was held one foot in front of him. An observer noted that the patient would read a few words when shown a newspaper headline but would not read the entire headline; he nevertheless seemed unconcerned about this situation.

Results of funduscopic examination were normal. In tests of visual acuity, the patient "purposefully reached for everything around the reading card, but strategically acted as if he could not find the card" (Juergens et al., 1986, p. 598), and he "refused" to read. He could track and follow the movements of the ophthalmologist but had a tendency to stare away and out the window. However, he was observed to eat his breakfast cereal deftly and to walk to the bathroom by himself.

A computed tomography (CT) scan revealed an old left parietal infarct, which was believed to play an insignificant role in the present clinical picture. The doctors' consensus was that the patient's vision was normal and that he was most likely suffering from an acute conversion disorder. The depression, the stressful home situation he was facing, the seeming *la belle indifférence*, the unchanged results of physical examination—all were taken to support the diagnosis of conversion disorder, and the patient was duly tranferred to the psychiatry unit.

The psychiatrists decided to repeat the neurologic consult, and this time they were unable to elicit a blink reflex or optokinetic response. Another CT scan was ordered and this one revealed a fresh right temporoparietal infarct, in addition to the old left parietal lesion. On further testing, visual evoked responses were found to be abnormal bilaterally, and Balint's syndrome was finally diagnosed.

Palinacousis was described by Jacobs and colleagues (1973) as a persistent or recurring auditory illusion in which environmentally produced sounds persist for a variable length of time after the initial stimulus has ended. The source may be a voice, music, or random noises, and the sensation is often indistinguishable from the original stimulus. This relatively rare disorder may be associated with seizure activity and may be differentiated from the auditory hallucinations of psychotic illness by the fact that palinacoustic events typically occur as exact replicas or fragments of the original sound. The sounds are generally neutral in content, and they characteristically occur in the absence of other psychiatric symptoms.

Malone and Leiman (1983) reported the case of Ms. A, who at age seventy-five began "hearing voices." She described them as consisting variably of her own voice, voices of people around her, or noises from the television or radio. She heard each voice or noise exactly as if it were being repeated to her in the room. The sensation would persist until another external sound occurred, at which time the new word, phrase, or noise would be repeated. Occasionally, this repetitive auditory sensation would eventually die away, but often it went on for long periods of time and disturbed her sleep. She described the voices or noises as seeming always to come from somewhere in the room, and she was surprised that other people failed to hear them. The content was always an exact reproduction of the external auditory event and never contained material of a self-referential or persecutory nature, as in many cases of psychotic hallucination.

Seven months after the symptoms began, Ms. A was hospitalized because of recurrent dizziness, vertigo, and nausea. The voices persisted. A neurologist diagnosed dysfunction of the vestibular system, a "mild organic brain syndrome," and palinacousis. A CT scan showed possible signs of degenerative change, although otherwise the results were within normal limits. Electroencephalogram (EEG) revealed some generalized slowing, with a sharp wave focus in the left temporal region, an indication of seizure activity. Accordingly, Ms. A was put on anticonvulsant medication, and on the thirteenth day she reported that the voices had stopped but that she did still hear occasional "whooshing" noises. By the eighteenth day she was asymptomatic, and a repeat EEG revealed some residual abnormality, this time without the left temporal sharp waves.

In the sense of vision, perception of an object or scene normally requires intact functioning of the primary visual cortex in the occipital lobe for the identification of the raw sensory parameters of that object or scene, as well as of the secondary visual cortex and higher order association areas for the interpretation of that percept as a meaningful object or scene. Accordingly, destruction of primary visual cortex usually produces *cortical blindness*, a loss of all visual sensation in the part of the visual field served by the damaged area of cortex.

Studies have shown that some subjects can locate a visual stimulus in space even when primary visual cortex in the occipital lobe has been damaged, or at least when stimuli are presented in the region of the visual field that is assumed to be blind according to conventional perimetric field examination (Poppel et al., 1973; Weiskrantz et al., 1974). The patient may swear that he is unable to see anything in the affected part of the visual field, but when induced by the examiner to "guess" the position of randomly presented stimuli, he is correct more often than chance would predict. In this so-called *blindsight*, there seems to be a dissociation between the brain mechanisms involved in localizing the position of a stimulus in space and those involved in identifying what that stimulus actually is—or even being aware that one has "seen" it at all (Zihl & Von Cramon, 1979).

What about such a localization–recognition dissociation in senses other than vision? At least one instance of a tactual analogue of blindsight has been described by Palliard and colleagues (1983) in the case of a fifty-two-year-old right-handed woman who was referred to a French neurological hospital for headaches and reading difficulties. Evaluation discovered an arteriovenous malformation (AVM), an abnormal tangle of fragile and inefficient blood vessels in the brain that can act as a tumor-like mass and also tends to bleed easily. During an operation to remove the AVM, some residual thrombotic material escaped from the tip of the needle and eventually obstructed the left posterior parietal artery. This led to destruction of the left parietal area, which was clearly visible on CT scan. A number of neuropsychological deficits resulted, most of which cleared up considerably in the ensuing weeks.

What did not disappear was an impairment in tactile sensibility— in touch, pressure, and pain—so severe that the patient could cut or burn herself without noticing it. Her face was affected to the point where she often forgot morsels of food between her right cheek and gums. Also affected was her leg: she twisted her ankle and missed steps going upstairs. However, she was able to distinguish hot from cold, and movement was essentially normal.

The most striking finding was a virtually total dissociation between localization and identification: despite this patient's inability to recognize or even detect any sense of pressure on her skin, she was able, to her own considerable surprise, to point approximately to where the stimulus was applied. Furthermore, she could discern gross differences in the size of objects manipulated by the affected hand, all the time insisting that she couldn't "feel" them. There was also evidence of improvement with practice: after several sessions of the localization test, she was able to localize stimuli more and more precisely—even though she was still unable to "consciously" identify having felt them.

In conceptualizing their case, the authors suggest that the preserved ability to localize may have been due to sparing of the *second somatosensory area*, or SSII (Woolsey et al., 1979). This represents a region on the medial surface of the cortex, outside the primary somatosensory area, that seems to be involved in more complex sensory processing than occurs in the primary sensory cortex. That is, the role of SSII may be as a bridge in the experiential chain beyond mere perceptual registration and iden-tification of a sensory stimulus. After the brain has analyzed the various sensory qualities of an object and determined what it is, SSII may then operate to evaluate how that information can be used in the present context to coordinate perception with action.

But if the intervening interpretive step is missing due to damage to primary and secondary sensory cortex, then the context-specificity function of SSII now operates intact but in a dissociated state: the brain knows how to *use* the information—that is, to localize—but not *what* that information actually is. We will return to consider SSII in more detail in a subsequent chapter when we deal with the neuropsychodynamic basis of hysterical conversion symptoms.

Disorders of Action and Volition

Marsden (1986) studied a series of patients with motor disorders whose very "hysterical"-looking presentations in both clinical phenomenology and supposed psychodynamic origin initially led to diagnoses of hysteria; these were only altered upon further medical investigation. Some rep-resentative cases follow, and the reader will note the startling similarities between these and some of the patients reported by Breuer and Freud.

A seven-year-old boy began to limp on the day he visited a severely disabled cousin. Hysteria was diagnosed, followed by many lengthy stays in psychiatric hospitals over the next ten years, until a revised diagnosis of generalized torsion dystonia, or dystonia musculorum deformans, was established. It turned out that the disabled cousin he had visited on that fateful day ten years earlier was similarly affected with the disease, as was one of his sisters.

A fifty-two-year-old man began to blink repetitively and then developed prolonged episodes in which his eyes would seem to force themselves shut against his will. Hysterical blepharospasm was diagnosed, and he became housebound over the next seven years, spending eighty percent of the day with his eyes closed. Surgical section of the upper branches of the facial nerve to denervate the orbicularis oculi muscles restored his vision to normal.

A forty-one-year-old opera singer began to falter on the high notes. Since spoken speech was normal, psychodynamically motivated hysterical self-sabotage of her singing career was presumed. Over the next ten years spoken speech itself became increasingly strained. She then began to experience severe, prolonged spasms of mouth opening, sufficiently violent on two occasions to cause spontaneous dislocation of the jaw. At this point, the diagnosis was revised to spasmodic dysphonia and oromandibular dystonia.

A twenty-two-year-old woman developed hour-long attacks of intense muscle spasms, accompanied by fear, sweating, and hyperventilation. Initially, she was sent to psychiatrists with the presumption of hysteria. Some six years after onset she fractured her femur in one such attack owing to the intensity of the muscle spasms. Her diagnosis was revised to progressive fluctuating muscular rigidity, also known as the "stiff-man syndrome."

A twenty-one-year-old medical student complained of sudden attacks in which his legs and arms would writhe uncontrollably for up to five minutes—sometimes on one side, sometimes on both—without loss of consciousness. These were thought to be hysterical pseudoseizures, perhaps a variant of the polysymptomatic "medical student's syndrome," until it was discovered that all such episodes were preceded by sudden movement, suggesting a diagnosis of paroxysmal kinesigenic dyskinesia. His attacks were abolished by treatment with anticonvulsants.

A fifty-three-year-old career seaman complained that every time he stood up his legs would shake, which was particularly distressing when he was called upon to do public speaking. Despite being a resolute Navy man with a long record of both wartime and peacetime achievements, his symptoms were dismissed as hysterical until he was discovered to be suffering from primary orthostatic tremor, a syndrome only first described in 1984.

Tics, twitches, tremors, and motor spasms dot the accounts of Breuer and Freud's cases; one thinks, for example, of Anna O's writhings or Frau

Emmy's clacking and stammering. Although, of course, unaware of the more recently identified motor syndromes, Freud must have been aware of *tic disorders* as a general syndromic class, since the neurologists of his day had already begun to take account of these phenomena by the time Freud began his medical practice.

Itard, in 1825, presented a case of a French noblewoman who suffered from multiple tics, including the explosive utterance of shrieks, "senseless" words, and curses. Sixty years later, Gilles de la Tourette (1885) reported nine cases of what appeared to be the same syndrome, thereby achieving eponymous clinical immortality. In his report, Gilles de la Tourette carefully described the onset and progression of symptoms and introduced the term *coprolalia* to refer to the utterance of obscenities.

More recently, Gilles de la Tourette's syndrome—or now simply *Tourette syndrome*—has become one of the more well-known neurologic entities. Neurologists define it as a lifelong condition with onset between two and fifteen years of age and characterized by multiple involuntary motor tics. Although the precise etiology is not yet fully understood— for many years it was considered a classic form of psychogenic syn-drome—the presence of neurological "soft signs," nonspecific EEG ab-normalities, and subtle findings of impairment on neuropsychological testing in more than half of all patients favors an underlying organic origin. Vocal tics are essential for the diagnosis, and coprolalia occurs in some sixty percent of cases, but other abnormalities of speech and phonation are not typically found.

Spastic, or *spasmodic, dysphonia*, more recently described, is an idiopathic condition in which the voice becomes hoarse, strained, tight, and oc-casionally tremulous (Lang & Marsden, 1983). It has been suggested that this is a form of focal dystonia involving the muscles of the larynx and usually leading to hyperadduction, or squeezing together, of the vocal cords. A minority of patients suffer from abduction (pulling apart) vocal cord spasms, distinguishing features being intermittent aphonia, breathy phonation, and marked breathlessness with sudden drops in pitch. This disorder is often associated with other forms of focal and generalized *dystonias*, which are involuntary abnormal postural movements that may affect various parts of the body and are believed to be related to disorders of the extrapyramidal motor system, the brain network that deals with postural, background, and automatic movements.

Shapiro and Shapiro (1977) reported a dystonic variant of Tourette syndrome with features partially resembling blepharospasm, torticollis, and writer's cramp. More recently, Lang and Marsden (1983) described a patient with Tourette syndrome who developed spasmodic dysphonia while being treated with haloperidol, a condition that persisted for fifteen months despite cessation of the drug. The case involved a twenty-two-year-old man who had been born after an uneventful pregnancy and delivery. He had had some early swallowing difficulties and speech delay, but both of these functions normalized during his childhood. At age six he developed recurrent throat noises; later, these were accompanied by a variety of focal and generalized motor tics. At age thirteen, Tourette syndrome was diagnosed, and he was given haloperidol (Haldol), an antidopaminergic medication.

By age nineteen his speech had become strained and quiet, at times disappearing altogether, and his mouth and throat would become "tense" while speaking. Examination disclosed classic features of spasmodic dysphonia with a hoarse, strained voice of low volume and high pitch, accompanied by tensing of the jaw and larynx during phonation. At this point, the haloperidol was stopped, but nine drug-free months later, occasional grunting was still noted. Fifteen months later, the patient said that he felt better, but his voice appeared unchanged, still hoarse and strained, and his jaw and larynx were still tense; this was now accompanied by occasional tics of the right shoulder.

According to Frankel and Cummings (1984), blepharospasm and gaze abnormalities are common manifestations of extrapyramidal movement disorders such as Huntington's chorea, idiopathic basal ganglia calcification, dystonia musculorum deformans, Meige's disease, progressive supranuclear palsy, Sydenham's chorea, and Wilson's disease. In addition, the eye movement abnormalities of some Tourette patients would suggest an anatomic and functional link to these disorders. In their series, the authors found neuro-ophthalmic symptoms in twenty-nine of their Tourette cases. Twenty-eight of these had blepharospasm, and nineteen had other eye tics that included forced staring and involuntary gaze deviation, similar to the neuro-ophthalmic abnormalities found in known disorders of the basal ganglia, the group of brain structures involved in the involuntary, supportive, postural, and motivational aspects of movement (part of the extrapyramidal motor system mentioned earlier).

Frankel and Cummings observed two types of involuntary gaze disturbance in the Tourette cases they studied. The first type included forced gaze deviation occurring as part of complex oculogyric tics and eye rolling that were similar to, but less sustained than, the oculogyric crises of postencephalitic Parkinson's disease or the forced gaze deviations of acute dystonic reactions induced by neuroleptic drugs. The second type of gaze disturbance consisted of involuntary staring that had a forced, compulsive quality to it and that, when mistaken for willful voyeurism, often got the victim into trouble. Similar "compulsory" motor acts are common in postencephalitic parkinsonism and the parkinsonian state that occurs with manganese poisoning.

Up to now we have been concerned mainly with organic neurologic disorders that reproduce some of the "classic" symptoms of hysteria, as described by Breuer and Freud. The other side of the coin—"organic"-

looking symptoms with no confirming neuropathological signs—can be seen in a case presented by David and Bone (1985). Margaret, an eighteen-year-old woman, had begun to experience episodes of altered consciousness five years earlier, at age thirteen. Observers witnessed a generalized, or grand mal, seizure that began with twitching around the mouth and spread to involve all four limbs in a tonic–clonic fashion. An EEG showed sharp-wave and occasional spike-and-slow-wave activity, independently and bisynchronously, and a diagnosis of idiopathic epilepsy was made.

At age seventeen Margaret was assessed by ambulatory EEG monitoring, which indicated that some attacks were feigned. Margaret had "fits" at a rate of about once a month while receiving anticonvulsant medication until at age eighteen, after failing to take her medication appropriately, she was admitted to the hospital in status epilepticus, a state of continual seizures. She was having generalized convulsions, was in a confusional state, and developed what looked like a flaccid paralytic quadriplegia, usually indicative of severe nervous system dysfunction.

The puzzling piece to this picture, however, was that her neurologic exam was essentially normal. Although Margaret was "paralyzed" by day, a concealed video camera recorded normal coordinated movements during sleep. During light sleep Margaret scratched the side of her head, pulled up the sheets, and turned over; the authors speculate that perhaps some "inhibitory influence" was switched off during reduced "cerebral vigilance"—compare the types of interpretations offered by Breuer and Freud. A senior psychiatrist examined Margaret and found no evidence of psychopathology but commented on her "facile" attitude. In response to this examination, Margaret suddenly raised her arms in a jerky, uncontrolled way. She was then confronted with the fact that she could move during sleep, but this seemed to have little effect on her behavior or attitude. She was not shown the video.

Four months after first being admitted to the hospital, Margaret still had only gross arm movement and slight movement in the toes. Fits occurred monthly, and on one occasion she flung herself out of bed. "Treatment" programs consisting of admixtures of encouragement, reward, cajolery, intimidation, and other ploys were only slowly and modestly successful. Reminiscent of Breuer and Freud's efforts, abreactive therapy provided some diminution of the symptoms, but the effects were temporary. Margaret could be quite manipulative and eventually persuaded her parents—who, at any rate, disapproved of the authors' "psychological" treatment methods—to take her home.

Margaret was the youngest of three children from a lower-middle-class Roman Catholic family. Her father was an undertaker, a rigid, uncommunicative man, and her mother an affectionate, if overprotective, homemaker. Before Margaret's present illness, her parents had separated for a short time. Margaret had recently achieved her ambition to be a nurse, but this had been an uphill struggle: because of her epilepsy, she had applied to many colleges before being accepted to a program. However, she performed well in examinations and was liked by her colleagues and teachers. At age eighteen, she was sexually inexperienced, solitary, and studious—in fact, very much like Anna O. There was no family history of epilepsy or psychiatric illness, no "neuropathic heredity," to use Breuer and Freud's term.

In conceptualizing their case, David and Bone (1985) note that Margaret moved her arms and legs during sleep, under the influence of drugs, and in the course of an epileptic fit, yet no action was carried out consciously. They therefore raise the obvious question: was the paralysis due to a problem situated in the "unconscious"? Or was the volitional, "conscious" part of the brain or mind somehow unable to carry out her wishes?

With regard to hysteria itself, the authors point out that true epilepsy is well recognized as a predisposing factor in the development of pseudoseizures (Ramani et al., 1980), as well as in other conversion reactions (Merskey & Trimble, 1979). They thus offer the following psychodynamic interpretation: Margaret was seeking to reunite her parents by focusing their attention on her illness rather than on their own difficulties. The mode of presentation, from the extreme muscular activity of the "convulsion" to total paralysis, could be seen as involving two aspects of the same process.

The authors also raise some philosophical issues: psychiatry, neurology, and philosophy, they note, seem to converge around the syndrome of epilepsy, where matters of volition and responsibility still abound. Questions arise when "unacceptable" behavior occurs in a setting of altered consciousness—as, we may note, in the case of Anna O. Such state-dependent behavior applies to Margaret's case as well, but here the abnormality, paralysis, existed only in clear consciousness and yet apparently was by no means freely willed. The authors therefore choose to postulate determinism at another level, hypothesizing a split between the "doing" and the "willing" parts of the brain. "Hysteria appears to be a lesion of the will" (David & Bone, 1985, p. 439), they say, adding that

> hysteria lies at the crux of the mind–body problem. Neurologists turn to philosophy seeking answers only to realize that beneath their question lies another, infinitely more profound. To explain hysterical paralysis (even the word suggests a split), we must first explain all voluntary movement, free will, volition, internal mental events, and so on: in effect, the mind–body problem. (p. 439)

In so saying, David and Bone in fact come close to the guiding thesis of this book: the "abnormal" phenomena seen in psychopathological states are merely extensions of the normal range of human experience that can be affected by permanent or transient alterations in brain functioning. These perturbations appear in boldest relief usually only in cases of extensive structural damage to the brain but may sometimes also occur—as in the present case—when the person's own neuropsychodynamic processes replicate these exaggerated brain states in the form of "hysterical" symptoms.

Disorders of Personal Recognition

As we have seen, part of Anna O's problem involved an inability to identify previously familiar people; indeed, apparently only Breuer's visage was immune to this peculiar perceptual deficit. Could organic factors produce such a syndrome of impaired interpersonal recognition that might, in turn, be replicated neuropsychodynamically in hysteria?

In 1923 Capgras and Reboul-Lachaux reported the case of a fifty-three-year-old woman who displayed what they called *l'illusion des sosies*, a delusional belief that the important people in her life—husband, children, neighbors, police, even herself—had been replaced by identical doubles as part of a plot to steal her inheritance. According to Berson (1983) and Wilcox and Waziri (1983), the clinical definition of *Capgras syndrome* requires the delusional belief that close relatives or familiar individuals, sometimes the patient him/herself, have been replaced by imposters who are nevertheless strikingly precise replicas of the "originals." The syndrome may be accompanied by psychotic symptoms, such as auditory hallucinations, delusions of persecution, ideas of reference, and paranoia; approximately half of the Capgras cases in Merrin and Silberfarb's (1976) series received a diagnosis of schizophrenia.

Explanations for this syndrome have ranged from the psychodynamic to the neurologic. Berson (1983) suggests that the Capgras phenomenon represents a form of pathological splitting in which the internalized object representations are divided into "good," consciously acknowledged, and "bad," unconscious, images. These images persist until a significant interpersonal event triggers an important emotional change, whereupon previously repressed feelings enter awareness, the "bad" image surfaces, and the patient is faced with conflict over incompatible good and bad images of the same person. Since the "real" person is so good, this "bad" person who stands before the patient must be an imposter, and so the Capgras patient asserts that one or more familiar people have been replaced by doubles. We may note that such replacement fantasies seem to have persisted in the popular mind-set throughout the ages, as evidenced by tales of demonic possession, zombie legends, and, in our own day, science fiction films and tabloid reportage dealing with extraterrestrial "mind invaders" and "body snatchers."

While some authors stress the psychodynamic aspects of the Capgras phenomenon, there is a growing body of literature examining the possible brain mechanisms involved. Hayman and Abrams (1977) have suggested that Capgras symptoms stem from dysfunction in the parietal lobes, mainly because of the relationship between parietal damage and the syndrome of *prosopagnosia*, the inability to recognize faces, particularly once-familiar faces. Theories vary as to the precise neurocognitive mechanisms of this disorder, with some authorities (Benton & Van Allen, 1972) attributing it to a selective memory disorder for faces while others (Whitely & Warrington, 1977) see it more as an impairment of visuoperceptual classification.

It may be that no single deficit uniformly underlies all cases of prosopagnosia but that some cases involve a memory disorder, others a problem in perceptual classification, and still others both (and perhaps other) kinds of impairment (Benton, 1980; Malone et al., 1982). Neuropsychological assessment findings of patients with prosopagnosia are consistent with at least some kind of associated visuospatial impairment, since these patients often show problems in visuoconstructive ability and visual memory (Malone et al., 1982; Benton & Van Allen, 1972; Kay & Levin, 1982), as well as deficits in the recognition of famous faces (Benton & Van Allen, 1972). Nearly all patients with prosopagnosia have been found to have left upper quadrant visual field defects (Meadows, 1974), and analyses of postmortem and CT scan data have consistently implicated lesions of the bilateral occipitotemporal areas, which are important for visuoperceptual memory (Damasio et al., 1982).

In addition to prosopagnosia, Capgras syndrome may also be related to the phenomenon of *reduplicative paramnesia*, first described by Pick in 1903 and generally considered to be a limited disturbance of memory wherein the patient believes that certain familiar places or persons are duplicates of their originals. It has been suggested (Alexander et al., 1979; Benson et al., 1976) that the organic basis for reduplicative paramnesia is related to pathology of the right hemisphere and frontal lobe structures.

Wilcox and Waziri (1983) described the case of a thirty-two-year-old right-handed married woman from a rural area who had no history of brain disease but had several psychiatric hospitalizations for paranoid delusions over the previous ten years. She came to clinical attention this time by claiming that she and her husband were having problems at home and that he was accordingly planning to do her in, his murderous intent being the reason she now sought sanctuary at the hospital. She also believed that people were poisoning her food and that her parents had been killed in an accident and had been replaced by imposters. She claimed, however, that she had learned to differentiate the imposters from her real parents by noting subtle changes in gesture and expression. She showed no other apparent perceptual problems on the ward and seemed to get along well with both patients and staff.

On mental status examination the patient's speech was logical and goal-oriented, she was not hallucinatory or otherwise overtly psychotic, and her affect was somewhat flat but generally appropriate. Her memory appeared intact, and arithmetic calculation skills were good. However, she did show deficits in visuospatial functioning, as evidenced by her defective copies of drawings. More extensive neuropsychological assessment was then ordered. The results indicated that overall IQ was in the borderline range. Verbal functions appeared within normal limits, but visuospatial reasoning, visual perception and integration, and visuospatial memory were all impaired. Orientation for time was intact, but line orientation, facial recognition, and right–left discrimination were impaired.

The neuropsychological report cited in Wilcox and Waziri's (1983) case study attributed the aforementioned findings to "diffuse organic cerebral dysfunction." However, my own analysis of their test data suggests that these results might represent a pattern of selective right hemisphere impairment, as evidenced by significantly poorer visuospatial intellectual functioning and impaired visuospatial memory and reasoning in the presence of intact verbal functioning in these modalities.

Indeed, in their own conceptualization of this case the authors point out that patients with predominantly right parietal lobe lesions are liable to develop an impairment in their ability to recognize familiar faces, that is, prosopagnosia (Hecaen & Angelergues, 1962). Reduplicative paramnesia has also been associated with lesions of the right hemisphere and frontal lobe structures. Since the right hemisphere is involved in the analysis of visuospatial material, disturbances in this hemisphere may lead to misperceptions of faces. In a nonpsychotic patient these deficits will most likely be recognized and reported without delusional content whereas a less reality-oriented or psychotic patient might embellish the perceptual disorder with delusional ideas or beliefs.

Morrison and Tarter (1984) report the case of a thirty-seven-year-old right-handed woman with a sixteen-year history of psychiatric disturbance and a recent diagnosis of chronic paranoid schizophrenia. Upon admission she appeared unkempt and dirty and spoke in a very vague manner, claiming that her parents had died and were replaced by doubles who had changed their names to that of their own parents. These doubles were reportedly now threatening her and, as a result, she feared for her safety.

Here, too, psychological and neuropsychological testing was carried out. Personality assessment by means of the Minnesota Multiphasic Personality Inventory (MMPI) showed no evidence of florid psychosis or other severe psychiatric disorder, although there were indications of depression and paranoid symptomatology. Her formal IQ score fell in the borderline range, but a more culture-fair form of assessment found her intellect to be toward the average range.

Neuropsychological assessment showed marked deficits in planning and visuomotor sequencing. On language testing, fluency of verbal output was slow and comprehension was impaired, but confrontation naming, responsive naming, simple paragraph reading, and sentence writing were all intact. Memory functions were quite poor, and the patient's performance on perceptuomotor and visuospatial tests varied according to the complexity of the task. Where the test required spatial integration, her performance was substantially impaired. Motor functions were mildly slowed and perceptuomotor speed was also somewhat reduced, although basic auditory and visual capacities were unimpaired. Of particular interest is the fact that the patient's performance on a facial recognition test was in the organically impaired range.

According to Morrison and Tarter (1984), these neuropsychological findings indicate a frontotemporal pattern of cerebral dysfunction. The frontal region of the brain, the authors point out, is particularly responsible for subserving the so-called executive functions of planning, evaluation of the situation, self-regulation, and implementation of behavior programs. Furthermore, the frontotemporal area subserves oral language fluency, comprehension, memory, sequencing, and attention. In contrast, spelling, reading, perception, and spatial orientation—processes that are generally thought to be subserved by the more posterior parieto-temporo-occipital region—were found to be intact in this patient.

The authors acknowledge that whether the obtained neuropsychological impairments influence the development of the Capgras syndrome or are merely correlated features cannot be ascertained from the present data. The fact, however, that the personality profile was not grossly disturbed suggests that the observed cognitive deficits are not simply the product of psychotic disorganization but, rather, appear to be part of a relatively stable dispositional pattern of impairment that underlies the delusion.

The authors suggest that in a person already prone to paranoid thinking, the superimposed neuropsychological deficits would result in the adoption of a delusional syndrome that is determined by the specific dimensions of the cognitive impairment, which in this case involves memory, spatial analysis, and evaluative capacities. The understandably negative response of a familiar person to being regarded as a stranger creates a vicious cycle that further ferments the Capgras delusion.

A third case of Capgras syndrome, involving an etiology that appears unequivocally organic, comes from Bouckoms and colleagues (1986). Mrs. B was a sixty-six-year-old right-handed high school graduate, a widowed housewife and mother of two daughters, one of whom, Mary, lived with her. One day, while cleaning her car, Mrs. B suddenly experienced a crashing headache and telephoned Mary for help. Mary rushed home to find her mother holding her head and sweating, her face flushed. Mrs. B was admitted to the hospital in a drowsy but arousable state. A CT scan confirmed that Mrs. B had suffered a stroke with bleeding into the brain and a resulting rise in intracranial pressure, the result of a hemorrhage from a long-standing small right middle cerebral artery aneurysm. The patient underwent a ventriculovenous shunt and simultaneous clipping of the aneurysm, and she was discharged with expectations of a good recovery.

Mary had taken a leave of absence from work of several months to care for her mother. A few days after arriving home, Mrs. B complained that a younger girl masquerading as her daughter Mary had come into the house, had stayed for dinner, but then had been sent away. She could tell the imposter was not Mary by the difference in voice, although the physical resemblance to her "real" daughter was remarkable. At one moment she would speak to Mary and tell her about the new "sister" who looked almost exactly like her, and at another moment she would actually believe that Mary was the imposter.

When questioned, Mrs. B would try to separate the two Marys by the tone of their voices, their height, or the color of their hair, but none of these differences were identified as stable distinctions. The imposter was always seen within the body of Mary, never as a separate visual hallucination. This confusion of identities remained limited to the daughter with whom she lived; otherwise, she seemed to maintain good reality contact with her own identity, as well as with that of other people.

Neuropsychological assessment suggested significant impairment in frontal lobe functions, particularly problems in establishing, maintaining, and shifting conceptual sets; a tendency to perseverate; and decreased verbal fluency. Mrs. B's ability to plan and reason out the logical significance of details was below expectation for someone her age, and she was generally very concrete in her thinking. Interestingly, she showed a tendency to draw inappropriate conclusions to account for the details she found confusing, and she was unable to keep information in the correct temporal sequence; that is, although she could remember certain facts, she recalled them out of context and within a jumbled time frame. For example, in drawing she took one design and incorporated it into her recollection of a previous design; nevertheless, her constructional abilities as a whole were relatively well preserved, and there was only mild overall impairment in verbal and visuospatial memory and in language functions.

Thus, Mrs. B's main problems were concreteness and inflexibility in thinking, perseveration, and impairment of conceptual reasoning—all deficits associated with frontal lobe dysfunction. The end result was seen clinically as a difficulty in organizing available information in a meaningful emotional and conceptual context. Over the next year there was gradual abatement in Mrs. B's delusional thinking. The imposter belief, while still present, had ceased to preoccupy her. A CT scan one year after the surgery demonstrated some ventricular dilatation and asymmetry, with the right frontal horn being larger than the left, suggesting possible loss of neural tissue in the right frontal lobe.

For Bouckoms and colleagues (1986), their case demonstrates that the specific delusional belief of Capgras syndrome may result from right frontal hemispheric pathology, at least in the context of more diffuse cognitive impairment. Mrs. B showed no reduplicative paramnesia or prosopagnosia, and there were no specific parietal lobe signs. Her sensorium was alert and clear, ruling out a generalized state of delirium, and there was no evidence of psychosis, either currently or by history.

Although the phenomenology of this Capgras case can be understood on a neuropsychological basis without having to invoke any functional, or psychogenic, *cause*, the authors nevertheless attempt to put things in a psychodynamic framework with respect to the *expression* of the neuro-psychopathology. They hypothesize that Mrs. B experienced a sense of loss over something very important to her, in this case the very integrity of her own cognitive functioning. Loss of clear thinking is a major stress to anyone, particularly an elderly person, and Mrs. B identified the loss with something else she knew was important to her, namely, her daughter Mary. The daughter was chosen because, in the context of the forced regression imposed by the illness, there was ambivalence toward the very person on whom she was forced to depend. In other words, the loss was *displaced*, a mechanism that is different from dissociation, projection, splitting, paranoia, and autistic isolation, as seen in typical cases of functional psychosis.

The lesson from cases like Mrs. B's, say the authors, is that "organic brain disorders are subject to the same heterogeneity of expression as functional psychotic syndromes" (Bouckoms et al., 1986, p. 487). I would go further to add that in many cases of brain damage-induced changes in thought, feeling, and behavior, organicity provides the mechanism while psychology shapes the content; in still other cases, however, organicity may determine the content as well. We will return to this theme several times throughout this book.

Disorders of Language

In prosopagnosia, we have seen, patients lose the ability to recognize familiar faces, such as those of close friends, family members, and famous personalities, whereas their ability to discriminate between two unfamiliar faces may remain intact. While such a dissociation between facial recognition and facial discrimination has become well known in neuropsychology, an equivalent impairment of voice recognition and discrimination has only recently been reported by Van Lacker and colleagues (1988), a syndrome they term *phonagnosia*.

The investigators identified five patients with injuries to the right parietal region of the brain. Using familiar and unfamiliar voices as stimuli, they found a marked difference between the ability to recognize familiar voices and the ability to discriminate between unfamiliar voices, suggesting that these abilities represent separate neuropsychological functions and can be differentially affected by cerebral injuries to different parts of the brain. It appears from this study that recognition of familiar voices is dependent on the right lateral parietal area whereas discrimination of unfamiliar voices seems to be affected by temporal lobe lesions of either hemisphere. Such a dissociation of language functions might well be taken as evidence of hysteria.

Recall Anna O's curious peregrinations among different languages in speaking, reading, and writing. By Freud's day it was accepted as part of clinical aphasiology and neurolinguistics that if someone knows more than one language, brain damage will affect the later-learned or less familiar language to a greater degree than the native tongue. This later came to be known as *Ribot's law*, after the French neurologist who in 1883 first formulated the "rule of primacy" with respect to memory, including memory of languages. According to this rule, any damage to memory functioning will affect the oldest material less than that which has been acquired later. Actually, it was Pitres (1895) who applied this principle specifically to the recovery from aphasia seen in polyglots. Such a multilingual patient, said Pitres, usually first regains comprehension of his native tongue, next his ability to speak it, and, finally, the ability to comprehend and then speak other languages he has acquired. It is this "last hired, first fired" model of language recovery that has come to be associated with Ribot's law.

In clinical reality, Ribot's law has proven to be not much of a law at all. In many cases of aphasia in bilinguals or multilinguals, the patient recovers one language earlier than another—but not necessarily the first-learned one. In some patients, one language recovers, but the others never do while still other patients enjoy temporary recovery of one language only to have it regress as another takes its place. And in a few cases the same patient shows a different type of aphasic syndrome in each of the different languages (Albert & Obler, 1975; Obler et al., 1975).

Apropos of some of the language phenomena that Breuer and Freud observed in their hysteria cases, de Zulueta (1984) provides an intriguing review of the psychodynamics and neuropsychology of bilingualism. Recall of "lost" languages under hypnosis seems to have been a rarely reported clinical phenomenon since Breuer and Freud, but de Zulueta has discovered two relatively recent reports of successful recovery, under hypnotic age-regression, of an early language that was presumed by the subjects themselves to have been forgotten.

The first case, reported by As (1963), concerns an eighteen-year-old student who had spoken Swedish until he was five years old, when his family moved to the United States. With the mother's remarriage, English became the predominant language at home, and after the student reached six years of age, Finnish was the only second language spoken in the house. The experimenter composed a series of questions in Swedish applicable to a five-year-old. He found that before being hypnotized, the student understood six out of fifty-six questions and partly understood five. After five sessions of training in hypnotic age regression, he was able to answer twenty-five questions correctly and did not understand twenty-six.

Fromm (1970) described the case of a twenty-six-year-old Japanese-American man born in the United States who, as an adult, knew no Japanese. When hypnotically age-regressed below the age of four, he unexpectedly and spontaneously spoke in Japanese; he only spoke English when age-regressed above four years old. After the hypnotic session the patient could not completely understand the tape made of his Japanese conversation. He recalled, however, that his lips had moved in "funny shapes," and that his mouth and other muscles of speech seemed to move without his volition. The experimenter only then discovered that when the patient was a few months old, the family had been sent to a World War II relocation camp, where mostly Japanese was spoken, although his parents would also talk some English to him. Back home after the war, the child had trouble communicating with the local English-speaking children, so his parents stopped talking to him in Japanese. From then on, English became the only language he spoke. In therapy, the patient gradually recovered his lost Japanese and the posthypnotic amnesia disappeared.

Aside from hypnosis, de Zulueta (1984) also brings to light a little-known literature on the relationship of bilingualism to psychoanalysis and psychotherapy. Buxbaum (1949) psychoanalyzed two women who had left Germany during their adolescence to live in the United States. They were fluent in English and generally refused to speak in German. However, during their psychoanalytic therapy they recalled childhood memories only when they were induced to speak in German.

Greenson (1950) reported a similar case in which English was the second language of a German-born female patient. When the analyst switched to using German in the treatment, he observed a marked facilitation of the patient's recollection of childhood memories intimately linked to her mother. The patient also reported that she experienced herself as having two different identities in the two languages. Similarly, Ruiz (1976) noted how, in group therapy, the speaking of two languages in bilingual patients appeared to bring out different personality traits in the speakers, and Carlson (1979), describing the psychotherapeutic treatment of three bilingual cases in their primary language—again German—emphasized how this greatly aided the therapeutic process.

Following Salamy (1978), de Zulueta (1984) proffers the neuropsychological hypothesis that in early development, progressive myelination of the corpus callosum and anterior commissure enables an increasingly efficient callosal transmission. According to this view, there is no evidence of commissural transmission before the age of three and a half years old, and its full maturation takes place only at about ten years of age or later. This implies that in the first three and a half years of life, children have "split brains" analogous to those of commissurotomy patients but, of course, at an earlier developmental stage. Since basic language is already established prior to the onset of commissural transmission, this type of interhemispheric separation might provide a basis for the dissociative phenomena seen in hypnotic states. Carrying the Salamy–de Zulueta argument further, we can speculate that such functional disconnection phenomena—*intra*hemispheric, as well as cross-callosal—might provide a basis for the many "hysterical" symptoms observed clinically.

As subsequent chapters will show, hemispheric hypotheses in one form or another have been proposed to explain virtually all psychoanalytic phenomena—dreaming, repression, the unconscious—with variable degrees of success. For now, however, we continue to focus on hysteria, and having discussed the neuropsychological analogues that might help explain some of its manifest phenomenology, we now turn to a consideration of the brain dynamics that may be involved in its etiology and expression.

CHAPTER 4

Hysteria: The "Freudian" Theories

Among the first neuropsychodynamic theories of hysteria were those of Freud himself. In this chapter we look at his ideas about the brain's role in the development of hysterical conversion symptoms, and in the following chapters we will see how a number of more modern conceptions compare in both quality and scope.

The Comparative Study

In 1893, two years before *Studies on Hysteria* appeared, Freud wrote a theoretical paper entitled *Some Points for a Comparative Study of Organic and Hysterical Motor Paralyses*. Although less well known than the Breuer and Freud tract, this prior exposition reflects the basic neuropsychodynamic orientation that colored Freud's conception of nervous system functioning—that defined the model of Freud's brain—and that is in line with the neuropsychodynamic approach of the present book.

In an earlier work on the aphasias, which we will examine in more detail in a Chapter 13, Freud tried to account for the differences between disturbances of sensorimotor function due to injury of the spinal cord and impairment caused by damage to the cerebral cortex. In the case of spinal innervation, said Freud, there is a more or less direct correspondence between points in the body periphery—the sense organs and muscles— and the cell groups in the spinal cord that are either the terminations of the nerve fibers (in the case of sensation) or their origin (for motor functions). This accounts for the facility and regularity with which clinical localization of pathology within the spinal cord can be determined, based on an analysis of the particular pattern of anesthesia and/or paralysis. Indeed, long before the age of CT scans and evoked potentials, adept

45

neurologists were able to quite precisely localize sensorimotor pathology using only a careful clinical examination of the patient and their own knowledge of functional neuroanatomy; Freud himself apparently was quite skilled at this kind of neurodiagnostic localization.

But no such neat point-for-point connectivity exists between the neurons of the spinal cord and their eventual termini in the cerebral cortex. Here, Freud argued in the *Comparative Study*, the principle of convergence and divergence rules. That is, a single cortical locus may receive converging information from a number of spinal tracts representing many points at the sensory periphery, or, alternatively, a single muscle group at the motor periphery may be represented at numerous points of origin within the cortex. Freud, following the British neurologist John Hughlings Jackson, realized that, unlike a simple, spinally mediated sensation or reflexive movement, a more complex percept or motor act was in reality a dynamic "construction" involving multiple levels of the nervous system and different parts of the brain, not a static, punctate linking of outer and inner states.

In Freud's neurology, damage to the motor neurons in the grey matter of the spinal cord produced what he called a *projection paralysis*, that is, the muscle groups affected directly correspond to the damaged parts of the cord's grey matter. However, the complex arrangement of information between the cord and the cerebral cortex means that the impression at the cortical level is really more in the manner of a representation of the motor innervation at the periphery, rather than a direct projection. Accordingly, primary motor impairment produced by damage to the motor cortex of the brain was termed by Freud a *representation paralysis*.

Now hysterical paralysis, Freud went on to say, certainly bears little resemblance to projection paralysis because the symptoms rarely correspond to the spinal representation of the body musculature: adjacent muscle groups that should be affected by a true organic lesion of a particular segment of the cord are often miraculously spared while muscles remote from this hypothetical locus might be just as mysteriously impaired. Rather, hysterical paralysis is more akin to the representation paralyses that have their origin higher up in the nervous system and are thus more complexly organized—but, in the case of hysteria, with a special kind of "representation."

That is, hysterical paralysis typically shows two important characteristics that differentiate it from representation paralysis with a true organic basis. The first such characteristic Freud called *precise limitation*, that is, the tendency for a specific limb, part of a limb, or other segment of the body to be paralyzed while immediately surrounding areas operate perfectly normally. In true organic paralyses this almost never happens because the distribution of muscle groups within the body, and their innervations, do not delimit discrete regions.

For example, if the right hand is paralyzed by damage to the motor cortex, parts of the rest of the right arm and other regions of the right half of the body will probably also be affected to a greater or lesser extent, producing various degrees of weakness and loss of function on that side of the body and perhaps elsewhere. Both the way the cortical motor representation is organized and the patchy, irregular nature of most forms of organic pathology—stroke, tumor, missile wound, and so forth—make it virtually impossible that the paralysis would be sharply demarcated at the wrist or any other convenient body landmark.

The second characteristic of hysterical paralysis that Freud identified, *excessive intensity*, is related to the first. Here, whatever areas of the body are affected are affected totally, that is, are completely paralyzed. No gradations of impairment are seen, as is ordinarily the case with true organic paralyses. Thus, the hysterically paralyzed right hand becomes a totally inert blob while an organically impaired hand might show partial strength and mobility in a finger or two, or be capable of some movement in one direction or form but not in others.

Some of Freud's colleagues were tempted to ascribe hysterical symptoms, such as paralysis, to a "hysterical lesion," reasoning that if organic paralyses were produced by structural impairment of the brain in the appropriate locus, then hysterical paralyses must result from some less serious form of lesion that selectively affects the appropriate cortical motor representation. This might be something like edema or anemia that transiently and variably affect brain functioning but cause less permanent damage than, say, an ischemic stroke or severe blow to the head. Freud (1893) disagreed:

> I, on the contrary, assert that the lesion in hysterical paralyses must be completely independent of the anatomy of the nervous system, since in its paralyses and other manifestations hysteria behaves as though anatomy did not exist or as though it had no knowledge of it. (p. 169)

Freud preferred to use the term *functional*, or *dynamic*, *lesion* to mean an alteration in the state of excitability of neurons, rather than a destructive or degenerative change in the physical matrix of the brain itself, as might be caused by a stroke or head trauma—that is, a functional rather than a structural impairment. No lesion need operate in the organic–structural sense as long as something could produce a change in the neurodynamics involving the brain area related to the symptom. Freud was already familiar with the several classes of neurologic disturbances that could produce such transient, paroxysmal, functional changes in brain metabolism—drug states, epilepsy, and migraine, for example. Here he proposed one more such class of functional brain-altering influences: emotion-laden ideas.

The genesis of hysterical conversion symptoms, then, lies not in any special hysterical pattern of brain pathology or neuroinnervatory pathway interruption but, rather, asserted Freud, in "the sphere of the psychology of conceptions" (p. 171). Freud theorized that if the conception of a body part, say an arm, becomes imbued with a large quota of affect, it loses its accessibility to the free play of other associations. The arm will then be paralyzed in proportion to how completely the affect "fills up" or co-opts the neuroconceptual space. By the same token, if this affect is "drained away" from the conception of the arm, the innervatory mechanism is freed up and the paralysis recedes.

And where might this affect come from? Why, of course, from unconscious association with the memory of a traumatic event. That is why psychotherapeutic abreaction of such traumata frequently results in the amelioration of hysterical symptoms: as the affect is "drained away," the conceptual–associational "space" is freed to replenish itself with the normal ideational innervatory processes that govern the intact motor actions of the limb.

> This is the solution of the problem we have raised, for, in every case of hysterical paralysis, we find that the paralyzed organ or lost function is involved in a subconscious association which is provided with a large quota of affect and it can be shown that the arm is liberated as soon as this quota is wiped out. Accordingly, the conception of the arm exists in the material substratum, but it is not accessible to conscious associations and impulses because the whole of its associative affinity, so to say, is saturated in a subconscious association with the memory of the event, the trauma, which produced the paralysis. (Freud, 1893, p. 171)

Every experiential event, Freud explained, is provided with a certain quota of emotion, or affect, of which the ego divests itself either by an appropriate motor activity or by associative linkage to other psychological processes; that is, the emotional charge is either "blown off" in activity or reassimilated into the neuropsychical network. If, for some reason, the subject is unable or unwilling to rid himself of or diffuse the surplus affect in either of these two ways, the memory of the experience attains the status of a trauma and becomes the cause of permanent hysterical symptoms. This is especially true when the impression of the experience remains unconscious, so that the path to psychical divestiture is blocked. Thus, Freud (1893) argued that the lesion in hysterical paralyses consists in nothing other than the inaccessibility of the organ or function concerned to the associations of the unconscious ego; that this purely functional alteration (even the conception remaining unimpaired) is caused by the fixation of this conception in a subconscious association with the memory of the trauma; and that this conception does not become liberated and accessible so long as the quota of affect of the psychical trauma has not been eliminated by an adequate motor reaction or by conscious psychical activity. (p. 172)

It was this 1893 account of the genesis of hysterical motor paralyses that set the stage for Freud's later, more general theory of the origins of hysterical symptoms that appears in *Studies on Hysteria*. More specifically, some of the main points of the *Comparative Study* were incorporated into a separate paper, coauthored by Breuer and Freud, that also appeared in 1893 and two years later was used as the opening monograph to the *Studies*, a paper entitled *On the Mechanism of Hysterical Phenomena: Preliminary Communication*.

The *Preliminary Communication*

In the *Preliminary Communication* Breuer and Freud (1895) begin by affirming the relationship between hysterical symptoms and precipitating trauma—some in the quite remote past—and by adumbrating the variety of hysterical symptomatological phenomena that have their origin in this process.

The symptoms which we have been able to trace back to precipitating factors of this sort include neuralgias and anesthesias of various kinds, many of which had persisted for years, contractures and paralyses, hysterical attacks and epileptoid convulsions, which every observer regarded as true epilepsy, petit mal and disorders in the nature of tic, chronic vomiting and anorexia, carried to the pitch of rejection of all nourishment, various forms of disturbance of vision, constantly recurrent visual hallucinations, etc. The disproportion between the many years duration of the hysterical symptom and the single occurrence which provoked it is what we are accustomed invariably to find in traumatic neuroses. Quite frequently it is some event in childhood that sets up a more or less severe symptom which persists during the years that follow. (p. 4)

In other cases, say Breuer and Freud, the connection between a hysterical symptom and a psychical event "is not so simple" (p. 5). Rather, here the relationship between the precipitating cause and the pathological symptoms appears to be a *symbolic* one, similar to the relationship formed by healthy people in dreams. For example, a physical neuralgic limb pain might follow upon some excruciating mental pain, or vomiting might follow a feeling of moral revulsion. We have already seen the way in which several of Breuer's and Freud's patients, most notably Anna O and Frau Cäcilie, employed symbolic conversion of this type.

In still other cases, however, the genesis of the hysterical symptom cannot be easily discerned, since the connection to a particular prior event or the symbolic relationship is not immediately apparent. But Breuer and Freud (1895) now report a novel technique that they—principally Freud, in any systematic sense—devised and refined for the clinical exegesis of hysterical symptoms:

> We found, to our great surprise, that each individual hysterical symptom immediately and permanently disappeared when we had succeeded in bringing to light the memory of the event by which it was provoked and in arousing its accompanying affect, and when the patient had described that event in the greatest possible detail and had put the affect into words. Recollection without affect almost invariably produces no result. The psychical process which originally took place must be repeated as vividly as possible; it must be brought back to its status nascendi and then given verbal utterance. Where what we are dealing with are the phenomena involving stimuli (spasms, neuralgias and hallucinations), these reappear once again with the fullest intensity and then vanish forever. Failures of function, such as paralyses and anesthesias, vanish in the same way, though, of course, without the temporary intensification being discernible. (pp. 6–7)

These observations on the connection between buried past events and current hysterical symptoms are what moved Breuer and Freud to make their now-historic pronouncement that "hysterics suffer mainly from reminiscences" (p. 7). They concluded:

> It may therefore be said that the ideas which have become pathological have persisted with such freshness and affective strength because they have been denied the normal wearing-away processes by means of abreaction and reproduction in states of uninhibited association. (p. 11)

The key point made by Breuer and Freud about the effectiveness of this kind of abreaction in alleviating hysterical symptoms, about why a "talking cure" works, has to do with the role of *language* in the human psyche. Language, the authors assert, can serve as a substitute for action, action that would ordinarily be involved in discharging the emotional impact of a traumatic experience, as Freud pointed out in his *Comparative Study*. That is, by recounting verbally the traumatic event responsible for setting up the hysterical symptom, it becomes unnecessary to actually relive it; the abreaction is accomplished almost as effectively by the proxy of symbolic language.

> It will now be understood how it is that the psychotherapeutic procedure which we have described in these pages has a curative effect. It brings to an end the operative force of the idea which was not abreacted in the first instance, by allowing its strangulated affect to find a way out through speech; and it subjects it to associative correction by introducing it into normal consciousness (under light hypnosis) or by removing it through the physician's suggestion, as is done in somnambulism accompanied by amnesia. (Breuer & Freud, p. 17)

Next in the *Studies* follows the discussion of the individual cases that I presented in Chapter 2. Following their case history section, Breuer and Freud each continue to elaborate their own, mostly independent, theoretical formulations of hysteria.

Breuer's Theory of Hysteria

Breuer begins by asking the question, Are *all* hysterical phenomena ideogenic? That is, are they all the result of ideas, fears, affects, and wishes repressed from consciousness and emerging as somatic symptoms? As would many writers a century later, Breuer here endeavors to differentiate between symptoms that arise in the absence of physical pathology—that is, symptoms that are purely ideogenic—from those that have a true organic basis and are simply amplified and exacerbated by psychological factors.

For example, says Breuer, suppose someone sustains a slight injury to a joint and this later develops into a severe arthralgic syndrome. No doubt there is a psychical element here: the worried patient's relentless concentration on the injured part "intensifies the excitability of the nerve tracts concerned" (Breuer & Freud, 1895, p. 190). It can hardly be said that the joint pain is "ideogenic" but only that preoccupation with the effects of the original injury have magnified the patient's subjective distress all out of proportion.

But what defines a phenomenon as hysterical for Breuer is not that it is the result of "ideas" but that psychological factors play upon a particular constitutional trait, an abnormal excitability of the nervous system, which accounts for the misperception and amplification of otherwise physically insignificant symptoms. It is this nervous system instability, too, that makes hysterics particularly susceptible to suggestion. So, says Breuer, with every voluntary motor act it is the idea of the result to be achieved that initiates the relevant sequence of muscular contractions. If the idea that such muscular activity is impossible occurs in hysteria or is implanted by hypnotic suggestion, the movement is impeded: the limb is "ideogenically" paralyzed.

In the Breuerian scheme, then, those individuals prone to the development of hysterical symptoms have been constitutionally endowed with nervous systems of abnormally labile excitability. This permits a much greater range and intensity of influence by both internal, intrapsychic factors and external, suggestive ones. This hysterical predisposition, in turn, is simply one of a range of individual differences in predisposition to different forms of psychopathology, founded upon different patterns of nervous system excitability and resultant temperamental style.

> We are familiar with great individual variations which are found in this respect: the great differences between lively people and inert and lethargic ones, between those who "cannot sit still" and those who have an "innate gift for lounging on sofas" and between mentally agile minds and dull ones which can tolerate intellectual rest for an unlimited length of time. These differences, which make up a man's "natural temperament," are certainly based on profound differences in his nervous system—on the degree to which functionally quiescent cerebral elements liberate energy. (Breuer & Freud, 1895, pp. 197–198)

Breuer next considers the phenomenon of hysterical conversion. For most people, he asserts, such everyday visceral functions as are involved in regulating the circulation and digestion behave autonomously and remain out of awareness, "separated by strong resistances from the organs of ideation" (p. 203). This is as it should be; one does not want to have all one's conscious efforts taken up by directing bodily processes from moment to moment. However, people vary in terms of the degree to which their bodily functions are affected by their thoughts and feelings.

In certain particularly susceptible individuals, emotional states may become linked to bodily processes and influence them, much in the way that for most people fear or joy causes the heart to pound or the stomach to churn. But for most of us, when the acute situation has passed, such processes return to physiological baseline because we know that the cause of the emotional perturbation is now absent. And if we do not "know" this ourselves, we may be convinced or shown, as by visual proof, rational argument, or psychotherapeutic insight. However, if the ideational component becomes totally divorced from the affective component, the normal diffusion of the emotional state by association with ideas is now impossible. The emotion takes on a life of its own. And if the emotion has become linked to a bodily state or process, there is now no way for reason, persuasion, or insight to "break into" the cycle and alleviate the psycho-biological disturbance.

One of the prime characteristics of persons predisposed to develop conversion symptoms is, according to Breuer, the propensity to fall into *hypnoid states*. These are periods of diffuse consciousness and relaxed vigilance, similar to what is ordinarily experienced under hypnosis. Essentially, Breuer says, hypnoid states represent a form of spontaneously occurring autohypnosis in which affects may be introduced into a "habitual reverie." The emotions take advantage of the hypnoid states to slip into the psyche, unfettered by their normally accompanying ideational baggage, and thereby ensconce themselves firmly in the back seat of consciousness, from there to direct their mischief upon the body.

At this point, all this talk of "consciousness" and "the unconscious" seems to make Breuer uneasy. In a metapsychological aside, he expresses concern that his readers might begin to regard the unconscious as representing an actual locus in the brain or "space" in the mind. We are compelled to use such spatial metaphors, Breuer explains, because sometimes it is the only way we can understand and talk about abstruse concepts of mental functioning. But, even in this pre-"Freudian" account, Breuer was already worried about premature reification:

> It is only too easy to fall into a habit of thought which assumes that every substantive has a substance behind it—which gradually comes to regard "consciousness" as standing for some actual thing; and when we have become accustomed to make use metaphorically of spatial relations, as in the term "sub-conscious," we find as time goes on that we have actually formed an idea which has lost its metaphorical nature and which we can manipulate easily as though it were real. Our mythology is then complete. (Breuer & Freud, 1895, pp. 227–228)

This off his chest, Breuer then goes on to discuss Janet's (1894) theory of hysteria, with which Breuer pointedly disagrees. For Janet, all normal mental activity depends on the capacity to unite disparate mental elements into a unified complex. This is what happens, for example, when various sense perceptions, memories, ideas, and so on are combined to produce a stable and coherent picture of the world in which the person lives. It is precisely this kind of synthetic mental activity, says Janet, that is impaired in hysterical patients. According to Janet, the "splitting of personality" that underlies hysterical phenomena rests upon an innate psychological weakness, or *insuffisance psychologique*. For hysterics, separate mental elements remain in varying states of disparity, and their world is thus only dimly perceived and understood.

Certainly, this description hardly applies to Anna O and many of the other hysterics Breuer and Freud worked with. If anything, a number of these patients possessed particularly keen intellects, large funds of knowledge, and well-cultivated abilities in thought and language, although such "psychological insufficiency" could be said to have been a feature in some of the more modern cases encountered in the last chapter. To explain the discrepancy between Janet's and his own types of cases, Breuer invokes what today would be called the problem of selection bias. That is, Janet's patients were typically drawn from the indigent, feebleminded populations of public hospitals and institutions; they were patients who "have not been able to hold their own in life on account of their illness and mental weakness caused by it" (Breuer & Freud, 1895, p. 232). By contrast, Breuer worked mainly with the hysterical faction of the Viennese bourgeoisie—well-bred, educated, and thoroughly middle-class. That such variations in patient demographics and individual patient characteristics may account for differences in the expression of certain psychopathological states and the brain mechanisms that underlie them is a concept that continues to be ignored or dismissed by psychological theorists even today (see Miller, 1986b, 1990).

So while rejecting Janet's idea that there is but a single uniform species of feeble-witted hysterogenic type, Breuer still held firm to the belief that hysteria develops in those with an innate predisposition for it. But if not Janet's "psychological insufficiency," then what? "An excess," argues Breuer, "rather than a defect" (p. 240). Individuals, usually adolescents (and, typically, female), who are later to become hysterical tend to be lively, gifted, and full of intellectual interests before they fall ill. Their determination and force of will in carrying out intellectual pursuits is often remarkable, as, for example, in individuals who (like Anna O and Margaret, the young woman of David and Bone's [1985] case, mentioned in the last chapter) might be possessed of great intellectual precocity.

In fact, far from regarding hysterics with clinical contempt, as did many of his colleagues (even Freud, as we have seen, was not above a bit of gratuitous carping about the weak-willedness in some of his patients), Breuer's opinion of them seems to have bordered on the romantic: "The overflowing productivity of their minds has led one of my friends to assert that hysterics are the flower of mankind, as sterile, no doubt, but as beautiful as double flowers" (Breuer & Freud, 1895, p. 240).

What accounts for the liveliness and restlessness of hysterics, their craving for sensations and mental activity, their intolerance of monotony and boredom? Breuer offers the following hypothesis: The nervous systems of hysterics, even at rest, liberate excess excitation. This nervous activity needs to be used up somehow, and this is what drives the seemingly incessant activity of many hysterics. And the oft-noted association of the onset of hysteria with adolescence is due to the exacerbating effects of pubescent sexuality on this production of nervous energy.

This surplus of excitation, Breuer explains, may itself give rise to pathological phenomena in the motor sphere. For example, the excess energy might come out in the form of tic-like movements, which frequently begin in some localized area like the eyes or face and spread to involve multiple parts of the body. In the extreme case, speculates Breuer, motor convulsions may occur when an unusually large sum of this excess nervous energy is explosively discharged in an epileptic fit. Such cases would then represent a nonideogenic form of hysterical convulsion.

Breuer's theory of hysteria, then, was an ideogenic one but with certain important neuropsychodynamic qualifications. Psychical forces could determine the timing and perhaps the form of expression of hysterical symptoms, but the process could only operate on a particular type of hysterical predisposition and personality, or temperamental style; this, in turn, depended on a certain constitutional state of nervous system excitability and reactivity, which provided the raw material with which the psychogenic mechanisms could fashion their clinical manifestations. Hysterical symptoms, in other words, usually happened to hysterical people. We will return to the theme of hysterical symptoms and hysterical personalities in a subsequent chapter.

Freud's Theory: "The Psychotherapy of Hysteria"

The account provided here of Freud's portion of the *Studies'* theoretical section will be a brief one because we have already extensively considered Freud's views on this subject in his *Comparative Study* of 1893 and in the *Preliminary Communication* of the *Studies*. However, several points are raised in this section that are relevant to the neuropsychodynamic model as a whole.

Freud begins by reaffirming his belief in the primary role of sexuality in the psychogenesis of true hysterical symptoms. But some symptoms of this type, he acknowledges, may indeed have an underlying organic basis. Yet psychotherapeutic procedures are often effective in alleviating them. Why should this be?

> The solution lies in the fact that some of these non-psychogenic symptoms (stigmata, for instance) are, it is true, indications of illness, but cannot be described as ailment; and consequently it is not of practical importance if they persist after the successful treatment of the illness. As regards other such symptoms, it seems to be the case that in some roundabout way they are carried off along with the psychogenic symptoms, just

as, perhaps, in some roundabout way they are after all dependent on a psychical causation. (Breuer & Freud, 1895, p. 265)

So at this point, Freud still seems unsure about the precise relationship between organicity and psychogenicity. That, however, does not prevent him from offering some therapeutic suggestions. Freud points out that the psychotherapeutic enterprise is facilitated to a greater degree when repressed memories return in the form of pictures rather than thoughts. Hysterical patients, who tend as a group to be more of the "visual" type, are thus easier to treat than, say, obsessives, for whom ideation, not imagery, is the main cognitive process. Furthermore, the psychotherapeutic process typically involves a translation of these memory-images into verbal form.

Once a picture has emerged from the patient's memory, we may hear him say that it becomes fragmentary and obscure in proportion as he proceeds with his description of it. *The patient is, as it were, getting rid of it by turning it into words.* We go on to examine the memory picture itself in order to discover the direction in which our work is to proceed. (Breuer & Freud, 1895, p. 280)

The patient can only free himself from the hysterical symptom by a linguistic articulation of the pathogenic impressions that caused it, impressions that have persisted in repressed memory primarily in the form of images. It is the patient's difficulty or reluctance to make this imagistic-ideative translation that constitutes a greater part of the *resistance* and in the handling of which the therapist's personal influence is often an important factor. Thus, both doctor and patient must battle mightily in search of the psychodynamic truth that, when freed of its repressive associative links through the medium of thought and language, may consequently unfetter the patient from his/her hysterical state.

When I have promised my patients help or improvement by means of a cathartic treatment I have often been faced by this objection: "Why, you tell me yourself that illness is probably connected to my circumstances and the events of my life. You cannot alter these in any way. How do you propose to help me, then?" And I have been able to make this reply: "No doubt fate would find it easier than I do to relieve you of your illness. But you will be able to convince yourself that much will be gained if we succeed in transforming your hysterical misery into common unhappiness. With a mental life that has been restored to health you will be better armed against that unhappiness." (Breuer & Freud, 1895, p. 305)

And finally, as a footnote not only of the text but to psychoanalytic history itself, the editor of the present edition of the *Studies* lets us know that in the German editions prior to 1925 the term "mental life" in the last sentence of the above citation originally read "nervous system." In the early Freudian model, it would seem, mental states and functional brain states were one. Did psychoanalytic therapy, as originally conceived, boldy and grandly set out to alter the functional state of the brain itself? Was this the practical clinical mission that naturally flowed from this early theoretical model of Freud's brain?

CHAPTER 5

Paroxysmal Neurologic Disorders: Toward a Mechanism of Hysterical Symptoms

As we have seen, the sometimes strange neuropsychological manifestations occurring after organic brain damage may be replicated by the clinical symptomatology of hysteria, thereby providing the basis for a phenomenological model. But it is unlikely that such drastic and often relatively permanent brain changes can account for the actual neuropsychodynamic mechanisms of the typically fleeting and changing patterns of hysterical and hysterical-like symptoms. Instead, we must look for those forms and causes of neuropsychological impairment that by their very nature produce changes in brain state that vary over time, what are commonly referred to as "transient," or "paroxysmal," disorders.

Migraine

Although not generally regarded as very important by Freud scholars, migraine can rightfully claim a prominent place in the history of psychoanalysis. For one thing, Freud frequently referred to it in his hysteria cases, for example, that of Frau Emmy von N. Around the same time, in 1895, he outlined the draft of a theory of migraine (not surprisingly, he proposed a sexual etiology) in a letter to Wilhelm Fliess (Masson, 1985). In addition, migraine was of more than academic interest to Freud because he suffered from the malady himself. Characteristically, as he did with the other products of his introspection, he incorporated the observations of his own neuropsychological state changes—the states of Freud's

58

brain—into the evolving corpus of psychoanalytic theory. Such observations led him at one point to articulate what is perhaps the best expression within Freud's own work of the neuropsychodynamic model that informs the present book:

> The mild attacks of migraine from which I still suffer usually announce themselves hours in advance by my forgetting of names, and at the height of these attacks, during which I am not forced to abandon my work, it frequently happens that all proper names go out of my head. Now it is precisely cases like mine which could furnish the grounds for an objection on principle to our analytic efforts. Should it not necessarily be concluded from such observations that the cause of forgetfulness, and in particular of the forgetting of names, lies in circulatory and general functional disturbances of the cerebrum, and should we not therefore spare ourselves the search for psychological explanations of these phenomena? Not at all, in my view; *that would be to confuse the mechanism of a process, which is of the same kind in all cases, with the factors favoring the process, which are variable and not necessarily essential.* (Freud, 1901, p. 21; emphasis added)

Historically, Sacks (1985) credits Edward Liveing (1873) with the first comprehensive description of the syndrome of migraine and with pointing out the virtually limitless physical and psychological manifestations that this syndrome can produce. Liveing proposed his own theory of "nerve storms" to explain the sudden or gradual metamorphoses that characterize many migraine attacks. Later, Gowers (1907) conceptualized migraines, faints, vertigo, sleep disorders, and similar occurrences as lying in the "borderland of epilepsy," all such paroxysmal manifestations being inter-transformable, if mysteriously, among themselves. Sacks also comments on Lennox and Lennox's (1960) more recent concept of "migralepsy," which draws a similar parallel between migraine attacks and seizure-like disorders.

Migraine involves a disturbance of the cerebral metabolism and circulation and may produce a variety of symptoms, most commonly head pain and nausea—the famous "sick headache" of the hapless migraineur. Often, depending on which areas of the brain are affected by the metabolic and vascular changes, the headache is preceded or accompanied by other symptoms, such as disturbances in vision or tactile sensibility, weakness or disorders of movement, mood changes, or cognitive deficits. In the overwhelming majority of cases the deficits are transient, which is, after all, part of what qualifies migraine as a paroxysmal disorder. When these nonheadache phenomena precede the headache itself, they are described as "migraine auras," by analogy to the auras of epilepsy, the transient sensory or emotional states that often precede the seizure itself. When the nonheadache migraine symptoms occur in the absence of the headache, they are commonly designated "migraine equivalents," and when a patient suffers only the headache phase of migraine, he/she is said to be suffering from "common migraine." In "classical migraine," there occurs the aura, followed by the headache, and accompanied by nausea and perhaps other symptoms.

Whitty (1967) described several patients who suffered transitory hemipareses, visual disturbances, or speech difficulties that he considered to be migraine equivalents based on the short, resolving course and a family history of migraine. Fisher (1980) also speaks of the "transient migraine accompaniment," which occurs independently of headache and represents essentially the same phenomenon as the migraine equivalent. Among the features of this syndrome Fisher observes a relatively slow progression over as long as thirty minutes, a preponderance of visual symptoms, and a topographic "march" of symptoms; that is, the tactile symptoms spread steadily out over the body surface as the different portions of the brain's sensory strip become progressively affected.

Sacks (1985) describes a number of his own migraine cases, the phenomenology of which bears a striking resemblance to many of the symptoms of Breuer and Freud's hysterics. One of Sacks's patients was a young man of sixteen who had been prone to classical migraines and isolated migraine auras since childhood and whose attacks took a number of different forms. Most commonly, they began with strange, unnatural sensations, or paresthesias, in the left foot that rose toward the thigh and, when they reached knee level, were joined by a second focus of paresthesia that began in the right hand. Gradually, these died away only to be replaced by a distortion of hearing like the roaring ocean sound one hears when cupping seashells over the ears. This was followed by bilateral scintillating scotomas (shimmering blind spots) involving the lower half of the visual field of each eye. On a number of occasions the patient experienced an "aura status" that lasted as long as five hours and that consisted of alternating paresthesias in the feet, hands, and face. At other times the aura began with a sensation of "tingling—like vibrating wires" (p. 96) that seemed to emanate from the upper digestive tract and that was accompanied by an extreme sense of foreboding.

Other attacks, which came on during sleep, would have a nightmarish quality, beginning at first with feelings of compulsion and restlessness: "I feel edgy—like I got to get up and do something" (p. 96). This was followed by a state of hallucinatory delirium in which the patient believed himself trapped in a speeding car or menaced by metalloid figures. As this delirious state abated, he became conscious of paresthesias and scotomas and usually then developed a crashing headache. This young man also suffered a number of fainting spells during migraine auras in which the hallucinations were followed by a simultaneous "fading away" of sight and hearing, a sense of faintness, and then loss of consciousness.

Another of Sacks's patients was a fifty-five-year-old man whose history of classical migraine and isolated auras began in childhood. Two or three days before each attack he observed "luminous spots" flitting across his visual field, a perception accompanied by a feeling of excitement and euphoria. In fact, Sacks reports, the man would describe his various auras with a certain fervor. "There is greater depth and speed and acuity of thought," he said; "I keep recalling things long forgotten, visions of earlier years will spring to my mind" (p. 97). He actually seemed to enjoy the auras, provided they were not followed by a migraine headache. His wife, however, was less amused; during these auras, she observed, her husband would walk back and forth and speak in a repetitive monotone, seemed to be in a trance, and was "quite unlike his usual self" (p. 97).

Still another case in Sacks's migraine series sounds even more quintessentially "hysterical." This was a normally self-possessed fifteen-year-old girl whose classic migraines did not occur often but were particularly severe when they struck. In Sacks's consulting room she experienced a migraine aura during which she giggled without interruption for forty-five minutes. During this time she developed an aphasia and reported strange sensations flitting from one limb to another. When she finally recovered, she apologized for her uncharacteristic behavior, saying "I don't know what I was laughing at—I just couldn't help it—everything seemed so funny, like laughing gas" (p. 97).

Levy (1988) studied a number of cases of what he termed "transient CNS [central nervous system] dysfunction" associated with migraine. The subjects were a group of young adult participants in a survey conducted at the Department of Neurology at Cornell Medical Center, and their reported symptoms consisted of documentable loss of neurological function that persisted for less than twenty-four hours. These included the following: (1) visual symptoms such as hemianopia, quadrantanopia, bilateral blindness, visual obscurations, scotomas, formed hallucinations, macropsia, vibratory distortions, and positive afterimages; (2) motor symptoms such as limb and/or face paresis and clumsiness; (3) language disturbances such as dysgraphia, dysarthria, and mutism; and (4) disturbances of equilibrium. A number of these cases are reported in detail, three of which are summarized below.

A thirty-two-year-old right-handed man was writing when he abruptly experienced difficulty manipulating the pen and forming letters. Both sensation and muscle strength appeared to be normal. He was able to walk and talk, and reading was unimpaired; however, he continued to produce large malformed letters when he tried to write. Within ten minutes or so, writing returned to normal. There was no headache this time, but on other occasions he did have headaches without any other neurologic symptoms. He has had no episodes like this since then and ten years later is still neurologically intact.

A twenty-eight-year-old man recalls going into a "trance-like" state at age sixteen during which he was unable to speak for approximately two minutes. Other than some vague emotional changes, there were no other disturbances. A similar event took place two years later, but this time it was associated with bilateral blindness. For the past ten years he has been well.

A twenty-seven-year-old right-handed man with a documented history of migraine headaches experienced a ten- to fifteen-minute episode of clumsiness and altered sensation in his right hand. He was unable to manipulate a pen or to write, and objects in the affected hand felt "different." Muscle strength was normal, and he was able to speak, walk, and do arithmetic calculations. A colleague who was with him at the time noticed nothing abnormal. Approximately forty-five minutes later he developed a headache.

Pain other than headache is not a commonly reported symptom of migraine, but it does occur. Liveing (1873) noted that pain may occur in the upper or lower limbs in association with the paresthesias of migraine. Gowers (1892, 1907) reported that migraine pain may radiate from the side of the head to the neck and arm, and Jeliffe (1906) described a patient with right-sided migraine associated with pain and numbness in the arm and numbness and weakness in the leg on the same side. Aches and pains of every description and in virtually every location pepper the accounts of Breuer and Freud's hysteria cases, and even today chronic pain is probably the commonest form of somatization symptom seen in clinical practice.

More recently, Guiloff and Fruns (1988) carried out a study of twenty-two patients who had limb pain as a prominent complaint associated with migraine headaches. In most cases the pain involved the arms, but several patients had leg pain as well. The pain was always on the same side and affected the same area of the body as the accompanying numbness, paresthesias, and weakness and was usually on the same side as the headache. In two cases there were minor swelling and bluish patches in the skin of the painful limb. Some typical cases are described in more detail below.

Since her adolescence a thirty-two-year-old woman had suffered one or two episodes a year of right-sided headache preceded by blurred vision and "dancing images" and associated with nausea and vomiting. However, she had been free of these attacks for eight years until, about a year prior to being seen, she began experiencing intermittent throbbing and stinging pain in the right eye, temple, and ear as well as "burning–numb" pain in the right arm and hand, especially the ring and little fingers, and in the right side of the chest. Especially severe bouts could be triggered by bright light, wine, and sudden turning of the head. "Splitting" right-sided headaches, accompanied by sharp pains in the right ear, regularly appeared premenstrually.

A twenty-five-year-old woman had, since age twelve, experienced regular headaches and vomiting that were preceded by a variety of symptoms. A typical attack began with severe pain in the left or right eye that spread to the side of the head. There followed dizziness, tinnitus, vomiting, and impaired vision. The ipsilateral or, less often, contralateral arm would become weak for about ten minutes as numbness and paresthesias spread from the hand to the elbow. This in turn was followed by severe shooting pains radiating from the shoulder along the ulnar side of the arm to the elbow. The arm would feel heavy for another fifteen minutes or so, and the headache could last from several hours to all day. The sensory symptoms and upper limb pains could also occur without the headache. On three occasions, the headache had been preceded by an olfactory hallucination (cf. Freud's Lucy R), which consisted of the smell of either peanut butter or her grandfather's cigar.

In conceptualizing these findings, Guiloff and Fruns (1988) note that lesions in the primary (SSI) and secondary somatosensory (SSII) cortices of the parietal lobe may produce symptoms of limb pain and that the pain typically disappears when the lesions are removed. Woolsey and colleagues (1979) were able to reproduce phantom limb pain (the perception of pain in a missing limb lost to traumatic or surgical amputation) in quite precisely localized areas of the hand, arm, leg, and foot by stimulation of the contralateral postcentral and supplementary sensory cortices. In the monkey, some SSI and SSII neurons respond to pain stimuli and have large receptive fields, that is, receive information from wide areas of the body surface (Kenshalo & Isensee, 1980; Mountcastle & Powell, 1959; Whitsel et al., 1969). Connections between SSI and SSII and between SSII and ipsilateral motor cortex have also been described in the monkey (Jones & Powell, 1969a, 1969b).

Pain is a frequent manifestation of epileptic seizures. In addition, paresthesias and motor symptoms may co-occur in the same distribution as the pain. Young and Blume (1983) propose that the probable sites of origin of the electrical discharges in painful seizures are the contralateral SSI and SSII areas and that decreased inhibition accompanying seizures interferes with the normal cortical pain control mechanisms. In their 1988 report Guiloff and Fruns extend this conceptualization to include migraine as another mechanism that can transiently disturb the cortical or subcortical processes involved in pain. This may occur, for example, by means of vasospasm-induced ischemia or a particular form of metabolic disturbance that is believed to occur in migraine called "spreading depression" of brain function (see Lauritzen, 1987, for a review). In addition, Olesen and colleagues (1981), using the regional cerebral blood flow (rCBF) technique, found markedly reduced posterior blood flow at the time of headache in a man with migraine and attacks of pain in the right arm.

Thus, migraine, in all its myriad and sometimes bizarre manifestations, may provide one type of model for the paroxysmal, or at least transient, events that might underlie the genesis of some kinds of hysterical and hysterical-looking symptoms.

Epilepsy

But the quintessential, the paradigmatic, paroxysmal neurologic disorder is, of course, epilepsy, a syndrome in which seizures are the salient symptoms. A number of main classes of seizure types exist, although all manner of intermediate gradations may be found, and one kind of seizure occasionally turns into another.

The most well-known seizure type is the *generalized*, or *grand mal, seizure*, which involves whole-body convulsions, incontinence, loss of consciousness, and a period of postictal confusion and paralysis. *Focal*, or *Jacksonian, seizures* (after the British neurologist John Hughlings Jackson, who described epileptic phenomena in great detail) usually involve only a single limb or part of the body at a time, although the spasmodic motor activity may spread progressively to other areas—the famous "Jacksonian march." In *petit mal seizures* there are brief lapses of consciousness but no significant loss of muscle control. The symptoms of *psychomotor*, or *temporal lobe, epilepsy* (also referred to as "complex partial seizure disorder") are stranger and more diverse and may include sensory distortions; illusions or hallucinations; dreamy or "twilight" states; feelings of depersonalization, déjà vu, or impending doom; "forced" thoughts or emotions; various disturbances of consciousness; repetitive, robotic movements called *automatisms*; and other manifestations.

Breuer and Freud made passing reference to epilepsy in several of their cases in the *Studies*, and the history of neurology and psychiatry has documented the close relationship between epilepsy and hysteria; for example, many hysterical phenomena, including hysterical seizures, resemble the phenomena seen in true epileptic (especially psychomotor) seizures, and the highest rate of hysterical pseudoseizures occurs in patients with true epileptic seizures.

One question is whether hysterical-looking seizures are more apt to arise from one part of the brain than another. Williamson and colleagues (1985) described ten patients with documented seizure activity originating in the orbital or medial frontal lobe. Seizure-induced motor symptoms that had initially been considered hysterical included kicking, rocking, thrashing, rubbing, scratching, rolling, chewing, stepping, bouncing, waving, patting, clawing, pelvic thrusting, genital manipulation, lip smacking, arm flailing, hand clutching, leg slapping, leg restlessness, head nodding and shaking, tongue protrusion and wagging, and the production of weird facial expressions. Vocal symptoms that were initially considered hysterical included making repetitive vowel sounds, monotonous humming, talking gibberish, moaning, whispering, whimpering, squealing, screaming, and shouting, including shouting obscenities.

The frenetic and bizarre behavior during these episodes, along with a rapid return to normal consciousness, was mainly what had led to the original presumptive diagnoses of hysteria. Also misleading in some cases were scalp EEGs taken between the episodes, which often failed to identify seizure activity at the surface level. What finally established the seizure diagnosis was the stereotyped pattern of the attacks and, especially, depth electrode recording, which gave unequivocal evidence of deep seizure activity.

In *status epilepticus*, seizure activity is continual: in the case of grand mal, the patient does not stop convulsing. A persistently beclouded state from continuous or recurrent psychomotor seizures is less frequently encountered as a manifestation of status epilepticus and may be difficult to recognize clinically, since the basic epileptic character of the EEG may not be evident—one thinks of Breuer's "hypnoid states" and Anna O's "clouds."

Drake and Coffey (1983) studied two patients with complex partial status epilepticus, using both clinical examination and EEG. Recognition of the true ictal character of the patients' behaviors was impeded by the presence of what at first seemed to be feigned or psychogenic unresponsiveness. The first case was of a seventy-seven-year-old woman, Ms. A, who entered the hospital for removal of a kidney stone and a tumor of the parathyroid gland. After the surgery she intermittently became confused and unresponsive, despite a normal neurologic exam. Lowered states of responsiveness were associated with grimacing, head posturing, eyelid fluttering and picking at her bedclothes. When completely unresponsive, Ms. A resisted eye opening or passive limb movement; when her arm was placed over her face, it hovered briefly and slowly descended to her side, a classic hysterical response (Weintraub, 1978). EEG revealed seizure activity, and a CT scan showed a mild widening of the left sylvian fissure. Ms. A was put on anticonvulsant medication, and her condition improved.

The second patient, Ms. B, was a thirty-year-old right-handed woman who had had psychomotor and grand mal seizures since age eight. She also suffered for years from peptic ulcers and finally underwent a total gastrectomy at her local hospital. Following the surgery she became confused and agitated and showed a curious alternation of behavior: at one moment she would be screaming and thrashing about, the next moment catatonically unresponsive with occasional grimacing and arm movements. She was unresponsive even with her eyes open, did not follow spoken commands, and would utter no word or sound. When her eyes closed spontaneously, she resisted anyone trying to open them. On some occasions she demonstrated so-called "waxy flexibility," her limbs remaining suspended in whatever position they were placed by the examiner; at other times she resisted anyone trying to move any part of her body. As with Ms. A, when this patient's arm was suspended over her face, it "hysterically" drifted to her side. Ms B's EEG was abnormal, as was Ms. A's, although her CT scan showed nothing remarkable. Her condition improved with anticonvulsants.

These two patients had prolonged impairment of consciousness due to psychomotor status epilepticus. The clinical state had all the earmarks of hysterical feigned unconsciousness, but the authors assert that their patients' impairment could be differentiated by the fluctuating character of the mental state and by the characteristic EEG findings. Like Anna O, Ms. A and Ms. B demonstrated an alternating pattern of unresponsiveness with stereotyped automatisms and a twilight state with partial responsiveness. Unlike Anna O, these two women lived in the age of EEGs, brain scans, and anticonvulsant drugs.

Stern and Murray (1984) describe a case of what they call *limbic epilepsy*. A thirty-six-year-old right-handed professional pianist was known to suffer from manic–depressive illness and temporal lobe epilepsy. She was admitted to the hospital after she had stopped taking her anticonvulsants, an act resulting in an increase in irritability and depression and the development of the paranoid delusion that her husband and children were trying to kill her.

On the day after admission the patient wandered off the ward and out of the hospital, saying that she felt "lost" and that her surroundings looked unfamiliar and frightening. She was observed to alternate between bouts of shouting and periods of calm conversation. On the third hospital day she felt a "rage" coming on and wanted to "burn the building down." She said she felt panicked and wanted to scream, whereupon she jumped up, ran into the bathroom, grabbed two wastebaskets, and threw one at a nurse, crying, "Everything is dead around me!"

Later that same morning the patient had an EEG, which showed intermittent bursts of abnormal electrical activity that were more prominent on the left side of the brain. This laterality pattern was further confirmed by neuropsychological testing, the findings being compatible with left temporal lobe dysfunction. For example, verbal learning was severely impaired whereas nonverbal learning was intact, a pattern consistent with what would be expected with localized left temporal lobe damage in a right-handed person. In addition, the patient's scores on tests measuring fund of information, vocabulary, verbal abstraction, and reasoning— functions that rely on the frontal and parietal but not necessarily temporal lobes of the left hemisphere—were all within normal limits.

From an exploration of the patient's history, it was discovered that at the age of two months she had fallen from a table and become temporarily unresponsive. For the next year her parents observed periods of eye rolling in their daughter, but, for reasons of their own, they never told her pediatrician or other physicians about the table injury. The patient had a lifelong history of psychiatric problems, including alcohol abuse, self-mutilation, masochistic relationships with men, religious and philosophical preoccupations, depression, and psychotic symptoms. Her various diagnoses at one time or another included schizophrenia, schizoaffective disorder, hysteria, borderline personality disorder, and temporal lobe epilepsy.

At times the patient lost her balance and became dizzy and confused. She complained of fugue-like memory lapses and was frequently found wandering about as if in a daze, occasionally naked. She developed numbness on her right side, as well as occasional decreased vision in her right eye. Her right hand eventually became so clumsy that she had to stop playing the piano. Familiar things looked strange and foreign to her, a phenomenon known as *jamais vu*. She was constantly anxious and suffered from panic attacks. She became paranoid that people were plotting to kill her, and she tended to compulsively repeat tasks again and again. She was alternately irritable, talkative, dependent, hypergraphic, and hyposexual, and her interest in philosophy grew more and more intense. Anticonvulsants seemed to partially ameliorate her compulsive behavior, and her overall condition improved somewhat under a combination of medications.

Sensory alterations in relatively clear consciousness are another feature of the hysterical presentation in Breuer and Freud's hysteria cases, as well as in some modern ones. Lesser and colleagues (1983) present the case of a man with a history of alcoholism and depression who first developed recurrent seizures at age fifty-eight. For thirteen months the seizures were controlled by anticonvulsants; then they began again, occurring several times a day. The spells consisted of a general sense of weakness or numbness that lasted for thirty seconds to a minute. There were no accompanying motor or sensory signs on examination. The weakness or numbness mainly affected the left shoulder, arm, and leg but sometimes involved the right leg and occasionally spread to the rectal area. About a third of these seizures ended with a strong unpleasant odor.

CT scan and angiography showed some mild, nonspecific abnormalities but nothing that would definitively account for the seizures. Neurologic and mental status exams were normal, except for decreased short-term memory and concreteness in proverb interpretation. Anticonvulsant medication was temporarily stopped, and two subsequent EEGs were normal.

At this point an attempt was made to induce one of these spells by hypnotic suggestion. One minute after beginning the suggestion protocol a typical seizure occurred, accompanied by an abnormal EEG recording over the left temporal area. Without further suggestion, seven additional episodes of altered sensation occurred spontaneously, all accompanied by the characteristic EEG pattern. The spells were described as consisting of a "vibe" or a "chill," beginning in the left knee and spreading to the left shoulder, arm, and hip, the rectum, and, finally, the right knee.

Medication was restarted, resulting in good seizure control. However, in the next three months the patient developed aphasia and right-sided paralysis. This time CT scan showed a mass in the left temporal area, which on biopsy proved to be a malignant brain tumor.

The unusual thing about this patient's seizures, the authors point out, is that they involved altered somatic sensation but no alteration in consciousness. Because of the vague descriptions of the symptoms, their bilateral presentation, the psychiatric history, and the fact that the spells could apparently be induced by suggestion, it would have been easy to dismiss these episodes as hysterical had it not been for the characteristic EEG findings. For this reason, the authors recommend that induction by suggestion not be used as a differential diagnostic criterion for hysterical symptoms. (They fail to raise the even more intriguing possibility that suggestion and allied techniques might have a therapeutic effect in controlling some "real" seizures, a line of recent research that is beyond the scope of this book.)

For Lesser and colleagues (1983), the bilateral sensory symptoms, as well as the repetitive left temporal epileptic discharges, suggest that these episodes originated in the second somatosensory area (SSII) of the brain, which is located below the primary sensorimotor strip on the upper bank of the sylvian fissure (and discussed earlier in connection with some migraine phenomena). Penfield and Jasper (1954) reported that stimulation of SSII during neurosurgery produces sensations on the face, trunk, arms, or legs of the opposite side, same side, or both sides of the body. The sensations themselves were variously described as pricking, tingling, shivering, crawling, cramping, numb, or hollow. The only two patients previously reported to have seizures originating in SSII were also reported by Penfield and Jasper (1954). One of these patients described tingling of the left half of the tongue, left little finger, and left heel; the other experienced a rising, chilly sensation, a humming sound, and a feeling of sadness, which were followed by automatisms, that is, stereotyped, repetitive, purposeless acts.

Numerals comprised the content of some of Anna O's hallucinations, and Freud was later to make much of the appearance of numerals and calculations in dreams. More recently, Gastaut and Zifkin (1984) reported three cases in which seizure-induced perceptual alterations specifically involved numerals. The disorder began at age eight for the little girl in the first case, when the water tap in the bathtub began to take on frightening shapes. From ages nine to fourteen she experienced *adversive seizures*, in which the head jerks to one side, in this case to the right. If anyone attempted to prevent this turning, the girl would exclaim, "Let me see!" However, she was never able to describe what she saw because she would lose consciousness after twenty seconds, with subsequent amnesia for the event. Postictally, a headache in the right temporal area typically lasted about two hours. After age fourteen, these adversive seizures disappeared; they were replaced by visual hallucinations of small and very bright numerals in the center of the visual field. This was sometimes followed by bilateral blind spots that began at the edges of the visual field and moved progressively inward, leading to complete but temporary loss of vision. On five occasions, a grand mal seizure followed the attack. The EEG showed seizure activity in the left occipital area, the part of the brain involved in processing visual information.

The seizures of the girl in the second case began at age five with brief losses of vision that occurred every several days, often followed by a headache that lasted only fifteen minutes. By age eight her seizures were occurring every few months and consisted of an initial hallucination of geometric figures or numerals, which was followed by confusion, mouthing movements, and other automatisms. During these episodes she would draw the figure 6 or 0 on any flat surface she could find and then just as quickly try to erase it. As in the first case, the EEG typically showed seizure activity in the left occipital area.

The third case involved a boy who had two seizures at age nine. Both began with an hallucination of a numeral surrounded by tiny red spots in the right visual field. He could not recall the numeral in the first seizure, but in the second attack he called out, "The number!" Both seizures progressed to automatistic behavior during which the boy gestured and walked around. The EEG showed bilateral occipital seizure activity.

Gastaut and Zifkin (1984) point out that epileptic attacks may begin unilaterally in either of the two primary occipital cortices, but to produce a bilateral or central formed and changeable visual hallucination, the visual association area, which surrounds the primary visual area and is responsible for higher order visual perception, of one or both sides must also be involved, especially if there is some change in behavior related to the content of the hallucination. This is because each primary visual cortex lacks direct contact through the corpus callosum to its counterpart in the opposite hemisphere. The authors further speculate that the subsequent emotional experiences, automatisms, and behavior related to the hallucinations probably reflect the spread of the seizure activity from the occipital cortex to the limbic structures of the temporal lobe.

We have seen that Anna O liked to read and write; in fact, Breuer made a special point of her intellectual precocity and predilection for literary pursuits, such as poetry. Could a preoccupation with written language have any connection with some hysterical-like phenomena seen in neuropsychopathological states?

In *primary reading epilepsy*, first described by Bickford and colleagues (1956), the patient characteristically experiences myoclonic jerking of the jaw while reading; this may progress to a generalized convulsion. If an EEG is taken while the patient is resting, it is typically normal whereas during reading epileptiform discharges may be clearly observed. Although many cases of this disorder have been described, its pathophysiological nature remains elusive.

Ramani (1983) described the case of a thirty-year-old right-handed electrician who complained of a tightening sensation and jerking of his jaw that occurred while reading. His problems in this area began at age eighteen, when he suffered a grand mal seizure following a period of prolonged bookwork. Since that episode he had noticed recurring transient auras of tightening and jerking of the jaw during reading, but only on three occasions did these attacks progress to generalized convulsions. He learned to avoid further seizures by recognizing the auras in time to tear himself away from the reading material.

The electrician had no seizures at work and did not experience auras when studying electrical circuit diagrams or while watching TV or playing cards at home. But reading novels or magazines would set off his jaw-jerking episodes, which were accompanied by anxiety and a feeling of pressure in his head. Prolonged reading, physical fatigue, emotional stress, or sleep deprivation seemed to heighten his susceptibility to these attacks. The patient's father had also suffered from the same kind of seizures for a number of years but had managed to keep these to a minimum simply by avoiding excessive reading.

To obtain a more objective and systematic evaluation of his seizure disorder, the patient was asked to read material of increasingly complex subject matter: (1) items of general interest, such as advertisements from popular magazines; (2) magazine articles presented in order of increasing complexity, concerning sports, national politics, world economy, and an editorial essay; and (3) technical articles from a medical journal. Reading was done both silently and aloud, and the patient was asked to try to understand the material he was reading.

Ramani found that the greatest number of seizure discharges occurred when the patient was reading the editorial essays or medical journal articles. That is, the seizures occurred with increasing frequency when the subject matter became more complex and difficult to comprehend. Here was a case, it seemed, where seizures were triggered specifically by the cerebral activity associated with complex visual–linguistic interpretation and comprehension.

Of course, one of the things that make Breuer and Freud's hysteria cases so interesting—indeed, what in large part accounts for the generally widespread fascination for "Freudian" ideas among professionals and laymen alike—is the proposed connection with sexuality. Can paroxysmal disorders shed light on the nature of human sexuality and its role in psychopathology?

Penfield and Jasper (1954) noted that sexual manifestations sometimes occur as part of the clinical picture of psychomotor seizures and might take the form of sexual automatisms, emotions, or genital sensations. Spencer and colleagues (1983) argue that the sexual aura in such cases probably originates in the temporal lobe, the genital somatosensory phenomena in the parietal lobe, and the sexual automatisms in the frontal lobe. These authors then go on to describe two such cases of their own.

The first case involved a man who had his first and only grand mal seizure at age twenty. While he never again had such a generalized convulsive attack, he did experience episodes of kicking, screaming, punching, and falling. At times he would pound the wall while mouthing obscenities; other times he was seen stalking about, exposing and grabbing his genitals. He had no aura and no recollection for these spells. At age thirty-six he began to periodically experience "strange feelings" in his stomach and "visions" of a man's head that persisted for about fifteen seconds. These occurred alone and were never followed by the other types of seizures. But these other types now announced their onset by impelling him to suddenly seize his groin with both hands, turn, thrash about, and curse. He would continue to play with his penis, then smack his lips, snort, and grimace for two minutes. This display was followed by a five-minute period of postictal confusion from which he emerged unable to recall the whole episode.

Not surprisingly, for years these quite hysterical-looking disturbances were thought to be psychogenic. Bilateral cerebral angiography showed the patient's brain vascularity to be normal. Psychological testing revealed him to be of average intelligence, to show impulsive action and self-indulgent behavior, and to have a long-standing personality disorder characterized by "insufficient thinking" (cf. Breuer's description of Janet's views on this subject). Depth electrode recording showed that subclinical seizure discharges arose from the right frontal region; the seizures with sexual automatisms were found to originate in the medial part of the right frontal lobe, with a visual aura arising in the right temporal region. Finally, a right frontal lobectomy confirmed the presence of glial scarring, which often acts as an irritative focus for seizures.

The second case was of a woman, born after an uncomplicated pregnancy and delivery, whose seizures began when she was two days old and consisted of tremulousness and twitching of the left side of the face. On phenobarbital she remained seizure-free until age five, when she began to have episodes of altered states of consciousness. These were sometimes accompanied by a frightened appearance and stamping of her feet. EEG and angiography were normal, but a skull radiogram revealed calcification in the right frontal lobe. At age eight, generalized convulsions became more frequent and were preceded by a "vague" abdominal sensation.

In the next few years there were episodes, sometimes lasting for hours, of focal twitching on the left side of her body, accompanied by an inability to speak. At age fourteen some of these seizures were preceded by a "strange feeling," whereupon she would turn on her stomach and thrash and roll about in her bed. Shuffling movements of the legs and feet were seen, along with pelvic thrusting, but the EEG showed no evidence of convulsive activity. Other seizures consisted of posturing of the left arm and extension of the head and neck to the left side; this time, abnormal EEG activity was picked up over the right hemisphere. The patient then underwent surgery, and a marble-sized tuberous sclerotic mass was removed from her right frontal lobe.

What these cases demonstrate, the authors point out, is that while sexual automatisms frequently take place in the presence of preceding sexual feelings, they may also occur without them and may consist of such histrionic—"hysterical"—features as writhing, pelvic thrusting, rhythmic fondling of the genitals, and exhibitionism. In such cases, with the preceding aura of sexual feelings absent, the patient may have no knowledge of the sexual aspects of the seizure itself because of postictal amnesia: the sexual acting-out is "ego-dystonic." Sexual manifestations of seizures can take a variety of forms. The emotional sexual aura may originate in the temporal lobe whereas genital sensations, including pain, may be of parietal lobe origin. In other cases, such as this one, the sexual automatisms themselves, that is, the behavioral component, may originate in the frontal lobes.

Still other seemingly bizarre phenomena, similar to those observed in Anna O and the other cases of Breuer and Freud, may be seen in association with different types of seizure states. The Klüver–Bucy syndrome, as originally described, was produced in monkeys by bilateral removal of the anterior temporal lobes (Klüver & Bucy, 1939). Several characteristic behavioral anomalies were seen in these neurosurgically altered creatures, and these have come to define the syndrome: (1) prominent oral tendencies, or "hyperorality," in which virtually all items that the monkey comes in contact with are mouthed indiscriminately; (2) emotional blunting, or excessive tameness; (3) altered dietary habits, with the animals eating inedible objects like nuts and bolts as readily as real food (this may be related to the hyperorality); (4) hypersexuality, in which male monkeys ceaselessly attempt to mount and copulate with other monkeys, male or female, with other animals (one early photo depicts such a prurient assault on a hapless chicken, another on a surprised-looking cat), with the experimenter's head or hands (no known photographic documentation exists in this case), or even with inanimate objects; and (5) visual and auditory agnosia, in which the monkey seems unable to appreciate the meaning or significance of previously important stimuli; again, this may be related to the indiscriminate mouthing, eating, and sexual mounting.

Following the original studies with monkeys, equivalent human cases have been reported, etiologically related to a variety of spontaneously occurring cerebral disorders (Hooshmand et al., 1974; Terzian & Ore, 1955). In general, the syndrome has been observed in conditions that tend to involve the temporal lobes bilaterally, such as herpes simplex encephalitis, Pick's disease, and head trauma; furthermore, there may be partial forms, or *formes frustes*, of the syndrome that show only a few of the classic features.

While most of these reported cases involve observable lesions of the brain that damage important temporal lobe structures, Nakada and colleagues (1984) describe a case of human Klüver–Bucy syndrome associated with psychomotor status epilepticus. The patient was a forty-six-year-old right-handed alcoholic man who was admitted to the hospital with pneumonia. He had a history of posttraumatic seizure disorder, which had begun after a head injury two years previously and had been well controlled by anticonvulsant drugs. Three weeks into his hospitalization, the medication was inadvertently discontinued, and a week later the patient was noted to be having numerous episodes of confusion and strange behavior. He seemed awake and alert but almost mute and oddly lacking in facial expression. He would grab for objects on his bedside table, masturbated in front of the nursing staff, placed all manner of objects in his mouth, chewed on tissue paper, and attempted to drink from his urine container.

EEG activity pointed to the right frontotemporal region. The following day the patient's mental status returned to normal, and he had no recollection of his bizarre behaviors. CT scan showed old bifrontal contusions, unchanged from the CT scan performed two years earlier. The authors point out that each of the two temporal lobes on either side of the brain, especially its medial portion, has extensive connections with the contralateral temporal lobe. Epileptogenic activity in one temporal lobe often spreads to the contralateral side without necessarily involving the entire brain. With repeated cross-hemispheric spread of seizure activity, such a temporal lobe spike focus may sometimes induce a so-called "mirror focus" at the equivalent site in the opposite hemisphere. Therefore, temporal lobe seizures may also produce bitemporal dysfunction and, with it, an epileptic version of the Klüver–Bucy syndrome.

Certainly, not all hysterical symptoms are produced by seizures, and most seizures are not mistaken for hysteria. Rather than an either–or kind of conceptualization, how might we approach the relationship between paroxysmal brain events and hysterical symptoms?

Seizures, Pseudoseizures, Kindling, and Hysteria

If, as I have been arguing, hysterical symptoms are not exactly the *same* as epileptic (or migraine) symptoms, could their genesis nevertheless be related to a seizure-like, or "functional paroxysmal," process that shares some neurodynamic mechanisms with a seizure but is not quite equivalent in the pathophysiological and syndromic senses? That is, what known neurophysiological process might explain Freud's concept of the "dynamic lesion" in hysterical symptoms, which he described in the 1893 *Comparative Study*?

As we have seen, true seizures and pseudoseizures often go together. Fenton (1986), in reviewing the topic of hysterical pseudoseizures, presents a model that describes pseudoseizures as attacks of sudden unconsciousness that are usually, but not invariably, associated with dramatic motor manifestations and that simulate epileptic attacks to a varying degree. Actually, Fenton disapproves of the term *pseudoseizure*, since it conveys the impression that the seizure is not a *real* seizure. Instead, he prefers the term *pseudoepileptic seizure*, since it acknowledges the occurrence of seizures and their resemblance to genuine epileptic fits but avoids the implication that there are equivalent physiological mechanisms in epilepsy and hysteria. According to Fenton, pseudoepileptic seizures are not an infrequent manifestation of hysteria, and he reiterates the point that genuine epilepsy and pseudoepilepsy can coexist in the same patient. Pseudoepileptic patients also frequently display many other features of personality disorder and psychopathology.

It has been noted that organic brain disease occurs in up to half of all patients with hysteria and seems to facilitate the use of hysterical mechanisms (Merskey, 1978; Merskey & Buhrich, 1975; Roy, 1980; Slater, 1965; Whitlock, 1967). Although, as Slater (1965) observed, hysteria can herald the onset of CNS disease, preexisting organic brain disease is, conversely, a common predisposing factor to the development of hysterical symptoms. The brain dysfunction tends to be acquired early in life, usually before age fifteen, and is often accompanied by cognitive impairment. Side effects of anticonvulsant drugs may be another factor.

Precipitating stress factors are frequently present in hysterical pseudoseizures (Standage & Fenton, 1975), and an illness-rewarding situation is often apparent. Previous episodes of unconsciousness, including epileptic fits either experienced personally or observed within the family or work environment, may provide a model for the choice of pseudoepileptic seizures as the hysterical manifestation. Among modern authorities, unconscious symbolic processes are not usually regarded as important in choice of hysterical symptoms, including hysterical seizures, although generalized anxiety and depressive mood change are reported to be common, as is other evidence of psychological maladjustment. The gender distribution, at least with regard to those cases that come to clinical attention, is—now, as in the past—predominantly female.

Post and colleagues (1986) have described an experimental neurophysiological paradigm and corresponding clinical syndrome that they term *kindling*, after the analogy that wood must be heated to a certain critical temperature before sustained combustion occurs. First described experimentally in rats, kindling refers to the repeated application of a stimulus (typically, an electrical pulse) to the brain, each individual application being insufficient in itself to evoke a seizure (i.e., subthreshold) but, when repeated over an optimal sequential time pattern, cumulatively able to kindle or "ignite" a full-blown attack (Goddard et al., 1969; Racine, 1978).

The brain structure most susceptible to kindling, because of its naturally high degree of excitability, is the *amygdala*, a limbic system structure that sits bilaterally in the anterior portion of each temporal lobe. It was subsequently discovered that certain drugs administered to the brain could also produce a progressive kindling-like increase in neural excitability, so that the final dose—too small in itself to produce a seizure—would act like the proverbial straw that broke the camel's back and precipitate a full-blown seizure. The kindling model of drug action has been used to explain some cases of cocaine psychosis and other human addictive phenomena (Post & Kopanda, 1976; Post et al., 1982).

It is the intermittency of the input that appears to be the critical factor in seizures kindled by amygdala stimulation (Goddard et al., 1969; Post, 1980; Racine, 1978). Continuous stimulation or stimulation at relatively short intervals—say, every two to five minutes—does not result in kindling; instead the animal habituates to the stimuli, and no seizures are produced. However, if the intervals are extended to once every several hours or days, such habituation or tolerance does not occur; on the contrary, there occurs a *sensitization* response, and such subthreshold stimuli eventually summate to produce a full-blown motor seizure.

Post (1980; Post et al., 1986) regards this time-based pattern of either tolerance (habituation) or sensitization as having implications for the development of pathological behavior in response to other kinds of intermittent stimuli—such as psychological stress. For example, severe depressive states that seem to come "out of the blue" following a string of apparently successful coping attempts may reflect the summation, occurring over a critical period of time, of depressogenic influences on brain mechanisms mediating mood. Any one or several of these challenges might have been handled adequately on an individual basis or if their time-based pattern of occurrence had been different. But many such stressors, occurring repeatedly over certain critical intervals of time, may summate to produce a full-blown kindled depressive disorder.

Kindling lasts. It seems to represent a relatively permanent change in neural excitability, and rats kindled in their youth retain convulsive excitability into adulthood. But higher up on the evolutionary scale, for example, in primates, kindling to the point of actual motor convulsions seems to be increasingly difficult to achieve. Instead, what may be successfully kindled are more of the behavioral changes associated with nonconvulsive seizure activity, including that whole range of phenomena subsumed under the rubric of psychomotor, or temporal lobe, epilepsy (Adamec, 1975; Post, 1981; Post et al., 1984).

After many repetitions of kindled seizures, an animal may exhibit what is called *spontaneity*; that is, seizures or seizure-related behavioral changes can now develop in the absence of any external stimulation. In fact, about one-third of kindled animals show such spontaneous cycling in their seizure patterns (Post, 1981). Post and colleagues (1986) suggest that the kindling model might explain how stress-induced mood alterations become so sensitized that they occur spontaneously, providing one possible model for bipolar, or manic–depressive, illness.

The kindling model, according to Post, may even account for how symbolic, or psychodynamic, influences can affect the biological bases of mental disorder. The sensitization–conditioning pattern of kindling suggests that the symbolic aspects of previous events that have set off a depressive response might be learned or conditioned so that they later come to elicit the depression even in the absence of the original stress or loss. If this response pattern is sufficiently conditioned, anticipated stresses or imagined losses, as much as real ones, may eventually be capable of producing the behavioral, physiological, and biochemical alterations of a full-blown depressive episode.

For example, a song or a smell that reminds a person of a lost loved one—or perhaps even of some psychical trauma from the remote past—may be sufficient to bring the whole emotionally painful episode flooding back into consciousness, kicking off a sustained bout of depression. Post thus sees the kindling model as providing a bridge between psychoanalytic concepts of symbolic psychogenesis and the biological–endogenous bases of depression. Further, some psychodynamic theorists have postulated that manic responses may emerge as a defense against depression. In the present kindling formulation, the repeated experience of depressive episodes might progressively bring into play biologically triggered compensatory mechanisms that not only serve to terminate the depressive episode but cycle the mood state into a manic phase.

Although Post and his coworkers deal mainly with depression, I propose that we can use the kindling model to understand hysteria as well. In this formulation, kindled representations of pathological psychical or somatic symptom states—either through personal experience with illness or observations of others—could, in the susceptible brain, set up a repetitive pattern whereby states of stress would induce the sequence of paroxysmal neuropsychodynamic events that lead to symptom formation. Individuals with a "neuropathic heredity," as Breuer termed it, might thus be characterized by a particular sensitivity to kindled neuropsychodynamic tranformations.

However, if such a paroxysmal, kindling-like, process provides the neurophysiological impetus for the generation of at least some kinds of hysterical symptoms, what might be the actual brain mechanisms by which a symbolic representation is transmuted into a bodily symptom? That is, how does hysterical conversion actually come about? It is to this question that we now turn.

CHAPTER 6

The Neuropsychodynamics
of Hysterical Conversion

From Hippocrates to Freud to the modern framers of the ever-changing *Diagnostic and Statistical Manual of Mental Disorders* (DSM) compendium, clinicians have groped for an adequate conceptualization of hysterical conversion, that is, of how ideas in the mind can produce symptoms of the body. For the most part, the various interpretations have depended on what was at one time or another considered "organic" and what "psychological," on what was "body" and what was "mind."

Hysterical Conversion and Organic Disease

The beginning of the modern psychodynamic concept that ideas can cause bodily symptoms is attributed by Merskey (1986) to Sir John Russell Reynolds, who in 1869 described three cases of "paralysis dependent upon an idea," apparently the first systematic discussion of the ideogenic basis for hysterical symptoms. Freud's early mentor Charcot (1889) was impressed by Reynold's conceptualization and proceeded to produce symptoms in his own hysterical patients by hypnotic suggestion—literally, an implantation of an idea causing a physical symptom to sprout. But Charcot was not a pure ideogenicist, for he also believed that hysteria was a functional neurologic disease and that only individuals with nervous systems already predisposed could develop the syndrome (Marsden, 1986), a notion similar, in fact, to Breuer's conception of individual innate vulnerability to hysteria.

An early theoretical integration, which approaches the neuropsychodynamic model of the present book, was offered by Gowers (1892) in

78

the second edition of his classic textbook of neurology. According to Gowers:

> A rough division is often made into two broad classes of "organic" and "functional" disease. The first class, that of "organic diseases," comprehends those in which there is always a visible lesion, manifesting sometimes only the ultimate degree or result of that process. The second class, that of "functional diseases," is less definite, comprehending 1) those diseases that consist only in the disturbance of function, and are therefore properly so designated; and 2) many diseases which have this in common with true functional disease, that they are transient and not permanent, that they are not known to depend on organic changes. (quoted in Marsden, 1986, p. 277)

More recently, Slater (1965) noted that there is virtually no hysterical symptom that cannot also be produced by well-defined, nonhysterical, medical causes. For example, acute intermittent porphyria, systemic lupus erythematosus, and psychomotor epilepsy are all commonly misdiagnosed as hysteria, especially in their early stages. Woodruff and colleagues (1971) have observed that patients with unexplained hysterical-looking symptoms often go on to develop other illnesses. Similarly, in a nine-year follow-up study by Slater and Glithero (1965), some sixty percent of patients originally diagnosed as hysteric had died from, or developed signs of, physical disease during the interim and a high proportion suffered from disorders of the central nervous system.

According to Whitlock (1967), organic correlates of hysteria are quite common. One study (Currie et al., 1971) found that gross hysterical symptoms were more frequent in a series of patients with temporal lobe epilepsy than in patients with schizophrenia. In Whitlock's (1967) series over sixty percent of patients with hysterical symptoms suffered from significant preceding or coexisting organic brain disorders, compared with about five percent of a control group. Similarly, Merskey and Buhrich (1975) found that many of their hysterical conversion patients had some organic diagnosis; of these, about half had pathology directly or systemically affecting the brain. In Whitlock's (1967) series more female than male hysterics showed evidence of organic brain disorder and hysterical symptoms were more frequently preceded by organic brain disorders in younger than in older patients. However, there was no correlation between any particular kind of organic brain disorder and a particular class of hysterical symptom.

MMPI patterns in patients with multiple sclerosis are often indistinguishable from those of hysterical patients (Ziegler et al., 1963). This is no doubt due to the fact that an "organic" disease that is notorious for producing multiple and often transitory somatic symptoms will prompt the same kinds of questionnaire responses as a syndrome in which "psychogenic" somatization phenomena are the hallmark. This was reinforced by Cripe's (1988) study that found elevations in MMPI scales measuring hypochondriasis, depression, hysteria, psychasthenia, and schizophrenia in neurologic patients without any other significant psychopathology. In this regard, it is of historical interest that much of Charcot's work on hysteria was informed by his experience with multiple sclerosis patients.

Roughly half of all hysterical conversion symptoms involve some disorder of movement (Marsden, 1986; cf. Breuer and Freud's cases and the more recent cases discussed in Chapters 3 and 5). In both idiopathic torsion dystonia and the dystonias secondary to phenothiazine-induced tardive dyskinesia, the muscular spasmodic activity may increase or remit in response to emotional stress or verbal suggestion, which may lead to a diagnosis of hysteria (Angus & Simpson, 1970). In fact, a wide variety of hysterical-looking motor symptoms can be produced by torsion dystonia, including spasmodic torticollis, writer's cramp, blepharospasm, and spasmodic dysphonia (Engel, 1970). In Marsden's (1986) clinical experience fifty percent or more of such patients are diagnosed initially as hysterics, yet of over four hundred dystonia patients seen personally by Marsden only five had a rigorous diagnosis of hysteria finally confirmed.

Marsden's (1986) concern seems to be a legitimate one: as we have seen in previous chapters, many "hysterical" symptoms are later shown to have a true "organic" etiology once the proper diagnostic tools are employed or new organic disease syndromes are identified and studied. If symptoms that were yesterday called hysterical are today considered to be (at least partly) organic because our modern knowledge of pathophysiology is greater than in the past, might not today's hysterical symptoms just as naturally become tomorrow's medical syndromes as our knowledge continues to grow? Not necessarily, Marsden points out, because the discovery of new diseases probably cannot go on forever, and such new diseases certainly will not account for many of the one percent (Marsden's figure) of neurological patients presenting with bona fide hysterical symptoms.

For this reason, I think it is time to abandon the strict dichotomy between organic and hysterical and to begin to conceptualize conversion within a broader, more comprehensive neuropsychodynamic framework. The first step is to examine how—if we may be forgiven for abusing the homuncular metaphor—the mind might use the brain to affect the body.

Neurophysiological Mechanisms of Conversion

Whitlock (1967) speculates that when sufficiently stressed or damaged, almost any person's central nervous system will develop reactions of the kind exemplified by hysterical symptoms; as we saw in the last chapter, kindling-like neurophysiological processes may contribute to this. Merskey and Buhrich (1975) suggest that there exists some causal relationship between organic cerebral dysfunction and hysterical manifestations, although the relationship may be indirect. On the other hand, Whitlock (1967) feels that in some cases the effects of psychogenic disturbances may summate with the effects of a brain lesion to produce hysterical symptoms. In either case, what might the mechanism be?

In a kind of protosociobiological theory of hysterical conversion, Kretschmer (1926) argued that most forms of hysteria could be regarded as manifestations of two instinctive reaction patterns that, he believed, are prevalent throughout the animal kingdom and that represent mechanisms of biological adaptation to dangerous or threatening situations. The first, Kretschmer characterized as the *violent motor reaction*, exemplified by the wild flailing response many animals show when trying to escape injury, capture, or confinement. The counterpart to this in human hysteria can be seen in fugue states, convulsive paroxysms, and violent emotional attacks with subsequent amnesia and tremors—exactly the kind of wild activity popularly and often pejoratively labeled "hysterical."

The second kind of reaction Kretschmer called the *sham death* or *immobilization reflex*, in which inactivity and seemingly stuporous features predominate. Animals and humans often "freeze" when confronted with a threat; this immobilization serves to obscure the identity or whereabouts of the threatened party or to convey a message of innocuous nonchallenge, which will, hopefully, deflect a risky confrontation. Human hysterical analogues to this second pattern, Kretschmer said, might include twilight and dreamy states, "spells," blindness, deafness, analgesia, paralysis, movement disorders, and speech impairment.

More recently, Kretschmer's (1926) formulation has been revived and expanded by Ludwig (1972). The latter posits a natural tendency for animals and humans to react in progressively more primitive ways when confronted with potentially dangerous and inescapable situations. Under such conditions, organisms readily and automatically resort to behaviors appropriate to prior developmental stages, behaviors that appear regressive or "childish." These include urinary incontinence, babbling, rocking, head bobbing, crying, vivid fantasizing, and so on—the kinds of reactions often associated with "shell shock" or catastrophic stress reactions. This type of regressive activity contributes to the posture of helplessness and defenselessness that, like Kretschmer's (1926) sham death–immobilization reflex, passively wards off attack. In addition, the resulting alteration in consciousness blurs reality testing and thereby provides a certain psychological insulation from the dangerous situation. In the case of human hysteria, if any of these ontogenetically primitive behaviors are reinforced by their success in actually removing or escaping from the danger or threat, they will more than likely be resorted to automatically under similar circumstances in the future.

Ludwig (1972) places attentional dysfunction at the pathological core of the hysterical conversion syndrome. In this view, the hysteric experiencing, say, a sensory-loss conversion reaction suffers from a dissociation between brain systems responsible for mediating the raw perceptual data, that is, the informational or content part of the incoming stimulation, and those that deal with the individual's ability to attend to that input in the first place.

Neurophysiological research has shown that the conscious appreciation of a particular sensory impression, whether sight, sound, smell, or body sense, depends not just on the sensory pathway conveying that sensation but also on the participation of a separate, collateral, but facilitatory route called the *reticular activating system* (RAS). This chain of neural structures and connections is responsible for literally directing attention to incoming sensory information at different levels of nervous system processing. Damage to the RAS produces a condition in which the sensory areas of the brain may process the information normally (as shown, for example, by the EEG), but the person remains subjectively unaware of the stimulus; it simply does not "register." Normal sensory perception, then, depends on the coordinated activity of the neural systems conveying the incoming sensory data themselves *and* the reticular mechanisms governing appropriate attention to and registration of that information (Brodal, 1969; Grossman, 1967; Thompson, 1975).

Even intense stimuli, like the pain from a serious battlefield wound, which under ordinary circumstances would certainly consume all of a person's interest, may be relegated to the fringes of consciousness if more pressing concerns—like figuring out how to escape from the immediate threat to life and limb—supervene. Also, it is frequently difficult for a person to pay attention to some trivial external situation or material— say, a magazine article—when he/she is preoccupied by some more pressing inner concern, for example, agonizing over possible biopsy results in the doctor's waiting room.

However, in most circumstances, individuals possess a certain conscious flexibility and volitional control over attentional processes. A student can "force" himself to concentrate on boring academic course material in favor of a much anticipated ballgame on TV in the next room if he knows he is having an important test the next day. Similarly, a person may "force" his attention away from exceedingly unpleasant thoughts or feelings related to painful experiences such as a recent disappointment, injustice, humiliation, or obsessive worry. In some cases this serves the adaptive function of permitting constructive action to take place by keeping the mind from being totally swamped by unpleasant affect; we try not to dwell on painful thoughts in order to allow ourselves to move on to other things.

But there are certain people who seem to make a habit of turning their attention away from unpleasant things, even when they can or should do something about them, and many of these people come to clinical attention as hysterics with conversion symptoms. According to Ludwig (1972), in hysterical conversions that involve derangements of sensory processing and movement (because normal motor activity depends on adequate sensory feedback from movements), there occurs a dissociation between attention and certain sources of incoming stimulation. Attention to a symptom of disability, like anesthesia or paralysis, is usually necessary for there to be any degree of concern over it. Thus, the inhibition of reticular attentional mechanisms that is involved in the disability itself may also account for the blithe unconcern around it, *la belle indifférence*, which has been noted for a century to be one of the hallmarks of the clinical picture of hysterical conversion.

Moreover, posits Ludwig (1972), there exists in hysterical conversion an *ideomotor schism* that renders it virtually impossible for the hysteric to consciously and volitionally mobilize attention toward the symptom. The patient cannot, therefore, "willingly" remedy the dysfunction. Ludwig proposes that hysterical conversion may be due to the action of attention-inhibiting impulses brought about by particularly intense emotional experiences. The awareness of bodily function is, as it were, shouted down by the emotional cacophony that competes for reticular attentional mechanisms. In line with this, temporary improvement or disappearance of the symptoms would be most likely to occur during periods of relaxed vigilance or under conditions, such as hypnosis or the use of barbiturate drugs, that selectively inhibit the reticular formation (French et al., 1955).

Several studies have, in fact, confirmed the existence of neurophysiological and psychophysiological changes in hysterical conversion reactions, and attempts have been made to demonstrate abnormalities in cerebral arousal and physiological reactivity in patients with so-called "somatoform disorders" (Miller, 1984a). Rosen (1951) characterized conversion patients as manifesting "physiological negativism" on the basis of their responses to the cold-pressor procedure. In this technique, the subject immerses his hand in a receptacle of ice water, the usual response to which is a significant rise in blood pressure as peripheral blood vessels reflexively constrict. In Rosen's study, conversion hysterics were observed to show a significantly lessened blood pressure response to this procedure, suggesting that their nervous systems are characteristically underresponsive to physiologically activating stimuli.

A seemingly opposite result was obtained in a subsequent study by Meares and Horvath (1972), which found greater than normal physiological activity in the form of higher heart rate, sweat gland activity, and muscle activity in patients with chronically debilitating conversion symptoms, poor interpersonal and occupational coping skills, and long histories of multiple medical complaints. Together, these two studies hardly confirm any consistent direction in hysterics' physiological reactivity. However, they do seem to suggest that hysterics may show an unusually greater *lability* of physiological reactivity to certain stressful stimuli.

Lader (1973) took the results of such studies to indicate that patients with conversion symptoms have a consistently high anxiety level. Earlier, Lader and Sartorius (1968) had compared hysteria patients with chronic anxiety patients and found that the hysterics actually rated themselves as more anxious than did the anxiety patients. However, the ratings of the examining psychiatrists were in the opposite direction; that is, they rated the hysterics as less anxious than the anxiety patients. When recordings were made of the subjects' levels of psychophysiological arousal, the physiological readings agreed with the patients, not the doctors; that is, the hysterics displayed greater physiological signs of arousal than did the anxiety patients.

Could this mean that *la belle indifférence*—the seemingly bland unconcern that characterizes hysterics with conversion reactions—could in fact be masking a deeper inner anxiety that is not observable on the surface during a cursory clinical interview? Finally, this study found that conversion symptoms tended to persist longer in those hysteria patients who had both high anxiety self-ratings and greater recorded physiological arousal, supporting the view that greater lability of arousal mechanisms may be associated with a more pronounced susceptibility to hysterical conversion.

The work considered thus far has focused on the body's response to neurophysiological processes, but what about the response of the brain itself? One technique that has been used to study the brain's reaction to arousing stimuli is the *cortical evoked response*. Here, a visual, auditory, or tactile stimulus is delivered to one of the senses, and the activity "evoked" in the brain as it processes the incoming sensory data is detected by means of recording electrodes. In this manner clinicians or researchers are able to determine the electrophysiological state of brain activity as the brain deals with certain kinds of information.

The first studies of the evoked response, carried out by Hernandez-Peon and colleagues (1956), were with cats. These researchers reported that evoked responses to stimuli in one sensory modality, like hearing, could be blocked by presenting salient stimuli to other sensory modalities, such as smell or vision. That is, the brain activity of a cat showing strong and reliable evoked responses to a tone would become virtually silent when the smell of fish or the sight of a live mouse was introduced at the same time as the tone. Fish and mice, being generally more important to cats than the electronically produced noises of the experimenters, overrode the evoked response to the tone. In essence, the cat's attention was diverted from the tone to the fish or mouse, and this was reflected in the brain's activity.

From these results the researchers concluded that sensation and perception are not passive processes but that the brain actively regulates the amount and type of incoming information arriving through the different sensory pathways by means of reticular attentional mechanisms. Could such an influence over incoming sensory information exerted by reticular mechanisms somehow be associated with the hysteric's seeming out-of-touchedness with his/her own body and its functions?

One early application of the evoked response technique to the study of hysterical conversion was carried out by the Hernandez-Peon group themselves (Hernandez-Peon et al., 1963). The case involved a fifteen-year-old girl with *glove-and-stocking anesthesia* over the left side of her body. This syndrome is so named because the patient complains of complete loss of feeling in the hands or feet that abruptly ends at some point midarm or midleg, exactly as if the zone of sensory loss were precisely defined by the contours of a glove or sock.

Organic brain dysfunction that produces sensory loss virtually never involves such a sharply demarcated zone of impairment bordered by completely normal sensation. Instead, the sensory loss over a given area of body surface tends to have irregular borders and a graded severity, with completely anesthetic areas surrounded by regions of lesser impairment and shading gradually outward into normal sensibility; Freud, as we saw, described this well in his *Comparative Study* of 1893. In rare cases, toxic–metabolic damage to peripheral nerves in the limbs themselves may produce a syndrome resembling glove-and-stocking anesthesia, but this is typically accompanied by other symptoms, such as pain and sometimes motor dysfunction, that distinguish it from its hysterical counterpart.

The hysterical girl in Hernandez-Peon's study showed clear-cut evoked responses from the somatosensory areas of the brain that process input from the normal right forearm. However, when the conversion-impaired left forearm was stimulated, no definite brain response was seen. It appeared as if this patient were suffering from an impairment of attention related to perception of the hysterically anesthetic limb.

Levy and Behrman (1970) studied a forty-three-year-old woman with right-sided hysterical hemianesthesia. This time, two levels of sensory stimulation were used, high and low. In addition, the experimenters varied the location of the stimuli: on some trials the stimulus was applied to the skin surface of the forearm, other times directly to the ulnar nerve that conveys sensory information from the arm to the central nervous system. The investigators found that high-intensity stimuli applied to the ulnar nerve on the hysterically anesthetic side of the body produced evoked responses equal to those obtained upon stimulation of the nonaffected side. With low-intensity stimulation, however, the response to stimulation on the affected side was less than that of the nonaffected side. When the stimuli were applied to the skin of the forearm, the evoked responses from the affected side were diminished, compared with the nonaffected side, and this was true both for high and low levels of stimulation.

Thus, the hypothesized cortex-to-reticular inhibition can apparently be overriden if the sensory stimulation is intense enough *and* if it is applied directly to the sensory nerve, as opposed to having to be processed as a normal skin sensation. These findings were subsequently replicated with several other patients having hysterical anesthesias (Levy & Mushin, 1973). Moreover, in cases where the hysterical conversion went into remission, the differences in evoked responses between the normal and the formerly affected side seemed to disappear as well; that is, the electrophysiological brain activity was observed to change in accord with the clinical course of the hysterical conversion syndrome.

Thus far, the attentional component of Ludwig's (1972) theory of hysterical conversion appears to have some support: the process of conversion apparently takes advantage of corticoreticular mechanisms in a way that for most people is foreign to ordinary waking consciousness. The hysteric appears to be able to allocate attention in a special and abnormal way, so that bodily function and concern over the loss of that function are both "canceled out."

But what of the sensorimotor component of some hysterical conversion symptoms? Is there a structure or locus or network or region in the brain that could be responsible for deficits in the ability to consciously appreciate and use perceptual information in the presence of intact sensory pathways? That is, does there exist in the brain an identifiable system that may be involved in translating ideogenic unconscious influences into hysterical somatosensory impairment?

Second Somatosensory Area

This section will apply fairly specifically to hysterical sensory loss and simple sensorimotor conversion symptoms; the brain mechanisms involved in more complex motor phenomena, that is, actions, will be considered in greater detail when we deal with parapraxic phenomena in Part IV.

Neuropsychological research has shown at least one cerebral structural system to possess properties that would make it particularly appropriate for the analysis and evaluation of complex, meaningful patterns of somesthetic input. This is the *second somatosensory area*, or *SSII*, whose cortical representation in man lies on the upper bank of the sylvian fissure, adjacent to the insula (Brodal, 1969; Carpenter, 1976; Mountcastle, 1974).

Responses to stimulation of SSII have been found to be bilateral, although contralateral responses are more marked (Mountcastle, 1974; Ochs, 1965). The neuronal synaptic organization mediating somesthetic input to SSII appears to be less discrete and somatotopic—that is, having less of a point-for-point correspondence between different parts of the body and specific regions of the cortex—than in the postcentral primary somatosensory area, or SSI (Mountcastle, 1974). While modality-specific units—neurons that respond to only one type of somatosensory stimulus or from one part of the body—exist in SSII, most neurons in this area react to stimulation of both the body surface and internal visceral structures, and some neurons have large receptive fields, implying integration of more diffuse input from relatively wide areas of the body (Brodal, 1969; Mountcastle, 1974).

SSII appears to subserve information from lemniscal–epicritic, as well as from spinothalamic–protopathic systems (Brodal, 1969; Carpenter, 1976). The former, *epicritic*, carry somatosensory information relating to touch, light pressure, limb position, and more precise, localized kinds of body sensations, such as those that allow us to detect a fly crawling on our arm and swat it accurately without looking or to know that an object or surface is rough or smooth, course or fine, by feeling it. *Protopathic* sensory systems are concerned more with diffuse, less accurately localized sensations like pain, temperature, and deep pressure, such as a poorly defined ache in the abdomen or coldness in a limb. Other response characteristics of neurons in SSII include being both place- and modality-nonspecific, that is, responding to input from more than one source and of more than one type (Carpenter, 1976; Mountcastle, 1974), although SSII may play a special role in some forms of pain perception (Carpenter, 1976).

Experimental studies with monkeys have shown SSII to receive cross-callosal projections from contralateral SSI and SSII, while SSII sends projections only to contralateral SSII, but not to SSI (Jones & Powell, 1969a, 1969b). SSII is known to have reciprocal connections with the posterior thalamic zone that subserves protopathic sensation, including pain, and with the intralaminar thalamic nucleus, which is the chief subcortical representative of the reticular formation involved in regulating attention and arousal (Brodal, 1969; Ochs, 1965). Moreover, spinothalamic projections to the intralaminar nucleus are known to be bilateral (Carpenter, 1976), thus affording SSII, by means of its reciprocal thalamic connections, access to diffusely, nonsomatotopically represented, affectively and attentionally linked somatic information from relatively wide regions of both sides of the body.

In man, electrical stimulation of SSII has been found to produce sensations of tingling, numbness, and warmth, which are less subjectively localizable and more likely to be bilaterally referred than sensations produced by stimulation of SSI (Penfield & Faulk, 1955; Penfield & Jasper, 1954). Often, abdominal and gastric sensations are reported upon stimulation of SSII, and this is frequently accompanied by a concomitant change in gastric motility (Penfield & Faulk, 1955).

As we saw in a previous chapter, SSII and the areas surrounding it appear to play a role in the "pure" localization of somesthetic stimuli without appreciation of intensity or quality, the somatosensory equivalent of "blindsight," the seemingly uncanny ability of some otherwise totally blind people to correctly orient themselves in space (Palliard et al., 1983; Woolsey et al., 1979). As we have also seen, in at least one case, attacks of bilateral paresthesias with retained consciousness, initially diagnosed as psychogenic epilepsy, were found to represent true seizure activity whose most probable origin was SSII (Lesser et al., 1983). Stimulation of SSII has also been found to result in complex body movements and may thus play a role in sensory feedback, or "reafferent" sensory control of motor function (Brodal, 1969; Carpenter, 1976).

Thus, SSII, by virtue of its interactions with protopathic–sensory, affective–arousal, and attentional–motivational systems, may be one cerebral structural system intimately involved in the genesis of hysterical sensory conversion symptoms. Further, SSII may possess the type of information-processing characteristics that are functionally and descriptively related to what could be referred to as "unconscious" aspects of somatic apperception (Miller, 1984a, 1986a, 1986–1987). And inasmuch as normal voluntary motor control requires precise and accurate on-line feedback from sensory systems, functional alterations in SSII might account for some species of hysterical motor disorders as well (more about complex motor phenomena in Part III).

Perhaps in SSII we can begin to look for how an ideogenic entity can be translated into one kind of hysterical symptom: hysterical somatosensory impairment. With SSII as a nodal point in the symbolic–sensory transduction process, psychical forces may exert their effects on the functioning of the body. The entire process may be facilitated by a paroxysmally induced overlability of the functional state of the brain as a whole, as expressed, in some cases, in the form of altered states of consciousness (cf. Breuer's "hypnoid states"). And these states might be induced under conditions of external stress or inner turmoil by a subtle kindling-like mechanism affecting reticular, limbic, and cortical systems of the brain.

But having specified a neurophysiological mechanism (i.e., paroxysmal alterations in functional brain state) and a neuroanatomic system (i.e., SSII) as hypothetical substrates for at least one class of hysterical conversion symptoms, namely, hysterical somatosensory loss or alteration, we may be tempted to forget that hysterical symptoms typically occur not in neurological or psychological isolation but in a personological context. Even Breuer and Freud acknowledged that certain personality types are more susceptible to the manifestations of hysteria (Charcot was even more adamant about this), and indeed, clinicians frequently speak of the "hysterical personality" as well as of hysterical symptoms. Going several steps beyond hysterical conversion itself, what might be the neuropsychodynamic relationships between thought and feeling, perception and action, personality and symptomatology, that determine the clinical manifestations of hysteria in its broadest, characterological sense?

CHAPTER 7

Hysteria: Neuropsychology, Personality, and Cognitive Style

The term *cognitive style* was introduced by Klein (1954) to refer to the individual arrangement of general regulatory or mental control structures in the psyche of a particular person, such as native intelligence, verbal or spatial ability, proficiency of memory, capacity for sustained attention and concentration, and so on. These "cognitive controls," Klein suggested, may have a basis in the type of constitutional intellectual talents and deficits originally suggested by Hartmann (1939). The idea was that, in any given person, the direction of symptomatological and characterological expression taken by Freudian psychodynamics—unconscious conflicts, repressed fears and wishes, and so forth—is shaped by the particular cognitive style that the person is constitutionally endowed with. For example, a highly verbal and logical individual might express his neuroses through obsessive speaking and writing, someone with a more emotional or imaginal bent would be drawn to fantasy and the arts, the person with a poor memory might be prone to repression and confabulation, and so on.

The notion of cognitive style was subsequently adapted by Shapiro (1965) in his concept of *neurotic styles*:

> By "style" I mean a form or mode of functioning—the way or manner of a given area of behavior—that is identifiable in an individual through a range of his specific acts. By "neurotic styles" I mean those modes of functioning that seem characteristic, respectively, of the various neurotic conditions. (p. 1)

What are taken clinically as neurotic symptoms or pathological personality traits, says Shapiro (1965), regularly appear in the context of a

90

person's attitudes, interests, intellectual endowments, and even vocational aptitudes and social affinities. From this perspective the patient does not simply "suffer" a neurosis, as one suffers from a cold or a toothache, but actively participates in it and sustains it. His/her cognitive style is an integral part of his neurotic functioning, moving him/her to think, feel, and act in ways that both confirm and reinforce it. The way a person characteristically organizes his/her perceptions, thoughts, feelings, and attitudes is in large part determined by his/her particular cognitive style, and this style also influences the ways in which the person deals with life and with his/her own reactions to the world around him/her. Recently, the theory of personality and cognitive style has been extended and reconceptualized neuropsychologically by Miller (1990). Can this approach be applied fruitfully to the neuropsychodynamics of hysteria?

The Hysterical Cognitive Style

According to Shapiro (1965), the hysterical cognitive style is global, relatively diffuse, and lacking in sharp focus of attention and detail, in other words, highly impressionistic. The hysteric tends to respond quickly and impulsively and is highly susceptible to what is immediately striking or obvious. Hysterics' perceptions and conclusions are based on immediate, emotionally salient impressions, not on active analysis of situations. Their lack of intense intellectual concentration and their resulting distractibility and impressionability account for the largely nonfactual world—the "fantasy world"—in which hysterics typically live.

For the hysteric, the hunch or first impression is the guiding cognitive process. This explains the common clinical observation that hysterics are relatively lacking in intellectual curiosity, even the mundane inquisitiveness about events around them that most people display. Inasmuch as most intellectual pursuits require at least some degree of sustained, focused attention, the hysteric, poorly endowed in this area, shows a marked disinclination for cognitively demanding work, although, as we have seen, exceptions do exist, as in the case of Anna O and Margaret, mentioned in a previous chapter.

Hysterics are often remarkably deficient in everyday factual knowledge that has no immediate emotional impact or practical use. They may follow intently the lives of soap opera characters (or, in Breuer and Freud's time, the equally lurid "penny-dreadful" serializations) but be unable to name the current mayor of their city, to explain who fought the last great war, to tell what paper is made of, or give the correct freezing point of water. Hysterics are not necessarily dull-witted in the usual sense; they can learn skills or information when necessary for some particular purpose, such as a job or card game. Indeed, they often show reasonably good practical intelligence when it comes to dealing with everyday situations. But sustained intellectual concentration and a range of interests that transcend the immediate or personal are typically absent. Even the kinds of high-minded intellectual and aesthetic pursuits of the "romantic" type of Breuerian hysteric tend to be of a distinctly nonmundane, ivory-tower variety; one gets the impression that these people do not spend much time in the "real world."

According to Shapiro (1965), the hysterical style has a particular connection with the defense mechanism of *repression*, which may be facilitated by this style in two ways. First, the original thought or plan is not sharply and factually defined in the first place and is therefore not likely to be logically coordinated with other facts such as names, dates, places, and so on. Instead, the input itself is highly impressionistic and highly susceptible to displacement by, or fusion with, other previous or subsequent impressions. Even at the input stage, there is a failure of analysis, categorization, and cross-referencing of information with other incoming and already-stored data that might provide the necessary context for a stable mental representation. This, after all, is how we ordinarily form coherent personal histories; they evolve and develop as new experiences continue to be assimilated with previously formed self-conceptions throughout our lives. But the hysteric's input is amorphous, garbled, unanalyzed, and unarticulated, especially with respect to those forms of input that require any kind of sustained or focused attention.

Second, the relative incapacity for sharply focused attention and concentration, as well as the passive, impressionistic, and distractible nature of the hysteric's cognitive style, also affects the recollection of already-stored material. Thus, clear, sharp, factual recall of memories is difficult even under the best of circumstances. Remembering something ordinarily requires some measure of active, directed attention, a kind of internal search mode. This, in turn, is facilitated by a certain degree of analysis, categorization, and sometimes verbal labeling, which enable the rememberer to pull from the brain's numberless bits of stored data just those fragments of fact and experience that are relevant to the situation at hand.

But when such internal scanning is deficient, one memory blends fuzzily with the next. Scenes and events, persons and places, thoughts and reactions, are comingled in an undifferentiated mental mélange. Thus, the hysteric gives one version of a story one minute and a different version the next—not necessarily out of willful prevarication but because what is remembered is more dictated by the feeling of the moment than by any concentrated effort to produce a factual recall. How apropos, then, Breuer and Freud's (1895) famous comment that "hysterics suffer mainly from reminiscences" (p. 7).

The often-cited naïveté of hysterics is also understandable in light of their cognitive style. The hysteric's inability to become fully aware of unpleasant material lying at the periphery of awareness is abetted by an incapacity to clearly and sharply focus attention. This cognitive style also predisposes the hysteric to the idealized, romantic recollection for which the histrionic Sarah Bernhardts of stage, screen, and literary fiction are so renowned. Typically, the hysteric's recollection is conspicuously lacking in factual detail, and, as Shapiro (1965) notes, one sometimes gets the impression that, for the hysteric, a sober, dispassionate analysis of objective facts would "spoil" the story.

This same quality is evident in the hysteric's idealization of the object of his/her romantic love. Blindness to a beloved's objective flaws permits the creation of a perfect fantasy-image of the loved other. Conversely, immediate global impressions of revulsion, disgust, petulant jealousy, and wounded outrage come just as easily and with the same obliviousness to complicating details or extenuating circumstances. The hysterical-romantic view thus has its villains as well as its heroes—often the same person at different times or when the hysteric is in different moods.

The hysteric's romantic, fantastical, and nonfactual experience of the world may also extend to the experience of his/her own self. Hysterics often do not *feel* like very substantial beings with real and factual histories, that is, with stable identities. Indeed, the hysteric is often barely aware of his/her own life story, except to the extent that it exists in the form of what Shapiro (1965) calls a "romance-history," a story populated by impressionistically perceived, romantic, or idealized figures.

Related to the frequently cited overemotionality of hysterics, their abrupt and often explosive emotional displays (as in "getting hysterical"), are a relative absence of complex cognitive integration and a quick impressionistic mode of information processing. Easily triggered, these emotional displays erupt into consciousness as the final emotional product, just as the immediate global impression emerges as the final cognitive product. The emotion undergoes little mental elaboration before being expressed in its raw, elemental form. This tendency is, in turn, abetted by the hysteric's global, immediate, and impressionistic style: feelings are experienced all at once, in an all-or-none fashion, and responses to feelings are correspondingly immediate and intense. Hysterical outbursts thus complete the picture of the hysterical cognitive style.

Neuropsychology of the Hysterical Cognitive Style

Recall from the last chapter Ludwig's (1972) model of hysteria, which is based on anomalies of attention and memory due to alterations in reticular function. Bendefeldt and colleagues (1976) sought to examine Ludwig's memory-attentional dysfunction hypothesis more systematically by employing a battery of psychological tests. These were administered to a group of hospitalized psychiatric patients diagnosed as suffering from hysterical conversion reactions, as well as to a group of nonhysterical matched control subjects. The test battery included measures of memory, attention and concentration, suggestibility, and field dependency/independency (i.e.,the tendency for perceptual judgments to be affected by external influences rather than by autonomous decisions).

In comparison to controls, the patients with hysterical conversion disorders were found to be more suggestible and more dependent on outside environmental cues and influences in making perceptual decisions (i.e., more field-dependent), to have greater memory impairment, and to show diminished vigilance and attention. The findings, therefore, appear to support Ludwig's (1972) earlier cognitive conceptualization of the hysteric.

Of equal interest for our present purposes, however, is the similarity between the cognitive profile suggested by Bendefeldt and colleagues' (1976) data and Shapiro's (1965) delineation of the hysterical cognitive style. That is, the hysteric's approach to experience is one of global, impressionistic, uncritical receptivity. Paradoxically, despite the exquisite attentional—albeit "unconscious"—control that the hysteric seems to exert over internal bodily states, his/her attention to the external world at large is correspondingly fuzzy. Perhaps in this very moment-to-moment changeability of information processing lies the neuropsychodynamic clue to the hysterical cognitive style, just as the psychophysiological lability discussed in the last chapter might help us understand the nature of hysterical conversion.

An ambitious study that sought to compare cerebral laterality patterns in hysterical and obsessive personalities was carried out by Smokler and Shevrin (1979), based on Levy and Trevarthen's (1976) concept of *hemispheric metacontrol.* According to the hemispheric metacontrol model, different kinds of cognitive tasks are handled preferentially by the two cerebral hemispheres (e.g., analytic and verbal tasks by the left hemisphere, synthetic and visuospatial tasks by the right). Given a particular task or situation, a person would be expected to apply the most "appropriate" hemisphere to that job. Since few tasks are entirely unidimensional, each hemisphere will normally contribute its specific skills and talents to those components of the task for which it is best suited. At some level of processing, the brain "makes a decision" about how to allocate hemispheric responsibility for the solution of different problems or the handling of different kinds of material. In most cases, according to the theory, people can adaptively direct this sort of metacontrol in their own brains, albeit usually without awareness of anything other than just "figuring out" how to solve the problem or get the job done.

However, some individuals may characteristically opt to use the "wrong," or less proficient, hemisphere to solve cognitive tasks or deal with broader life situations, even though this results in less than optimal performance and adjustment. The reason for this may be that other processing characteristics of the preferred hemisphere—its overall cognitive style—may be relied upon for more general features of personality and may come to dominate behavior, resulting in less flexible overall functioning. Smokler and Shevrin (1979) reasoned that a strongly "left-hemisphere person" would be one who analyzes everything in a piecemeal analytic manner, even in situations where this might be inappropriate, whereas a strongly "right-hemisphere person" would deal with all situations in a global manner, rarely analyzing details in a direct way.

On the basis of their review of the personality literature, the investigators delineated what they considered to be the main features of the hysterical personality style: (1) a strong tendency to repress disturbing ideas, (2) emotional lability, and (3) a concrete, stimulus-bound approach to problem solving rather than a logicodeductive approach. The hysterical-style tendency toward repression of ideas, argued the authors, seems consistent with a right hemisphericity preference. That is, it is not that hysterical personalities entirely lack the ability to reason and think logically; rather, these modes of cognition seem to be avoided in favor of other, more preferred, ways of responding to situations. The emotional lability would be consistent with findings that suggest greater right-hemisphere participation in emotional functioning. Thus, in this model, the hysterical-style approach to problem solving most closely corresponds to the neuropsychologically identified metacontrol processing style of the right hemisphere.

Conversely, the investigators described the obsessive–compulsive style as characteristically (1) repressing disturbing affects, (2) treating everything in an ideational way, even when inappropriate (e.g., aesthetic or emotional experiences), and (3) favoring a logicodeductive approach to problem solving rather than a concrete, stimulus-bound approach. In this model, the paucity of emotion in favor of a preponderance of ideation—an earmark of the obsessive style—would be consistent with a left hemisphericity preference. Again, this is not to imply that obsessive–compulsives never use their right hemispheres, only that right hemisphere functions are used proportionately less even in situations appropriate to right hemisphere bias (for more extensive discussions of neuropsychology, personality, and cognitive style, see Miller, 1986a, 1988b, 1990, 1991).

To evaluate their theory, Smokler and Shevrin (1979) first gave a large group of subjects the Rorschach test and a self-administered form of the Wechsler Adult Intelligence Scale (WAIS) Comprehension subtest.

On the basis of an analysis of the Rorschach protocols, subjects were divided into three subgroups: those with hysterical personality styles, those with obsessive–compulsive styles, and those with neither style predominant. These subjects next underwent an examination of *conjugate lateral eye movements* (LEMs), which are believed to be an index of dominant hemisphericity for problem solving (Gur & Gur, 1975, 1977).

Studies have shown that a person's gaze typically deviates to one side or the other just at the end of hearing a question, prior to giving the answer. The direction of the LEMs may indicate which hemisphere is most activated by the question and by the cognitive work required to produce a response. Because of the way the brain controls eye movements, the shift is characteristically in the direction opposite the activated hemisphere. Accordingly, a particular LEM could be influenced by the type of question asked; for example, verbal or logical questions would result in a rightward shift (left hemisphere predominant) whereas spatial or emotional questions would cause a leftward shift (right hemisphere predominant). Or the direction of LEMs could be influenced by the type of processing style the person uses to handle most problems, regardless of type; for example, an overrational person would show a preponderance of right shifts (left hemisphere), regardless of the nature of the question, while an overemotional person would show a left-shift predominance (right hemisphere) under the same circumstances.

To examine the interaction of question type and personality on hemispheric activation, Smokler and Shevrin (1979) asked the hysteric and obsessive subjects a series of forty questions, divided into three types: spatial–emotional, spatial–nonemotional, and verbal–nonemotional. The investigators found that the subjects with hysterical personality styles tended to look to the left during questioning, indicating predominant activation of the right hemisphere. The obsessive–compulsives, on the other hand, looked predominantly to the right, reflecting a more highly activated left hemisphere. Further, the type of question had no effect on LEM shifts, suggesting that overall personality style had a greater impact than problem type on hemispheric activation. That is, the differences between the hysterical and the obsessive–compulsive cognitive styles—styles that seem so diametrically opposed at the clinical level—may have a basis in opposite patterns of hemispheric activation; that is, there may be a rigid fixing of the normally flexible hemispheric metacontrol mechanism in one mode or the other, resulting in two entirely opposite ways of dealing with reality.

A study with a similar premise was carried out by Magaro and colleagues (1983), who began with the commonplace observation of how people go about searching through their home or workplace for an object. Some people employ what may be called a *serial search strategy*; that is, they seem to explore carefully and methodically, considering each alternative hiding place in its turn, and although this approach may at times seem slow and labored, they usually end up finding what they are looking for. Others rely on a *parallel search strategy* and seem to "look everywhere at once," the search proceeding virtually at random; sooner or later all the possibilities are covered one way or another, sometimes with success, other times resulting only in further frustration.

In addition to their everyday applications, search strategies are also useful for solving certain specialized cognitive tests. Magaro and colleagues (1983) reasoned that an individual with a compulsive cognitive style would be more likely to demonstrate a serial search strategy on such tasks while someone with a hysterical cognitive style would characteristically use a parallel search strategy.

To test this, groups of compulsive, hysteric, and control subjects were administered a visual search task in which they had to scan arrays of fifty-five-letter rows for a predesignated target letter. Contrary to the investigators' expectation, it was the hysterics, rather than the compulsives, who were more likely to use a serial processing style, especially in situations requiring the greatest amount of such processing. Compulsives seemed to conform more to the actual demands of the task in processing the stimuli; that is, they used both serial and parallel strategies as the situation demanded and did not, as the theory would predict, exhibit a dominant personality-based processing strategy that overrode task demands. However, although the hysterics relied on a serial processing style, they did worse on the task than the compulsives or the controls; that is, they were significantly slower to scan and process the stimuli.

The investigators' interpretation of these seemingly paradoxical findings is that hysterics have great difficulty in focusing on specific elements in a stimulus field; thus, when they attempt a careful serial analysis of stimulus elements, they quickly run into difficulty. The results suggest that hysterics do not necessarily use parallel processing all the time as an exclusive preferred mode of response, as originally hypothesized; instead, they often do try to use a serial processing strategy but use it badly. The hysterics may have preferred a parallel processing strategy, but because they believed that this particular task demanded a serial approach, they used an unaccustomed and unfamiliar serial processing strategy, which resulted in inefficient performance.

Another approach to the neuropsychology of hysteria was taken by Flor-Henry and colleagues (1981). Ten patients who satisfied strict clinical criteria (Perley & Guze, 1962) for the stable syndrome of hysteria were administered an extensive neuropsychological test battery. Their performance on these measures was compared with that of a larger group of previously tested subjects who had no prior history of neurologic or psychiatric disorder. As an added control, ten patients with schizophrenia and ten others with depressive disorders were studied.

An analysis of the test pattern results showed that, on the one hand, hysterics exhibited findings consistent with bilateral frontal and right frontotemporal dysfunction when compared to controls. On the other hand, findings suggestive of disturbed left-hemispheric functioning were also present. Moreover, the neuropsychological impairment patterns of hysterics resembled to some degree that of schizophrenics. On the basis of these findings, the investigators suggested that hysteria as a stable clinical syndrome is fundamentally related to left-hemisphere dysfunction. In turn, the observed indices of right-hemisphere dysfunction relate not to the essential neuropsychological nature of this syndrome but to the associated clinical features such as female predominance, emotional instability, dysphoric mood, and the presence of asymmetrical conversion symptoms.

Flor-Henry and colleagues (1981) further argue, on the basis of family studies (Cloninger et al., 1975; Guze et al., 1971) as well as neuropsychological results, that hysteria in the female is the syndromic equivalent of psychopathy (antisocial personality) in males, in which predominant left-hemisphere dysfunction is typically indicated on neuropsychological testing (see Miller, 1987, 1988a, for more comprehensive accounts of the neuropsychology of psychopathy, delinquency, and antisociality). Moreover, the Flor-Henry group suggest that true syndromic hysteria may represent in the female a relatively benign variant of schizophrenia characterized by imprecise verbal communications and a subtle form of emotional incongruity, in addition to the conversion dimension.

Thus, to Flor-Henry and colleagues (1981), the core deficits in hysteria consist of the impairment in verbal communication, the incongruity of emotional responsivity, and the difficulty in processing endogenous somatic signals. These are the consequences of altered left-hemispheric functioning, which produces, when it occurs in the female, a secondary disorganization of the contralateral right hemisphere, which in turn determines the flamboyant facade of female hysteria—the "hysterical" quality—but which at the same time may mask its fundamental left-hemisphere substrate.

Probably, hysteria as a syndrome will prove to be a heterogeneous clinical entity with many subtypes, as is the case with many kinds of mental disorders and clinical phenomena in general, and the varying laterality and localization patterns found on neuropsychological testing no doubt owe some of their diversity to this factor. However, for now, we must ask if a neuropsychological conceptualization can help bring together the phenomena of hysterical symptoms and the hysterical cognitive style in order to develop a truly integrative neuropsychodynamic model of hysteria.

Hysterical Conversion and the Hysterical Cognitive Style

Neurologists have long observed that patients with damage to the non-dominant (usually right) cerebral hemisphere frequently display a syndrome of *contralateral neglect* in which the part of the environment and areas of the body that lie in the sensory field opposite the side of the lesion, that is, the opposite "hemispace," are ignored or otherwise abnormally regarded (Critchley, 1953; Heilman et al., 1978). In some cases dysfunctional body parts are denied ownership by the patient or even attributed to someone else; shallow rationalizations for these beliefs may contribute to the clinical picture (Critchley, 1953; Heilman, 1979; Feinberg et al., 1990). Bizarre delusional systems have been known to develop around the affected body part or area, some even including paranoid psychotic features (Nightingale, 1982). Although neglect and related disorders can occur with left hemisphere lesions (affecting perception of the right hemispace), left-space perceptual syndromes resulting from right-hemisphere damage appear to be both more common and more clinically striking (Hecaen & Albert, 1978). In addition, the right hemisphere seems to play a special role in the apperception of the affective qualities of somatic signals coming from the body as a whole (Galin, 1974; Heilman & Valenstein, 1979).

Conversion symptoms tend to show an asymmetrical pattern of distribution. That is, if the pattern of symptoms were randomly distributed from patient to patient, one would expect to see the anesthesias, paralyses, and so forth occurring equally on both sides of the body. Yet studies have shown that conversion symptoms occur more frequently on the left side of the body than on the right, and this seems to be as true for left-handers as for right-handers (Galin et al., 1977; Stern, 1977). Moreover, complaints of pain, including both hysterical, psychogenic, pain as well as pain due to bona fide organic disease, appear to be more frequently referred to the left side of the body (Merskey & Watson, 1979). In addition, the right hemisphere may be more important than the left for mediating the ability to endure pain sensations in general (Cubelli et al., 1984).

Right-hemisphere emotionality is seen to have important implications for hysterical conversion disorders by such researchers as Stern (1977), who emphasizes the right brain's importance for the development of emotionally or motivationally determined somatic symptoms. And among psychoanalysts, Ferenczi (1926) proposed that the left side of the body is naturally more accessible to unconscious influences than the right side, which he believed to be better defended against unconscious influences by virtue of its being, for most people, more active and skillful than the left.

A number of modern neuropsychologists have seized upon the idea of the nonlinear, holistic, multiply convergent, affectively salient, and verbally inarticulate right-hemisphere cognitive style as forming the cerebral substrate for unconscious processes in general. As we will discuss further in Chapter 18, Galin (1974) regards certain aspects of right hemisphere cognition as congruent with primary process-style thinking, and Hoppe (1977) compares features of isolated right-hemisphere functioning in commissurotomized patients to certain "pure" aspects of unconscious thought. Similarly, the reinforcement of early emotional reaction patterns at a developmental stage prior to sufficient maturation of the cortex of the left cerebral hemisphere is regarded by Joseph (1982) as precluding adequate verbal–rational mediation of early experience; this would form the basis for repression, which in this model involves a self-comprehensible inarticulability of infantile wishes, fears, and residual behavior patterns, that is, an inability to "explain" such motives to oneself.

This brings us back to the role of attention in the production and perpetuation of hysterical symptoms. Studies of both brain-damaged and normal individuals have prompted the suggestion that the right hemisphere plays a special role in mediating attention and arousal involved in the processing of stimuli from both sides of the body and in preparing both hemispheres for a response. At the same time, the right hemisphere appears to have greater reciprocal connections than the left with the reticular formation so that even when there is bilateral representation of somatic arousal, some degree of contralateral (i.e., left-body) predominance exists.

Attention, however, is an active process, and several investigators have stressed the importance of a corticothalamic–reticular arousal loop whose cortical representation in man is found in the dorsolateral portion of the frontal lobe (Nauta, 1971), the part of the brain most involved in directing and controlling mental processes, including attention. In addition, reciprocal mediobasal frontal–limbic connections are important in handling emotional and motivational aspects of information processing and adaptive behavior (Luria, 1980), and evidence exists for a predominant role of the right hemisphere in mediating these emotional aspects of experience and behavior (Tucker, 1981).

Thus, it is tempting to view the global, inattentive, nonfocused, nonfactual, overemotional, and paramnesic cognitive style of hysterics as having a right-hemisphere neuropsychological substrate. Indeed, many of the aforementioned studies support this association. But as a number of the same kind of studies suggest, this relationship is probably more complex than allowed for by a narrow localizationist syndrome-equals-hemisphere approach (Miller, 1986a, 1986b).

For example, does hysterical cognition involve an overreactivity of the right hemisphere or an overreliance on the "wrong" (left) hemisphere to solve the "wrong" kinds of problems? Also, what components of the hysterical syndrome relate to an overreactive right hemisphere versus a deficient left hemisphere? And Flor-Henry and colleagues (1981) are probably correct in emphasizing the potential separability, syndromically and neuropsychologically, of the cognitive components of hysteria and the associated conversion and emotional symptomatological manifestations, at least in some cases. But in other cases the cognitive, affective, and symptomatological aspects of hysteria may actually cohere to a much greater degree.

The right-hemisphere component probably has more to do with the reticular attentional process itself and with the heightened emotionality and conversion symptoms that hysterics display. After all, the right hemisphere has the greater role in emotion and bodily perception and the stronger link to reticular attentional systems, which are themselves reciprocally influenced by the frontal lobes and their limbic connections.

Thus, an idea—that is, some psychical force, however defined—acts in a given person upon a preexisting personality and cognitive style based, in turn, upon his/her particular intra- and interhemispheric functional pattern, which shapes and determines how that person processes information from within and without, including thoughts, feelings, perceptions, words, and so on. In the case of the hysterical cognitive style, the neuropsychodynamic bias is away from analysis and reflection and more in the direction of repression and confabulation, just the condition that Freud hypothesized would lead to the development of hysterical conversion symptoms.

The mechanism by which such ideogenic forces become translated into a hysterical symptom may be through SSII in the case of somatosensory phenomena and through other, equivalent—perhaps as yet still undiscovered—brain systems in other modalities. Here, the nonsomatotopic anatomical arrangements, in addition to rich connections with limbic–emotional, reticular–attentional, and cortical–ideative brain systems, might provide for the complex neuropsychodynamic processes involved in the translation of a repressed wish, fear, or need into an impaired limb or other bodily function.

Finally, the lability and episodic fluctuations in mood and consciousness seen as common features of hysteria may be mediated by some paroxysmal kindling-like brain process. This in turn might induce, or at least facilitate, the functional brain state changes that abet the genesis and expression of hysterical symptoms—not just the sensory and motor manifestations but the entire panoply of hysterical phenomena.

PART THREE

Dreams

Any disquisition upon dreams which seeks to explain as many as possible of their observed characteristics from a particular point of view, and which at the same time defines the position occupied by dreams in a wider sphere of phenomena, deserves to be called a theory of dreams. The various theories will be found to differ in that they select one or the other characteristic of dreams as the essential one and take it as the point of departure for their explanations and correlations. It need not necessarily be possible to infer a *function* of dreaming (whether utilitarian or otherwise) from the theory. Nevertheless, since we have a habit of looking for teleological explanations, we shall be more ready to accept theories which are bound up with the attribution of a function of dreaming.

—SIGMUND FREUD,
The Interpretation of Dreams

CHAPTER 8

Brain Theories of Dreaming: Then and Now

The Interpretation of Dreams, which first appeared in 1900, was always regarded by Freud himself as his seminal work, his masterpiece. Throughout the many subsequent revisions in psychoanalytic theory and practice that spanned nearly four decades and despite the gradually changing and evolving metapsychological models and clinical principles, Freud kept the text of this book essentially intact (Holt, 1989). In the preface to the 1932 third revised English edition, he exclaimed,

> This book, with the new contribution to psychology which surprised the world when it was published, remains essentially unaltered. It contains, even according to my present-day judgement, the most valuable of all the discoveries it has been my good fortune to make. Insight such as this falls into one's lot but once in a lifetime. (p. xxxii)

This section will attempt to extend this insight into the realm of the brain, a realm that played an important part in spawning psychoanalytic dream theory and that may ultimately yield the most important clues to its significance for daily life.

Sleep and Dreams

Freud (1900) begins the first chapter of *The Interpretation of Dreams* by laying out the territory of his investigation:

> I have had little occasion to deal with the problem of sleep, for that is essentially a problem of physiology, even though one of the char-

105

acteristics of the state of sleep is that it brings about modifications in the conditions of functioning of the mental apparatus. The literature on the subject of sleep is accordingly disregarded in what follows. (p. 40)

Today, however, such disregard would be irresponsible; indeed, we can hardly begin to talk about dreams without at least a brief discussion of the brain mechanisms involved in sleep. We now know that the typical nightly sleep period is marked by several approximately ninety-minute cycles during which the brain of the dreamer passes through various levels, or stages, of sleep, from light sleep, through deeper and deeper stages of sleep, to what has been called REM, or *rapid eye movement*, sleep. During REM sleep most of what we remember as dreaming takes place. There is a heightened electrophysiological activation of the brain at the same time that most of the body musculature is temporarily paralyzed—as if the brain were trying to keep the dreamer from acting out the dream itself. The relationship between REM sleep and the non-REM phases depends on a delicately oscillating balance of action among a variety of brain stem nuclei, most prominently the *raphe* and the *locus coeruleus* (Grossman, 1967; Kleitman, 1963; Thompson, 1975). This will become important in our later discussion of the neuropsychology of dreaming. What determines *what* we dream about, however, was the main concern of Freud's *The Interpretation of Dreams* and is likewise the main agenda for this application of the neuropsychodynamic model.

Freud begins his tome by reviewing the theories of dreaming prominent in his day. As we will now see, everything old may indeed be new again, because many of the modern neuropsychological theories of dreaming bear a striking resemblance to those of Freud's contemporaries a hundred years ago, even though they are now presumably operating with a century's worth of hindsight and, in some ways at least, a radically different conception of the nervous system and its functioning. That is why the present chapter will review these theories together, the old and the new, in order to provide a context for the neuropsychodynamic model of dreaming that will presently be elaborated. (Most of these modern theories focus on the role of REM sleep in adaptive functioning, but for an unusual neurobiological view of non-REM sleep and its relationship to Freud's later theory of the repetition compulsion and the death instinct, see Stern, 1988.)

Dreaming to Remember

A number of Freud's contemporaries were prepared to reduce dreaming to an epiphenomenon of memory. By this account the function of dreaming was to facilitate the consolidation of memory traces from waking life in order to provide for continuity of experience and consistency in personality—which might also involve what Freud would later call a "regressive" function. For example, Freud (1900) quotes Sully (1893):

> Now, our dreams are a means of conserving these successive, earlier personalities. When asleep, we go back to the old ways of looking at things and of feeling about them, to impulses and activities which long ago dominated us. (p. 93)

Several modern-day dream theorists have independently picked up the thread of the memory-consolidation hypothesis and woven it into their own neurophysiologically based models of dreaming. For example, Winson (1985) takes as his starting point two observations from neurophysiological research: REM sleep and the hippocampal theta rhythm. Winson notes that REM sleep, unlike the relative neurophysiological quiescence that occurs during most of sleep, is marked by a great deal of brain activity, physiological arousal, rapid eye movements, and dreaming. All mammals have REM sleep except a phylogenetically primitive group, the *monotremes*, or egg-laying mammals, of which the Australian duck-billed platypus and the echidna, or spiny anteater, are the only surviving representatives.

The *echidna*, a small burrowing insectivore, is unusual in another respect. For most mammals, position on the phylogenetic scale is associated with a higher ratio of frontal cortex to other brain regions. The frontal lobes are involved in such cognitive processes as reasoning, planning, judgment, and the integration of experience and knowledge about real-world contingencies, the better to modulate behavior in a situation-appropriate and adaptive way. Primates have a proportionately greater volume of frontal cortex than other placental (i.e., live-birth, non-egg-laying) mammals, and humans have the largest proportion of frontal cortex of all. However, in the monotreme echidna the proportion of frontal cortex to the rest of the brain exceeds even that of man. What might this seeming paradox have to do with the fact that this animal lacks REM sleep?

For Winson (1985), the clue lies in the *hippocampal theta rhythm*. The hippocampus is a bilateral temporal lobe structure with a number of important functions, one of which is to fix ecologically relevant experiences (i.e., experiences important for survival) in memory, thus enabling the organism to learn and store new and valuable information. Hippocampal theta is observed mainly under two behavioral conditions. The first is when an animal is actively engaged in the processing of important species-specific and survival-relevant behaviors; this involves the assimilation and integration of ecologically relevant response patterns that are important to the adaptation of the species. Kittens, for example, show a great deal of theta activity when learning to kill prey, proper predation techniques obviously being an important lesson for cats to learn. However, the echidna shows very little theta activity except during some types of burrowing behavior, which are naturally important to a ground-dwelling insectivore. The second condition in which hippocampal theta is observed in most mammals is during REM sleep, a state echidnas appear to lack as well.

Sparse hippocampal theta, absence of REM sleep, and an oversized frontal cortex in the echidna—these are the preliminary neurobiological data on which Winson's (1985) theory is built. Winson notes that the frontal lobes are crucial for putting together information about internal drives, adaptation-relevant past experience, and perceptions of the current state of the organism in the particular moment-to-moment environment. The frontal lobes use this information to allow the individual to formulate behavioral strategies that will facilitate the best possible adaptive behavior at any given moment. This process depends a great deal on learning that occurs during *critical periods*, specific developmental stages of an organism's young life when its nervous system is especially primed to receive, process, and integrate species-relevant information, like predation for young cats or language for young humans.

In Winson's (1985) account, one of the main gateways from sensory systems of the brain to frontal cortex is the hippocampus, where the hippocampal theta rhythm is generated. This hippocampal–frontal cortex consolidation of experience and behavior during active waking life, which occurs with special intensity during early developmental critical periods, is what Winson—using a metaphor of the computer age—refers to as "on-line processing." The more complex the behavioral repertoire of the species, the larger the amount of frontal cortex required. Thus, the protomammalian monotreme forebears of the echidna, evolving more and more complex and flexible behavioral repertoires, also evolved bigger and more complex frontal cortices to process the necessary information on-line. The huge frontal cortex of the present-day echidna represents the culmination of this process in this comparatively advanced form of monotreme mammal.

The problem, says Winson (1985), is that the strategy of increased processing capacity through larger frontal cortex could be taken only so far in phylogeny: there are sheer physical limits to the extent of structure that can be used to subserve function. So as marsupial and placental mammals continued to evolve more complex and flexible behaviors, nature provided for some of the necessary species-specific information processing to occur "off-line." For this purpose, REM sleep evolved. Freed of the necessity for continuous on-line processing, brain evolution could cease relying on larger and larger frontal lobes and concentrate instead on other aspects of neurophylogenetic development.

Thus, in higher mammals, including man, the hippocampal theta rhythm occurring during REM sleep represents the off-line consolidation of ecologically relevant experience and behavior, continuing and extending the process that occurs in waking life during learning, especially during critical periods. That is why young mammals have more REM sleep than adults: they have more to consolidate off-line, just as they do on-line.

And during REM sleep we dream. Dreams are for Winson, as they were for Freud, the reflection of the lifelong pattern of experience and behavior consolidation that have occurred in the life of the individual. But where Winson parts company with Freud is in his view of the *function* of dreaming. The significance of dreams in the Winsonian model lies rather close to the surface; the stories dreams tell about our development are a rather straightforward reflection of past experience, even though the content of some individual dreams may at times not be readily comprehensible.

Dream symbolism, which for Freud represented the attempt to disguise consciously unacceptable psychical content, is for Winson simply a visual means by which the dream expresses an event or experience from the dreamer's life. The reason that "symbols" for different objects or ideas— cigars for phalluses, to cite a favorite example—seem so similar from person to person is because the perceptual representations of similarly shaped objects in general are situated in adjacent cortical columns in the sensory-perceptual areas of the brain (see, for example, Mountcastle, 1974).

Actually, the symbolic aspects of dream representation were discussed long before Freud, who in 1900 was apparently impressed with Scherner's (1861) earlier "proto-Freudian" account of dream symbolism:

> A dream caused by stimuli arising from the male sexual organs may cause the dreamer to find the top part of a clarinet in the street or the mouthpiece of a tobacco-pipe, or again, a piece of fur. Here the clarinet and the tobacco-pipe represent the approximate shape of the male organ, while the fur stands for the pubic hair. In the case of a sexual dream in a woman, the narrow space where the thighs come together may be represented by a narrow courtyard surrounded by houses, while the vagina may be symbolized by a soft, slippery and very narrow foot-path leading across the yard, along which the dreamer has to pass, in order, perhaps to take a gentleman a letter. (Scherner, 1861, cited in Freud, 1900, p. 118)

Symbolism aside, Winson's (1985) account of dreaming also defines his conceptualization of the unconscious. This he sees not as a thing or a place but as a process of ecologically relevant strategy-formation by association with past experience:

> I believe that the phylogenetically ancient mechanisms involving REM sleep, in which memories, associations and strategies are formed and handled by the brain as a distinct category of information in the prefrontal cortex and associated structures, are in fact the Freudian unconscious. (p. 209)

Many different types of experiences, says Winson (1985), along with their associated cognitive and emotional concomitants, will form relatively permanent traces in the brain and thus exert subsequent effects on behavior by virtue of their being consolidated during critical periods. That is why so many patterns of behavior, adaptive and maladaptive, appear so fixed and immutable in an individual's personality. Dreams allow us a glimpse at the neurobehavioral processes whereby, from early childhood on, behavioral strategies are laid down, modified, or consulted, a process that Winson calls the *unconscious personality*.

Another modern theory of dreaming that has experience-consolidation at its core is the *functional state shift hypothesis* of Koukkou and Lehman (1983). According to these authors, we should not be surprised that the content of dreams is often recalled with difficulty and in distorted form, since sleep—REM sleep in particular—constitutes a quite different functional state of the brain than waking consciousness.

It has been shown that information learned in one psychological state, for example, under hypnosis or while intoxicated, can be difficult to access in another state—the so-called *state-dependent learning* phenomenon (Bower, 1981). The functional brain state during sleep, say Koukkou and Lehman (1983), represents a "physiological regression to earlier stages of development" (p. 222) in both the individual and the species sense. The functional state shift in sleep is, in fact, similar to the state of consciousness that exists in early childhood and to the experiences of dreams that are difficult for the waking adult to recall: both early childhood consciousness and dream consciousness represent functional states different from what ordinarily exists in waking adults.

The repeated functional regressions to previous, ontogenetically more primitive functional stages that occur during sleep provide a mechanism by which an individual uses processing strategies and memory contents that are associated with earlier developmental periods. The cycles of REM sleep thus allow for a renewal of access to memory stores of more ontogenetically primitive stages of life, the better to foster an assimilation of new and old strategies of information processing.

The integration of new information into existing structures, the matching and linking of significant past and present events, has been proposed as the adaptive function of dreaming. This, if it occurs, would give the REM phase a special physiological significance for the brain's information handling—not only in the direct way of selecting, sorting and consolidating new experiences received during waking life, but also through optimizing the use and linking together of old and recent experience. (Koukkou & Lehman, 1983, pp. 227–228)

In this respect the Koukkou–Lehman model is similar to Winson's (1985)interpretation of dreaming. Like Winson, these theorists seek to account for some fundamental Freudian dream phenomena. For example, the access to more primitive content and lower order information processing strategies provided by REM sleep's functional state shift might correspond to Freud's (1900) *primary process*, the kind of primitive, concrete, basic instinct- or need-driven mode of thinking that characterizes the psychical life of young infants and that may appear in adulthood in pathologically regressed mental states or in dreams. This is contrasted with *secondary process* thinking, the more mature, rational, gratification-delaying kind of mentation that characterizes the psychological functioning of healthy adults (this is discussed further in Chapter 18). Also, the kinds of cognitive processing that go on in the functional states of sleep so alien to waking consciousness may account for what are retrospectively viewed as the mechanisms of condensation and displacement in the dream-work, which will be considered in more detail in the next chapter.

Dreaming to Forget

But dissenting views with respect to the dreaming-as-consolidation hypothesis appeared in Freud's time, even as they do today. In his 1900 review, Freud mentions the theory of Robert (1886), who described dreaming as a somatic process of "excretion," by which unneeded thoughts, images, and impulses that have been piling up since infancy are prevented from clogging the mental apparatus. In this view, dreams are essentially nothing more than a safety valve for blowing off psychic steam.

A man deprived of the capacity for dreaming would in the course of time become mentally deranged, because a great mass of uncompleted, unworked-out thoughts and superficial impressions would accumulate in his brain and would be bound by their bulk to smother the thoughts which should be assimilated into his memory as completed wholes. (Robert, 1886, cited in Freud, 1900, p. 111)

A modern neurophysiological incarnation of this theory is that of Crick and Mitchison (1983), who, using observations and data quite similar to those of the consolidationists, nevertheless arrive at quite different conclusions. Brain development, say Crick and Mitchison, necessarily involves the formation of countless synaptic connections and the processing of numberless bits of information, one side effect of which would naturally be the buildup of many "erroneous" connections. Like Robert (1886) a century earlier, Crick and Mitchison believe that this process results in the potentially dangerous accumulation of what they call "parasitic modes of behavior," that is, unadaptive patterns of perception, thought, feeling, and action that result from the random connections arising in a complexly developing human brain.

The function of REM sleep, then, is to allow the production of internally generated activity by the brain stem in order to "tune the cortical system" by exciting the inappropriate cortical–behavioral connections and thereby subjecting them to a "reverse learning mechanism." In effect, the purpose of REM sleep is to flush out and eliminate the parasitic modes of behavior by a sort of psychoneuronal chelation process. Thus, far from conceptualizing dreaming as the brain's way of impressing ecologically relevant experiences upon the memory store, Crick and Mitchison (1983) assert that "in REM sleep we unlearn our unconscious dreams. We dream in order to forget" (p. 112).

Those dreams that escape this nightly neural search-and-destroy mission and thereby insinuate themselves into our recall the next morning can, in this model, hardly be viewed as offering insight or aiding in adaptive learning. Rather, they represent residual manifestations of uneliminated parasitic modes of behavior, psychic detritus that has escaped the cleansing seine of sleep. The lesson is clear enough. "Attempting to remember one's dreams," caution the authors, "should perhaps not be encouraged because such remembering may help to retain patterns of thought which are better forgotten" (Crick & Mitchison, 1983, p. 114). For example, unhealthy psychic buildups resulting from defects in this reverse learning process might lead to a failure of cortical tuning and an efflorescence of dysfunctional associations in the brain. The result: the disordered thought, speech, and behavior of schizophrenia.

Even the echidna is again pressed into service, this time to support the dreaming-to-forget theory. Like Winson (1985), Crick and Mitchison (1983) believe that the relative absence of REM sleep in this creature is related to its disproportionately large allotment of frontal cortex. But while Winson posits that the echidna requires such enormous frontal lobes for on-line information processing, compensated later in phylogenesis by the evolution of memory-enhancing REM sleep, Crick and Mitchison assert that the echidna "needs such a large cortex because it cannot tune it up by the process of reverse learning" (p. 114). Since the echidna lacks REM sleep, there is no way of eliminating parasitic modes of behavior; thus, it needs a more capacious neural-waste storage and treatment facility to deal with the excess and keep it from adversely affecting the more adaptive associations.

Trauma sind Schauma

A popular expression among Freud's detractors was *Trauma sind Schauma*, or "dreams are froth," the idea being that a search for deeper, hidden meanings behind such commonplace nocturnal experiences constituted frivolous parlor-game nonsense at best, dangerous occultism at worst. And many of today's theorists, armed with the tools and data of modern neuroscience, would suggest that perhaps a purely neurophysiological theory of dreaming obviates any arcane hypothesizing as to psychological functions. That is, if we can explain *how* the brain makes dreams, do we really need to ask *why* dreams occur?

An early expression of this view is the account given by Binz (1878), which Freud (1900) included in his review. Binz recognized that dreaming tends to occur most heavily during the latter part of the night, toward early morning. The transition from the torpor of sleep to complete wakefulness is a gradual, not an abrupt, process, said Binz, because the "products of fatigue" that have built up in the brain and caused the onset of sleep in the first place dissipate from the brain's neurons only slowly. Since some groups of neurons recover before others during this gradual waking stage, the mental apparatus is temporarily functioning only with dissociated sets of neurons in varying degrees of functional integrity. And this accounts for why the interim mental activity is characterized by a bizarreness that is unlike anything occurring in waking life.

> This condition (of torpor) comes to an end in the early hours of the morning, but only by degrees. The products of fatigue which have accumulated in the albumin of the brain gradually diminish; more and more of them are decomposed or eliminated by the unceasing flow of the blood-stream. Here and there separate groups of cells begin to emerge into wakefulness, while the torpid state still persists all around them. The isolated work of these separate groups now appears before our clouded consciousness, unchecked by other portions of the brain which govern the process of association. For that reason, the images produced, which correspond for the most part to material impressions of the more recent past, are strung together in a wild and irregular manner. The number of the liberated brain cells constantly grows and

the senselessness of the dreams correspondingly diminishes. (Binz, 1878, cited in Freud, 1900, pp. 108–109)

A modern version of this view can be found in Hobson's (1988) and Hobson and McCarley's (1977) *activation–synthesis hypothesis* of dreaming. The main tenet of this theory is that during dreaming the brain generates its own information by a special neuronal mechanism in the pontine brain stem. Hobson hypothesizes that this internally generated sensorimotor information, which is partially random and partially specific, is then compared with already-stored sensorimotor data in order to synthesize the dream content. That is, the automatically activated forebrain synthesizes a dream by comparing information generated in specific brain stem circuits with information stored in memory. Specifically, the pontine brain stem is the generator zone for the dream sleep state. The *locus coeruleus* is especially important in mediating the spinal reflex inhibition that produces the motor paralysis occurring during REM sleep.

According to the activation–synthesis hypothesis, during dream sleep a mechanism in the reticular formation of the pontine brain stem is periodically turned on, with several results. First, the forebrain is tonically activated, probably via the midbrain reticular formation that is also responsible for its activation during waking; thus, the forebrain is made ready to process information. Second, the spinal reflexes are tonically inhibited, possibly via the brain stem reticular formation and the locus coeruleus; motor outflow is thereby blocked, despite high levels of activity in the motor cortex and other brain areas. Third, the oculomotor and vestibular systems are activated by the pontine reticular formation to produce eye movements. This system as a whole acts as an internal information generator that provides the forebrain with spatially specific but temporally disorganized information about eye velocity, relative position, and direction of movement. Information may similarly be derived from the brain stem generators of patterned motor activity. Fourth, at the same time that internal information feedback is being generated by the activation of various motor systems, input to sensory systems from the outside world is blocked. This may intensify the relative impact of the endogenous inputs to the brain, accounting for the intensity of dream imagery and preventing sleep disruption by excitation generated in the dreamer's surrounding environment.

In this model, symbol formation and the often bizarre juxtaposition of thoughts, images, and actions in dreams would reflect the heightened degree of simultaneous activation of multiple sensory channels that occurs in dreaming but usually not in waking. For example, in the classic chase dream, the dreamer who has trouble fleeing from a pursuer because he is frozen to the spot is accurately reading the activated state of his motor pattern generator and the paralyzed state of his spinal neurons: the forebrain says run, but the paralyzed spinal neurons keep him immobilized. No need for hypothetical inhibited "wishes" here.

Another example of this phenomenon is the flying dream. Here, says Hobson (1988), the central, automatic activation during sleep of the vestibular system, normally important for balance, posture, and coordination, may provide a substrate for endogenously generated specific information about body position and movement. Flying dreams may thus be a logical, direct, and decidedly unsymbolic way of synthesizing information generated endogenously by the vestibular system in dream sleep. Thus, Hobson regards it as "gratuitous" to appeal to a Freudian interpretation of the flying dream as having to do with anything sexual.

Dreaming with the Dual Brain

The Hobsonian approach seems to assume that focusing on the brain mechanisms that produce dream phenomenology must ipso facto eliminate the need even to consider the potential importance of a *function* of dreaming. For Freud (1900), however, one key feature of dreams was that they

> think essentially in images; and with the approach of sleep it is possible to observe how, in proportion as voluntary activities become more difficult, involuntary ideas arise, all of which fall into the class of images. Incapacity for ideational work of the kind which we feel as intentionally willed and the emergence (habitually associated with such states of abstraction) of images—these are two characteristics which persevere in dreams and which the psychological analysis of dreams forces us to recognize as essential features of dream-life. (p. 82)

Furthermore,

> the transformation of ideas into hallucinations is not the only respect in which dreams differ from corresponding thoughts in waking life. Dreams construct a *situation* out of these images. (p. 83)

The unquestioned preeminence of imagery in dreams has led a number of researchers to focus on the role of the brain's right hemisphere in generating the dream process and dream content. For example, Koukkou and Lehman (1983), whose functional state shift theory of dreaming we discussed earlier, see REM sleep as allowing an increased access of the adult left hemisphere to memory material stored in the right hemisphere in early childhood, before functional left dominance was established. REM sleep also allows the possibility of verbalization of material generated in the right hemisphere, which might be dominant during dreaming.

The idea of right-hemisphere dominance during REM sleep and dreaming finds perhaps its most ardent advocate in Bakan (1977–1978), who asserts categorically that "the right brain is the dreamer" (p. 285). Bakan points to some notable similarities between REM dream thought and the type of mentation that has been associated with the right hemisphere's cognitive style, especially the predominance of imagery, affect, and primary process types of thought. In Bakan's view, REM sleep represents a period of "cyclic ascendance in the functioning of a right hemisphere system during sleep" (p. 286) occurring as the result of a "functional disconnection" between the hemispheres during the sleep cycle. Dreaming, then, results from an imagistic, fanciful right hemisphere that is functionally disconnected during sleep from the more rational, reality-oriented constraints of the left.

Bakan uses his model to address the phenomenon of immobility during sleep. The right hemisphere's cognitive style, says Bakan, is a poor guide for overt behavior, and REM paralysis may allow right-hemisphere primary process dream activity to occur in all its cognitive, affective, and physiological manifestations while protecting the dreamer from the consequences that would befall him/her if this psychical activity were actually translated into action.

Further, the functional uncoupling of the right hemisphere from the left during REM sleep may have important consequences for normal development. The right hemisphere may require such periods of independent activity—of "exercise," as Bakan calls it—in order to impart its own unique contribution to information processing and problem solving. Thus, during these periods, the right hemisphere may be involved in the strengthening of such psychological functions as imagery, divergent thinking, perceptuospatial processing, and music—all important primary process components (the Freudian theory of the primary and secondary processes is discussed further in Chapter 18).

Dreams, Madness, and the Brain

In a section on "Dreams and Mental Diseases," Freud (1900) reviews the contemporary literature on the relationship of dreaming to mental illness. He concludes that when we speak of such a relationship, we may have any of three things in mind: (1) the etiological and clinical connection, as when a dream represents or introduces a psychotic state; (2) modifications of the dream-life itself as a result of the mental illness; or (3) intrinsic connections between dreams and psychoses, analogies pointing to their being essentially alike. In these latter instances, says Freud, the dreams are often regarded as merely representative of the etiology of the mental disorder, but it would be just as correct to say that the mental disorder made its appearance in dream-life, that it first broke through in a dream.

In some further examples Freud tells us that the pathological symptoms are contained in dream-life or that the psychosis is limited to dream-life. In cases of recovery from mental diseases it can often be quite clearly observed that, while functioning is normal during the day, dream-life is still under the influence of the psychosis. However, cautions Freud (1900), the close connection between dreams and psychosis should not be over-interpreted.

> The indisputable analogy between dreams and insanity, extending as it does down to their characteristic details, is one of the most powerful props of the medical theory of dream-life, which regards dreaming as a useless and disturbing process and as the expression of a reduced activity of the mind. Nevertheless, it is not to be expected that we shall find the ultimate explanation of dreams in the direction of mental disorders; for the unsatisfactory state of the knowledge of the origin of these latter conditions is generally recognized. It is quite likely, on the contrary, that a modification of our attitude toward dreams will at the same time affect our views upon the internal mechanism of mental disorders and that we shall be working towards an explanation of the psychoses while we are endeavoring to throw some light on the mystery of dreams. (p. 124)

Moving to the present, the potential affinity of mental disorders and dreams has not escaped Bakan's (1977–1978) theory. Following Bertini (1973), Bakan proposes that the organization of day residues (the representation of the previous day's events within the content of a dream) within the memory process requires a type of specialized right-hemisphere primary process activity. For a day experience to be optimally integrated into the memory system, at least some of the material processed in the ordinary, waking secondary process manner must be translated into primary process code. This requires a shift in the brain's functional organization that allows for regression to more primitive ways of thinking and perceiving. According to Bakan's model, the autonomous right-hemisphere functioning he believes occurs during REM sleep would fit just this requirement.

The system is not perfect, however, and defects in the hemispheric disconnection mechanism may account for some of the clinical phenomena seen in mental disorders, for example, schizophrenia. Schizophrenic mentation, posits Bakan (1977–1978), involves "a spillover of right hemisphere mentation into periods which should be under greater control of left hemisphere mentation" (p. 293). The hallucinatory, fantastic, and dream-like mental activity of the right hemisphere, which in normal persons is confined to REM dream periods, obeys no such constraints in the schizophrenic. Instead,

> the barrier which keeps right hemisphere mentation confined to dreaming periods breaks down and there is a spillover of right hemisphere mentation into the waking life where it can influence overt behavior and thus produce the bizarre behavior found in schizophrenics. This analysis suggests that at least part of the pathology in schizophrenia is pathology of the hemispheric functioning of the brain. (Bakan, 1977–1978, p. 293)

A theory that takes on not just dreams and schizophrenia but hallucinatory drug states as well is that of Fischman (1983), who identifies a "certain psychological process" that seems to provide a basic continuity of experience, giving each of us the sense of a coherent self. A disruption of this mechanism, which Fischman believes to be related to the suspension of secondary process thinking, occurs in dream states and in schizophrenia and can also be induced by the effects of hallucinogenic drugs. As a result, primary process thinking becomes preeminent:

> The decathexis of the self-representation in dreams, hallucinogenic drug states and acute psychosis results in a dichotomous experience characterized by a weakening of the ego's identification with the self. . . . It consists initially in a disruption of the ego's ongoing synthesis of the various self-representations into a continuous, coherent self. (Fischman, 1983, p. 78).

Conclusions

Several of the theories reviewed in this chapter address the role of REM sleep and dreaming in information consolidation and in adaptive learning and development. Winson (1985) stresses the necessity of REM sleep for off-line integration of adaptive behavioral strategies, a process that supplements the on-line adaptive functioning of the brain's frontal lobes during waking life. In contrast, Crick and Mitchison (1983) take a seemingly opposite view of dreaming's purpose: to forget or unlearn random, nonadaptive associations that could interfere with normal neurobehavioral functioning.

Winson's (1985) and Crick and Mitchison's (1983) theories are, however, potentially compatible if we accept that learning and ecologically relevant information consolidation require both the retention of useful associations and the winnowing out of maladaptive ones. What we call learning probably involves this combination of integration and elimination, out of which is hewn the person's own individual identity and knowledge base. REM sleep may contribute to this process by providing for the functional state shifts that allow assimilation of old and new strategies of information processing, as Koukkou and Lehman (1983) assert. In fact, the theories of Koukkou and Lehman and of Winson see REM sleep as providing access to ontogenetically primitive memories (a "regressive" function of dreams) in order to foster integration with new material.

The view that these shifts in functional state are associated with changes in interhemispheric activity is favored by both Bakan (1977–1978) and Fischman (1983). In this type of model the REM dream state involves a suspension of waking left-hemisphere dominance and the consequent disinhibition and relative autonomy of right-hemisphere activity. While normally a neuropsychologically salubrious process during REM sleep, maladaptive hemispheric release of this sort during waking life is thought by these authors to underlie psychopathological states such as schizophrenia. (Other authors, e.g., West, 1984, have proposed similar right-hemisphere theories of schizophrenia, which I have critiqued elsewhere; see Miller, 1984b.)

The relationship between dreams and psychosis is also mentioned by Crick and Mitchison (1983), and even Freud (1900) acknowledged that patients who show a rather direct and uneffortful understanding of dream symbolism are "often sufferers from dementia praecox" (p. 386). However, the hemisphericity and other neuropsychological issues with regard to schizophrenia itself are, at present, far from settled (Goldstein, 1978; Merrin, 1981; Miller, 1984b, 1986b, 1986c).

"Dreams are the *guardians* of sleep and not its disturbers," proclaimed Freud (1900, p. 267), and one mechanism by which this occurs may be the inhibition of motor activity during REM sleep by brain stem influences on the forebrain, as postulated by Hobson (1988; Hobson & McCarley, 1977). Brain vestibular and proprioceptive mechanisms may thus explain the ubiquity of dreams of falling, flying, and running, which Freud attributed to intrapsychic conflict and the influence of infantile memory residues of body movement.

As for dream symbolism, while contiguity between cortical columns mediating perception (Winson, 1985) may explain some of the commonalities of the images that constitute the perceptual component of dreams, such an explanation fails to account for similarities in dream story line or thematic content. Indeed, Freud (1900) criticized the cataloging of stock "dream symbols" based on raw similarities of content—an approach, he believed, that "seems to leave the door open to arbitrary interpretations"

(p. 259). And as subsequent chapters in the present volume show, many dream themes go beyond the level of mere image and may actually be more conceptual than perceptual.

Finally, with regard to Winson's (1985) comparison of off-line REM sleep information consolidation to an on-line function mediated by the brain's frontal lobes, the evidence suggests that the frontal lobes may be as integrally involved in dreaming as they are in waking life. This is elaborated upon further in Chapter 12. For now, let us consider the rest of Freud's dream opus more closely.

CHAPTER 9

"The Interpretation of Dreams"

Following the theoretical review in the first chapter of *The Interpretation of Dreams*, Freud (1900) proceeds with his own theorizing on the nature of dreams and the dream process. He describes how his method of dream analysis evolved from his first work with hysteria and the other neuroses. Freud recalls that if he traced a particular pathological idea back to its psychical origins, the symptoms would often go away and the patient would recover. Dreams came up in the process because the patients, pledged by Freud to communicate everything without censoring (i.e., the technique of free association), often reported dreams as part of this mental content. It was a "short step," says Freud, to treating dreams themselves as symptoms and applying to them the same kinds of analytic and interpretive tools as to the rest of the psychical material. This led Freud (1900) to an important—in his own view, *the* important—insight about dreams:

> If we adopt the method of interpreting dreams which I have indicated here, we shall find that dreams really have a meaning and are far from being the expression of a fragmentary activity of the brain, as the authorities have claimed. *When the work of interpretation has been completed, we perceive that a dream is the fulfillment of a wish.* (p. 154)

Freud goes on to discuss the distortions of normal perception, thought, and imagery that occur in dreams and makes the distinction between the manifest and latent content of dreams. *Manifest content* refers to the dream as experienced by the dreamer, that is, the raw, uninterpreted surface content of the dream, the thought and imagery typically recalled upon awakening and reported to others. The *latent content* of a dream is, simply put, what the dream really *means*, the vast skein of associations that must be painstakingly analyzed in order to determine a dream's underlying

121

significance, which usually can be traced back to some form of wish fulfillment.

Freud next turns to the material and sources of dreams. Events that may have occurred long ago in the dreamer's life retain their immediacy in the dream, analogous to what occurs when hysterical symptoms symbolically revivify conflicts from the patient's past. But any given dream, Freud acknowledges, is determined by a combination of outside stimulation, repressed psychical material, and random physiological states of the moment.

> All dreams are in a sense dreams of convenience: they serve the purpose of prolonging sleep instead of waking up. *Dreams are the guardians of sleep and not its disturbers.* (p. 267)

This conceptualization allows Freud to account for a host of dream phenomena. For example, dreams have no difficulty representing a wide variety of motor acts, both actual and imaginary, such as in dreams of flying. Further, a sensation of inhibited movement in dreams is produced whenever the particular context requires it. Unlike the latter-day theory of Hobson (1988; Hobson & McCarley, 1977), which sees dream content as essentially epiphenomenological to the brain stem REM-generating process that acts to inhibit voluntary movement during these sleep stages, Freud's view was that such motoric inhibition, whatever the origin, served a *function* in representing some aspect of a repressed wish.

With regard to the catalog of so-called "typical dreams," the kinds of dreams that almost everyone seems to have at one time or another, Freud cautions against the facile interpretation of dreams based solely on their generic content; the modern reader need only scan the shelves of his/her local bookstore to realize that modern versions of such fanciful "dream books" are still popular today. Although Freud has been accused of taking a rigid approach to dream interpretation, such stock cataloging of dream symbols was actually a product of a group of overzealous post-Freudians with a peculiar passion for imposing what they believed was scientific classificatory order on psychological phenomena, including dreams (a similar attitude led also at one point to the cataloging of psychosomatic symptoms according to their associated specific core conflicts, an approach that is just today beginning to yield to more integrative approaches).

Freud's own approach to dreams was rather more thoroughgoing than any such simplistic system. In *The Interpretation of Dreams* he goes to great lengths to emphasize that it is a knowledge of what a particular dream content or dream symbol means to the *individual person* that facilitates the interpretation in a given case. Looking up a dream's meaning in a dream codebook, Freud would assert, is a pathetic substitute for analyzing the whole patient.

Freud is particularly intrigued by dreams of flying and falling. He rejects many contemporary notions that these arise solely from tactile feelings during sleep or sensations of movement of the lungs or other bodily functions. In Freud's view, such sensations are themselves reproduced as part of the memory to which the dream refers; that is, they are a part of the content of the dream and not its source. But Freud was not afraid to admit that the precise nature of such dreams still eluded him.

> I cannot, however, disguise from myself that I am unable to produce any complete explanation of this class of typical dreams. My material has left me in the lurch precisely at this point. I must, however, insist upon the general assertion that all the tactile and motor sensations which occur in these typical dreams are called up immediately there is any psychical reason for making use of them and that they can be disregarded when no such need for them arises. I am also of the opinion that the relation of these dreams to infantile experiences has been established with certainty from the indications I have found in the analyses of psychoneurotics. I am not able to say, however, what other meanings may become attached to the recollection of such sensations in the course of later life—different meanings, perhaps, in every individual case, in spite of the typical appearance of the dreams; and I should be glad to be able to fill up the gap by a careful analysis of clear instances. (Freud, 1900, p. 307)

Freud then elaborates his concept of the *dream-work*, the unique individual pattern of manifest and latent dream content—the actual form the dream takes—from which we disentangle a particular dream's meaning for that particular person. Several processes contribute to the dream-work.

Condensation involves what Freud calls a "double phenomenon," or what today we might refer to as a form of reduplication. Not only are the elements of a dream determined by the dream thoughts many times over but the individual dream thoughts are represented in the dream by several elements. Associative paths lead from one element of the dream to several dream thoughts and from one dream thought to several elements of the dream (note the analogy with Freud's earlier account of the brain's representation of hysterical symptoms, as described in the *Comparative Study* of 1893). A "collective figure" can also be produced for purposes of dream condensation by uniting the actual features of two or more people into a single dream image; we have seen in an earlier chapter that such reduplication of faces was also one of Anna O's hysterical presentations, a clinical phenomenon resembling organically produced Capgras syndrome. In fact, says Freud, this construction of collective and composite figures is one of the chief methods by which condensation operates in dreams.

The work of condensation in dreams is seen at its clearest when words or names are involved. In dreams, words are treated as though they were concrete things, and for that reason they are apt to be combined in just the same way as representations of concrete things. The verbal transformations in dreams, Freud points out, greatly resemble those that are familiar in paranoia but that are also present in hysteria and obsessions. The linguistic tricks performed by children, who sometimes actually treat words as though they were objects and may even invent new "languages" and artificial grammatical forms, are related to the analogous phenomena observed in dreams and psychoneuroses alike.

Displacement, on the one hand, strips the elements that have a high psychical value of their intensity and, on the other hand, invests elements of low psychical value with new values of high intensity by means of overdetermination; these afterward find their way into the dream content. By this mechanism the psychical impetus is transferred from the original high-intensity idea, impulse, or image to one of ostensibly low valence, which is why in dreams seemingly neutral material is so often imbued with such high emotional impact. These mechanisms of condensation and displacement, Freud points out, constitute the prime forces that shape the dream-work.

Freud next considers the *means of representation* in dreams and notes that dreams seem to have no way of representing abstract or linguistic conjunctive concepts, such as "if," "because," "just as," "although," "either–or," and so on, that form the basis for normal, waking, spoken communication. Logical relationships between dream thoughts, then, are not given any separate representation in dreams. Some of the means of representation that *are* used in dreams are as follows.

In *identification*, two separate people with certain traits or attributes in common are linked by a kind of fusion within the dream-work. In the process, however, only one person's image is represented in the dream while the other is suppressed. This single "covering figure" appears in the dream in all the situations that relate to him and the personages he stands for. In *composition*, the dream image contains features that are peculiar to one or the other of the persons concerned but not common to both. The result of this combination is a new entity, a composite figure.

One feature of dreams that stands out in Freud's (1900) account is that "every dream deals with the dreamer himself. Dreams are completely egoistical" (p. 358). Even when there is no figure or other reference to the dreamer himself, he is always hiding in the personage of some extraneous dream figure, melded therein by the process of identification. In cases in which the dreamer himself does make an overt appearance, it is then some *other* person who lies concealed within the dreamer's identity. Then again, there are dreams in which the dreamer appears side by side or in interaction with other figures. The identifications in this case allow the acknowledgment of certain ideas whose acceptance would otherwise be forbidden by the psychic censorship.

> Thus, my ego may be represented in a dream several times over, now directly and now through identification with extraneous persons. By means of a number of such identifications, it becomes possible to condense an extraordinary amount of thought material. The fact that the dreamer's own ego appears several times, or in several forms in a dream is at bottom no more remarkable than that the ego should be contained in a conscious thought several times or in different places or connections—e.g., in the sentence "when *I* think of what a healthy child *I* was." (Freud, 1900, p. 358)

In some dreams a conflict of will is expressed as a failure to carry out a movement that occurs not simply as a situation but as an actual sensation of inhibited movement. The motor paralysis accompanying sleep, says Freud, is precisely one of the fundamental determinants of the psychical process during dreaming. Motor inhibition is the dream's way of saying no to an impulse whose nature and origin are of the forbidden (typically sexual) kind.

Freud next discusses the *considerations of representability* in dreams, which are responsible for the often fantastic absurdity in which dreams are disguised. This occurs because dreams have a knack for transforming colorless abstract thoughts into concrete images, pictures being the most appropriate mental medium for representation in dreams. Freud likens the dream's representation of an abstract idea to the work of a political cartoonist in rendering a point of social commentary in the form of a nonverbal illustration. However, to accommodate the often rich range of expression that language offers in waking life, the dreamer-cartoonist frequently finds his pictorial talents stretched to the limit and must come up with representations that are decidedly bizarre. Such verbal–imagistic interplays find a role not just in dreams (or cartoons) but also in a reverse direction in the form of poems, where imagistic hues and shadings are skillfully conveyed by means of language.

Freud next takes up the issue of *dream symbolism*. He points out that the patients most in touch with the symbolic aspect of dreams are precisely those with the severest mental disorder, that is, sufferers from dementia praecox. But because psychopathological states often occur in association with rich or bizarre dream symbolism, we cannot assume the opposite— that is, that creative dreamers necessarily suffer from severe psychopathology. Rather, says Freud, there are marked differences from person to person in the propensity to dream in symbols, just as there are individual variations in many other psychological traits (the neuropsychodynamic relationship between creativity and madness is a topic that I have considered more extensively elsewhere; see Miller, 1988b, 1990).

One of the few direct references by Freud himself to the relationship between dream phenomena and neuropathological states appears in an textual emendation made in 1925. Here, Freud describes the experiments of Betlheim and Hartmann (1924) on patients with Korsakoff's syndrome. Freud's mentor Wernicke (1881) had originally described what was at that time a new disease entity found most frequently in chronic alcoholics, whose symptoms consisted of persistent vomiting, drowsiness, stumbling gait, impairment of visual acuity, photophobia, ophthalmological and oculomotor dysfunction, delirium, disorientation, apathy, intermittent somnolence, nocturnal restlessness, and fright. Six years later Korsakoff (1887) gave the first comprehensive description of the unique amnesic syndrome that now bears his name. Korsakoff drew attention to the psychological symptoms—chiefly disorientation and memory disturbance—that frequently accompany alcoholic polyneuropathy, or peripheral nerve impairment, and pointed out that the psychological disturbance and the neuropathy represent two facets of the same disease.

The Wernicke–Korsakoff syndrome was originally thought to be inflammatory or toxic in nature, but some early authors made reference to a disturbance in nutrition, an idea that became generally accepted only after Funk (1911) developed the concept of vitamin deficiency. The nutritional etiology of the Wernicke–Korsakoff syndrome, in the modern sense, was established in the 1930s by such researchers as Bender and Schilder (1933), who argued that alcohol intoxication was not in itself responsible for the pathology of the disease; rather, an associated avitaminosis resulting from poor nutrition led to deteriorated, skid-row-type drunks. There followed a great deal of experimental and clinical research corroborating the effectiveness of thiamine (vitamin B_1) in treating the Wernicke–Korsakoff syndrome.

Today, Wernicke's disease denotes a neurologic disorder of acute onset characterized by nystagmus and other oculomotor disorders, ataxia of gait, and a global confusional state, occurring together or in various combinations. Korsakoff's syndrome more specifically describes an abnormal mental state that usually follows the acute Wernicke's phase and in which learning and memory are affected out of proportion to other cognitive functions in an otherwise alert and responsive patient. It is characterized by two key features that almost always occur together: (1) an impaired ability to recall information acquired over a variable period of time before the onset of the illness (retrograde amnesia) with, however, a relative preservation of very early memories, and (2) an impaired ability to acquire new information, that is, to learn or form new memories since the onset of the illness (anterograde amnesia). Confabulation, the filling in of memory gaps with fallacious material, may or may not be present, although many authorities regard it as an important feature of the syndrome. Korsakoff's syndrome almost always results from nutritional deficiency associated with severe alcoholism, but a few cases have been shown to follow other types of brain damage (Adams & Victor, 1977; Lishman, 1978; Strub & Black, 1981; Victor et al., 1971).

In the study cited by Freud (which impressed him particularly because it was carried out without using hypnosis), Betlheim and Hartmann (1924) read stories to Korsakoff patients and recorded the distortions that the patients produced when relating back these passages.

> They found that the symbols familiar to us from the interpretation of dreams made their appearance (e.g., going upstairs, stabbing, and shooting as symbols of copulation, and knives and cigarettes as symbols of the penis). The authors attached special importance to the appearance of the symbol of a staircase, for, as they have justly observed, "no conscious desire to distort could have arrived at a symbol of such a kind." (Freud, 1900, pp. 419–420)

Another group of typical dreams are those in which the dreamer finds him/herself flying, floating, falling, or swimming. No generic interpretation exists for this dream type, says Freud; rather, the meaning must be determined in each case. However, they appear to hark back to the games of childhood involving movement. Other typical dreams are those of fire, which Freud relates to an underlying recollection of the enuresis of childhood (interestingly, modern clinicians have observed that attention deficit disorder, enuresis, and fascination with fire often occur together in the childhoods of delinquent boys; see Miller, 1988a), and of landscapes, often associated with feelings of déjà vu. These latter places are invariably the genitals of the dreamer's mother: "There is indeed no other place about which one can assert with such conviction that one has been there before" (Freud, 1900, p. 435).

For the purposes of representation in dreams, says Freud, the spelling of words is far less important than their sound, the same principle holding for rhyming verse. Dreams referring to childhood may also be expressed by a translation of time into space, the characters and scenes appearing as if at a great spatial distance—for example, at the end of a long road or seen through the wrong end of a telescope.

"Dreams, then, are often most profound when they seem most crazy" (Freud, 1900, p. 480). With regard to the frequent absurdity of dreams, Freud points out that absurdity is one of the ways that the dream-work represents a contradiction. Absurdity in a dream, however, is not to be interpreted as a simple no. Rather, it is intended to reproduce the actual mood of the dream thoughts, which combines derision or laughter with the contradiction.

Freud then relates a dream of his own, a portion of which is reproduced here and will be considered again in the next chapter. The setting of the dream involves a medical pathology lab in which Freud worked as a student. In the dream he has been assigned a dissection task by one of his early mentors.

> Old Brücke must have set me some task; stangely enough, it is related to a dissection of the lower part of my own body, my pelvis and legs, which I saw before me as though in the dissecting-room, but without noticing their absence in myself and also without a trace of any gruesome feeling. Louise N. was standing beside me and doing the work with me. The pelvis had been eviscerated, and it was visible now in its superior, now in its inferior aspect, the two being mixed together. Thick flesh-colored protuberances (which, in the dream itself, made me think of hemorrhoids) could be seen. Something which lay over it and was like crumpled silver-paper had also to be carefully fished out. I was then once more in possession of my legs and was making my way through the town. (p. 489)

Dreams such as this one illustrate the dissociation or incongruency that may exist between ideas or activities in a dream and the affect or feeling-states that surround them. In a dream, says Freud, if the affect and the idea are incompatible in their character and intensity, the ideational material undergoes displacement and substitution whereas the affect remains unaltered. This is seen even more clearly in the neuroses than in dreams. In neuroses, the affects are always appropriate to the situation, in quality if not al   tensity. What this shows is that emotion and thought do no   oluble psychic entity but are separable under certain conditions—   point, dreams.

But the distortions and disguises that the manifest dream content employs in order to conceal the latent content, the repressed wish, are abetted still further, even when the dream is over, by the process of what Freud called *secondary revision*. Waking consciousness relies on its ability to structure the perceptual and interpretive worlds, to make the experiential universe conform to our expectations of an intelligible whole. It is this need for intelligibility that forces the dream material into the procrustean bed of waking cognition and accounts for the dream-work's necessary distortions and disguising of the dream's true meaning, as, for example, when we attempt to "explain" what happened in the dream, fully knowing that our waking faculties often grasp vainly at the dream's full impact.

It is in the famous Chapter 7 of *The Interpretation of Dreams* that Freud articulates his first fully elaborated theory of mental life, the first

Freudian metapsychology. He begins, appropriately enough, with the brain, drawing an analogy between dream phenomena and organic delirium or confusional states. Following the suggestion of Leuret (1834), Freud points out that even such deliria as are produced by brain damage may have psychodynamic meaning, a conclusion reinforced, we are told, by some of Freud's own observations of organic cases during his neurology days. In this view,

> deliria are the work of a censorship which no longer takes the trouble to conceal its operation: instead of collaborating in producing a new version that shall be unobjectionable, it ruthlessly deletes whatever it disapproves of, so that what remains becomes quite disconnected. (Freud, 1900, p. 568)

And even if we acknowledge that some organic mental phenomena are not so psychically determined, that they have a psychodynamically neutral life of their own due to strictly neurological factors, the analogues that appear in psychoneurotic states certainly follow no such random path.

> It may be that free play of ideas with a fortuitous chain of associations is to be found in destructive organic cerebral processes; what is regarded as such in the psychoneuroses can always be explained as an effect of the censorship's influence upon a train of thought which has been pushed into the foreground by purposive ideas that have remained hidden. (Freud, 1900, p. 568)

Freud turns next to the "regressive" function of dreams. Dreaming, for Freud, represents an example of regression to the dreamer's earliest life, a revival of his/her childhood, of the instinctual impulses that dominated it and of the ways in which these were expressed. Furthermore, says Freud (incidently, anticipating Jung in this regard), behind the individual childhood we see a glimpse of a phylogenetic childhood, a picture of the development of the human race, of which the individual's ontogeny is in fact an abbreviated recapitulation influenced by the chance circumstances of life.

Freud then returns to the theme of dreams as wish fulfillments. A conscious desire can only become a dream instigator if it succeeds in awakening an unconscious wish and in obtaining reinforcement from it. Thus, a wish that is represented in a dream must be an infantile one. In adults, it originates from the unconscious, while in the case of young children it may be an unrepressed, actually unfulfilled or only partially fulfilled wish from waking life, for example, for candy, toys, or Mommy's undivided affection.

Freud reiterates the connection between dreams and waking phenomena, this time with regard to their motivational aspects. Unconscious wishful impulses make themselves known in waking life in the form of psychosis and in the transference relationship in psychoanalytic psychotherapy, where the patient begins to act toward the analyst in ways that replicate his/her early relationship to parental authority figures. The censorship that keeps the unconscious material out of awareness therefore deserves, says Freud, to be recognized and respected as the veritable watchman of our mental health.

> The theory governing all psychoneurotic symptoms culminates in a single proposition, which asserts that they too are to be regarded as fulfilments of unconscious wishes. Our explanation makes the dream only the first member of a class which is of the greatest significance to psychiatrists, and an understanding of which implies the solution of the purely psychological side of the problem of psychiatry. (p. 608)

In his emphasis on the primacy of the wish-fulfilling function of dreams, Freud makes a point of rejecting alternative views that see dreams in more of an adaptive problem-solving mode, views similar to those in some of the modern theories considered in the last chapter. As for the views of Freud's contemporaries (as expressed in subsequent editions of *The Interpretation of Dreams*), Adler (1911), for one, asserted that dreams played an anticipatory role, a function of "thinking ahead." Maeder (1912) observed that some dreams contain attempts at solving conflicts, attempts that are later carried out in reality, and thus behave as though they were trial practices for waking actions. Maeder posited that dreams have a *fonction ludique*, or play function, and he drew a parallel between dreams and the play of animals and children, which he regarded as practice in the operation of innate instincts and as preparation for serious activity later on—a position we identify today with Winson's (1985) theory.

This, Freud (1900) will have none of:

> A little reflection will convince us, however, that this "secondary" function of dreams has no claims to be considered as a part of the subject of dream-interpretation. Thinking ahead, forming intentions, framing attempted solutions which may perhaps be realized later in waking life, all these, and many other similar things, are products of the unconscious and preconscious activity of the mind: they may persist in the state of sleep as "the day residues" and combine with an unconscious wish in forming a dream. Thus, the dream's function of "thinking ahead" is rather a function of preconscious waking thought, the products of which may be revealed to us by the analysis of dreams or of other phenomena. (pp. 618–619)

Next, Freud discusses the *primary* and *secondary processes*, the first representing the basic, instinctual, "irrational," and for the most part unconscious drives of the individual, and the latter referring to the component of the psyche that must deal with the real world in a practical sense, what we sometimes call colloquially the "rational" mind. In Freud's view, the primary process impels us in the direction of instinctual gratification whereas the secondary process tries to effect the best compromise it can between these wishes and the exigencies of reality. And part of the insight into the mental apparatus as revealed by dreams comes, says Freud, from the study of the psychology of the neuroses, particularly hysteria:

> We have found from this that the same irrational psychical processes, and others we have not specified, dominate the production of hysterical symptoms. In hysteria, too, we come across a series of perfectly rational thoughts, equal in validity to our conscious thoughts; but to begin with we know nothing of their existence in this form and we can only reconstruct them subsequently. If they force themselves upon our notice at any point, we discover by analyzing the symptom which has been produced that these normal thoughts have been submitted to abnormal treatment: *that they have been transformed into the symptom by means of condensation and the formation of compromises, by way of superficial associations and in disregard of contradictions, and also, it may be, along the path of regression.* In view of the complete identity between the characteristic features of the dream-work and those of the psychical activity which issues in psychoneurotic symptoms, we feel justified in carrying over to dreams the conclusions we have been led to by hysteria. (p. 636)

For Freud, the primary process is present in the mental apparatus from the first whereas it is during the subsequent course of life that the secondary process unfolds and comes to inhibit and overlay the primary process, reaching its full development perhaps only in adulthood. Because the secondary process develops so much later, the core of our being, consisting of unconscious wishful impulses, remains inaccessible to the understanding and inhibition of conscious volition; the part played by the latter is restricted to directing along the most expedient paths the wishful impulses that arise from the unconscious. "The unconscious," Freud thus declares, "is the true psychical reality" (p. 651).

Now is the time, therefore, to consider the neuropsychodynamic parameters of this reality and of the dreams from which we endeavor to discern its nature.

CHAPTER 10

The Dreamer's Brain in Health and Disease

Here, as in previous chapters, we use the evidence from pathology to construct a model of the normal, the usual, the typical, neuropsychodynamics of the phenomenon in question, in the present case, dreaming.

The Frenzied Muse: Epileptic Dreaming

In Part I we used the model of paroxysmal alterations in functional cerebral state as a basis for conceptualizing conversion symptoms, changes in mood, alterations of consciousness, and other hysterical manifestations. Perhaps the same types of brain activity apply as well to the generation of some species of dream phenomena.

Epstein (1967) explored the relationship of dreaming to seizures that occur during sleep. Previous studies had demonstrated a close connection between recurrent dreams and seizures in some patients with temporal lobe epilepsy. Epstein examined this further by studying two patients with recurrent dreams related to epileptic seizures that were believed to originate in the temporal or temporoparietal areas of the brain. Epstein was particularly interested in the role of the epileptic process in shaping the remembered events in the dream, what Freud would call the dream's manifest content. In both patients the content of the recurrent dreams—and in some instances of the seizures during waking life as well—involved alterations in body image and subjective body position.

The first case, whom we will call Ms. A, was a forty-one-year-old woman whose seizures had been present since infancy, at first as grand

132

mal and later becoming mainly psychomotor. No attacks involving disturbances in body sensation or body image occurred until the patient's fortieth year, when she reported several new sensations during a group of seizures, this time while awake, all taking place on the same day. "My leg felt big," she said of one attack (although she couldn't specify which leg); "I thought the towel [present in her room during the seizure] was my thigh. I wondered what happened to my leg, and I went over and felt the towel. I actually thought my leg was on the table" (p. 613). The general feeling-tone during these seizures was described as unpleasant.

More intriguing, however, are the dreams reported by this patient while asleep at night. While reading the following account, note the parallels to Freud's dissection room dream, described in the last chapter.

> I felt that I was looking at the cat. I felt like I was the cat and I was dying. I felt sorry for the cat. I was dying—but I was the cat. It was very real. When the feeling left me, I had a terrible headache for about three hours. I was sure the cat was dead.
>
> In the middle of the night I woke up. I felt my senses all mixed. I felt my eyes were protruding. I felt my eyes were dropping out. When I came out of it, I felt afraid to look in the mirror—I thought my eyes would be gone. Then I had a headache for three hours.
>
> I woke up. It was so real while it was going on. I felt like my whole body was disappearing. I felt my bust going down like it was disappearing. I actually felt it going down—like a balloon going down. I didn't have a headache this time.
>
> In the middle of the night I felt that my fingers were falling off; my bust was coming off; my eyes were out. I felt that I was dissolving. My fingers actually felt as if they were not there.
>
> I felt I was nothing but bones. All I could feel was bones. I felt my body shrinking more and more.
>
> I see a brain—skull. The brain is spongy. This spongy stuff was kind of falling off. Skull falling into pieces. My brain deteriorating. I said, thinking, "well, you won't have any more—oh, that's the reason for all these other feelings—the brain is going." Then I woke up. (Epstein, 1967, p. 614)

Epstein (1967) refers to these alterations in body image during the dreams as "illusions of corporeal transformation," in which the body or a part of it is viewed as changing in size. Also experienced was a sense of dissolution or loss of body parts. Of further interest is the fact that in this seizure-induced dream, the patient occasionally projected her self— her ego—into an extraneous being, the cat, and viewed the projected self as shrinking and undergoing dissolution. What type of primary process-induced latent content might underlie the seizure-induced manifest content of a dream like this?

On the basis of clinical presentation, Epstein (1967) hypothesizes that the localization of the seizure focus was in the temporal lobe. To support this, he refers to an earlier study of Arseni and colleagues (1966), who reported fourteen patients with paroxysmal seizure disorders involving body image, the majority with abnormalities in the parietotemporal region of the right hemisphere. Among the body-image disturbances described in that report were sensations of diffuse and localized bodily disintegration, hypertrophy ("hyperschematia"), and atrophy ("hyposchematia") of certain body parts. For example, during her seizures, one patient with a right parieto-temporo-occipital cystic astrocytoma experienced a sensation of enlargement of the left arm and leg and the left half of the tongue; in other seizures she had the impression that the left half of her body was falling to pieces, disintegrating like a "sheet of burned paper." A second patient, with diffuse EEG abnormalities and without a verified brain lesion, felt during her seizures that her breasts were growing in size.

Epstein's (1967) own explanation of his patient's cat dream is intriguing in light of its attempted integration of psychological and neurophysiological interpretations; he seems to be expounding the view of Freud that while physiology may shape the direction and form of a symptom, psychodynamics may influence the meaning, although his account lies psychologically closer to the surface, to the manifest content, than Freud's might be. Thus, in this seizure-dream, the woman's body was viewed as outside of herself and as existing in the cat. The idea of dying developed as an elaboration and may derive from the elementary sensation that the body is shrinking or undergoing dissolution. The cat (the projected self) was then viewed as dying. The emotion of sorrow can perhaps be more readily attached to the projected than to the true self, and thus the patient dreamed that she "felt sorry for the cat." This is as far as Epstein goes in his interpretation. Freud, we may be sure, would have continued to delve deeper, convinced, as we saw in the last chapter, that even organically-induced mental states owe their particular content to the psychodynamic forces active in the individual person.

Epstein's (1967) second case, Ms. B, was a twenty-year-old woman who had experienced nocturnal seizures since age thirteen. Several weeks before the onset of overt grand mal convulsions, a dream, distinctly unpleasant in quality, appeared and then recurred nightly:

My mother and father—they're both on different trains—coming the same way—toward me. They are both on the same track and coming to meet me. One is supposed to get there before the other. One of them is supposed to give me the ticket before the other. The wrong one is always getting there. I try to warn them. (p. 616)

This dream eventually disappeared. Subsequently, during waking, a complex series of sensations preceded the majority of Ms. B's grand mal convulsions:

> It feels as though my left leg is up in the air. I try to grab it. It seems like it is going up in the air. My leg has to go over my body and touch the floor. My whole body feels like it is turning over several times. It feels as though my leg is trying to touch the floor and also as though something is trying to hold it back from touching the floor. I have to roll over several times before touching. My leg has got to touch the floor. Every time I touch my foot to the floor, I feel a sense of relief. It feels wonderful. It feels like I look foward to it when my foot will touch. At the moment that my left leg touches the floor, I cross my fingers and yell out. I feel all right when I do that. But then I pass out. (p. 617)

With regard to localization, Epstein (1967) feels that the episodic paresthesias in the left leg and the occasional sense of absence of that leg tend to implicate the right parietal lobe; this is corroborated by the focal accentuation of the EEG abnormality in this area. In addition, the complex subjective experience of alteration in position and, specifically, of movement of the left leg and rotation of the body suggest a vestibular component, the cerebral representation of the vestibular system residing chiefly in the superior temporal gyrus, bordering the parietal lobe. On clinical grounds, therefore, Epstein believes that this patient's seizures arose from a focus in the right temporoparietal area.

Commenting generally on these two cases, Epstein (1967) asserts that the bulk of clinical evidence favors the parietal lobe and adjacent temporal region as the substrate for such complex disturbances of body image; this is an area, it may be noted, that lies in close proximity to and perhaps overlaps SSII, the area we conceptualized as playing an important role in the generation of somatosensory and body image disturbances in hysteria. In the two patients reported here, temporoparietal areas are implicated on clinical grounds, and in the second patient it is the right temporoparietal area that seems to have been involved; EEG data corroborated a parietal focus. Citing the contemporary literature up to the time of his report, Epstein notes the consensus that the right hemisphere more frequently than the left is the site of seizure discharge in temporal lobe epileptics with recurrent dreams.

Epstein (1967) then asks, If certain dreams are the product of abnormal cerebral activity, does their content have recognizable features? Earlier, Epstein (1964) had suggested that such "epileptic dreams" are usually recurrent and dysphoric, at times related to previous painful memories and other times containing visceral sensations. Manifest content motifs of such dreams include sensations and images of falling, colliding, and dying, themes related to the alterations in body position and body image noted in Epstein's 1967 case study. It would seem that during dreaming sleep, ideation is more accessible to the influence of certain neural systems than during the waking state. This, says Epstein, is a factor to be considered in the formation of dream content, perhaps not only in the "epileptic" dream but in a more general sense. As we will soon see, the modern data on cerebral hemispheric asymmetry of function may provide one kind of model for selective ideational malleability.

Morpheus Unchained: Narcoleptic Dreaming

In 1880 Gelineau described the case of a thirty-eight-old wine-barrel retailer who suffered repetitive attacks of sudden muscle weakness and sleep. These attacks, he reported, seemed to occur in association with intense emotional states. Gelineau termed the condition *narcolepsy*, the name that is still used for this syndrome. The symptoms of narcolepsy fall into four major groups, often referred to as the "narcoleptic tetrad," or sometimes "Gelineau's tetrad"; some, but usually not all, of the following symptoms are experienced by the patient with narcolepsy:

1. *Sleep attacks* are sudden episodes of irresistible drowsiness and sleep that occur at variable times throughout the day.
2. *Cataplexy* refers to sudden loss of muscle tone, occurring either alone or along with the sleep attack, in which the person may appear to abruptly crumple to the ground; this may be precipitated by an intense emotional state, such as fright or laughter.
3. *Sleep paralysis* are attacks of immobility upon falling asleep or waking up.
4. *Hypnagogic* and *hypnopompic hallucinations* are vivid, dream-like hallucinations that occur while falling asleep and, more rarely, upon waking up, respectively.

Narcolepsy is usually diagnosed by its clinical features, often assisted by an EEG pattern of sleep-onset REM, in contrast to the normal occurrence of REM later in the sleep cycle. While the etiology of narcolepsy is still unclear, it is thought to relate to dysfunction of the brain stem and other brain mechanisms normally controlling the sleep–wakefulness cycle; indeed, many narcoleptic phenomena (hallucinations, paralysis) appear to represent a kind of abnormal REM-sleep intrusion or disinhibition. Treatment typically consists of daily activity management and the use of stimulant or other medications to combat daytime sleepiness, although contrasting opinions exist regarding the latter (Larkin, 1984; Lishman, 1978; Regestein et al., 1983; Strub & Black, 1981).

Many narcoleptic patients report hypnagogic hallucinations and even recurrent dreams during regular sleep that are occasionally so bizarre and vivid that they may strain reality testing and be experienced as quite frightening (Ribstein, 1974; Sours, 1963). The content of these dreams typically involves being pursued by dangerous creatures, being pushed or impelled by some unknown force, or sensing an intruder in the house (Ribstein, 1974). Intense anxiety frequently accompanies these recurrent dreams, which have been related to awakening from sleep-onset REM (Roth & Bruhova, 1969).

In contrast to these frightening dreams, a less familiar type of vivid dream theme was noted by Krishnan and colleagues (1984) during a support group session for narcoleptic patients. Many of these patients described dreams with similar content: dreams of flying, of being airborne, or of floating. The dreams were recurrent in all individuals and were accompanied by nonanxious or even pleasant affect. Some examples follow.

The first case was of a fifty-three-year-old married man with a thirty-year history of EEG-confirmed narcolepsy with sleep paralysis and cataplexy, the latter appearing only with exhaustion or strong emotion. Occasional sleep attacks lasted for about fifteen minutes, and the patient benefited only moderately from medication. He reported recurring dreams of floating gently through the sky in an airplane. He believed these dreams occurred while he was asleep; that is, they were not waking hallucinations. The dreams were devoid of either intense positive or negative affect.

In the second case a fifty-seven-year-old man with narcolepsy for twenty years experienced cataplexy when excited or laughing and had EEG-documented narcoleptic attacks that occurred about ten times a day. Medication had little effect on either symptom. The patient reported a long history of pleasant dreams of becoming a bird and soaring or floating through the air with his arms spread out. He believed that these dreams occurred during the night, did not think them to be more prevalent during the early stages of sleep, and did not experience hypnagogic hallucinations.

In the third case, a sixty-four-year-old man had narcolepsy since age four; cataplexy developed during adolescence. The diagnosis had been confirmed by EEG, and the narcoleptic attacks were found to be related to REM sleep. Medication was of some value in treating the condition. The patient reported pleasant dreams of flying "like Superman" and floating through the sky. These dreams occurred during narcoleptic attacks and during nighttime sleep.

In conceptualizing these cases, Krishnan and colleagues (1984) refer to Van den Hoed and colleagues (1979), who noted flying sensations in their cases, especially when the patients did not try to fight off a cataplectic attack. They suggested that during the longer cataplectic episodes, REM sleep may intrude into wakefulness, with consequent mental clouding and heightened awareness of nonvolitional rapid eye movements, both possibly contributing to the flying sensations. One of Krishnan and colleagues' own patients noted that his dreams of flying intensified when the sleep attacks got worse, but other patients were unable to describe such a relationship.

Attack on the Brain's Dream Generators

Narcolepsy appears to be related to dysfunction in the subcortical brain mechanisms that regulate the sleep cycle. As discussed in a previous chapter, much of our present-day understanding of sleep and dream physiology has come from the study of these subcortical systems; indeed, as we saw earlier, Hobson (1988; Hobson & McCarley, 1977) bases his whole theory of dreaming on the actions of the brain stem dream generators, particularly the *locus coeruleus*.

The role of the locus coeruleus in sleep has been the subject of much controversy ever since Jouvet (1962) first proposed his neurochemical theory of sleep control. In Jouvet's model, noradrenergic neurons, with their cell bodies located in the locus coeruleus, control the generation of REM sleep and its related events. The original pontine tegmental lesion studies in cats demonstrated that REM sleep retains its basic characteristic despite the absent muscle atonia and the consequent release of overt behavioral repertoires, including head raising, signs of rage, and hallucinatory motor activity during dreaming sleep (Jouvet & Delorme, 1965).

Subsequent research revealed that loss of atonia was a necessary but not sufficient condition to disinhibit REM-sleep behaviors (Hendricks et al., 1982). Lesions in various pontine areas released stereotypical behaviors that formed four syndromes: (1) a minimal syndrome consisting of loss of atonia and unorganized head and limb movements; (2) a pattern of staring, orienting, head raising, reaching behaviors, and attempts at standing; (3) phasic episodes of attack behavior alternating with periods of quiet staring or searching movements; and (4) locomotion, that is, actually walking, stalking, or running around. Although subsequent studies failed to completely support these initial claims (see Vertes, 1984, for a review), the locus coeruleus has remained an area of great interest to sleep researchers.

Since virtually all of our understanding of the role of the locus coeruleus in sleep comes from electrical stimulation and lesion studies in animals, Kaitin and colleagues (1986) seized the unique opportunity to study the sleep and dreams of a twenty-five-year old man who had had a stimulating electrode surgically implanted in the vicinity of the locus coeruleus for the therapeutic relief of spasticity. Seven years after the implantation, the subject's sleep patterns were studied for five days in a sleep laboratory to observe the effects of locus coeruleus stimulation on sleep patterns. In contrast to the normal sleep patterns that occurred during the two nonstimulation nights, electrical stimulation of the locus coeruleus produced a profound disruption of sleep and significant reductions in the total amounts of REM sleep, non-REM sleep, and total sleep.

These results suggested that in man the locus coeruleus may make multiple contributions to the overall control of sleep, including maintaining the general balance between sleep and waking, as well as a more selective role related to the expression of REM sleep. The results also attested to the impressive resilience of the sleep cycle, considering that even after seven years of virtually continuous stimulation of this subject's brain, sleep patterns returned essentially to normal during the two nonstimulation nights.

Five patients with unusual sleep behavior were studied by Schenck and colleagues (1986). One representative case in this sample concerns a sixty-seven-year-old man referred for treatment because of violent behavior during sleep. He had slept uneventfully through adolescence in a small room with three brothers, but on his wedding night his wife was startled by his sleep talking, groaning, tooth grinding, and body movements. These persisted without undue consequence for over forty years until, one night, he found himself out of bed, attempting to carry out a dream.

This was the beginning of an increasingly frequent and progressively severe sleep disorder in which he would punch and kick his wife, lurch out of bed, lunge about the room, crash into objects, and injure himself. These activities seemed to correspond to what was taking place in the ongoing dream. For example, one night he dreamed that he was riding along on a motorcycle when another cyclist tried to pass him and run him off the road. The patient's response in the dream was to kick the other vehicle aside; in fact, it was his wife who was jolted awake by the sharp blow. On another night he dreamed he was running down a football field, deflecting tackles, and awoke to find the room in shambles. The other four cases in this series showed a similar pattern.

According to the researchers, cases like this document the existence of complex and clinically important behaviors during human REM sleep that resemble the REM-sleep behaviors observed in the original experimental studies with brain stem-lesioned cats. In conceptualizing their cases, Schenck and colleagues (1986) propose that the pontine tegmentum during REM sleep has responsibility not only for motoneuron inhibition causing atonia but also for inhibition of the brain stem generators of motor activity (Hendricks et al., 1982; Morrison, 1979). A lesion affecting the former mechanism would result in REM sleep without atonia whereas a lesion affecting both mechanisms would release REM behaviors as well. All of Schenck and colleagues' patients, including the "dream cyclist," had REM sleep that retained its basic features, despite variable muscle tone activity, and all had documented REM behaviors consistent with Hendricks and colleagues' (1982) experimental syndromes (1) and (2), as described earlier. In addition, four of the patients were documented to have syndrome (3), and their histories were consistent with syndrome (4).

Thus, the reported dream hyperactivity may have been another consequence of disinhibited brain stem motor drive, as would be predicted from Hobson and McCarley's (1977) activation–synthesis model of dreaming. Recall that this theory postulates that during REM sleep, specific brain stem generators activate motor, perceptual, affective, memory, and cognitive neuronal circuits that in turn feed their information to an integrating forebrain mechanism whose resultant product is the dream. Thus, increased activity of motor pattern generators might induce corresponding dream changes.

Lugaresi and colleagues (1986) report the case of a fifty-three-year-old Italian man who presented with progressive insomnia and disorders of the autonomic nervous system, which regulates visceral and metabolic functions. These symptoms included fever, increased sweating, pupillary constriction, and sphincter disturbances. At age fifty-two the patient, who had formerly slept five to seven hours a night and napped for thirty minutes in the afternoon, began to have nocturnal insomnia. Sleep became poorer, only two to three hours a night, and was at first associated with impotence and loss of libido and a month later with urinary difficulties, constipation, sweating, fever, and increased flow of saliva, tears, and nasal mucus. Two months later the patient could sleep for only one hour a night, and even this brief interlude was frequently disturbed by vivid dreams during which he would rise from his bed, stand, and give a military salute. When awakened, the patient recalled dreaming that he was attending a coronation.

Three months after the onset of symptoms, normal sleep became impossible and the dreaming episodes gradually became more frequent. Speech difficulties, severe fatigue, and fever forced the patient to retire from his job as an industrial manager. Six months after onset, breathing irregularities, gait clumsiness, and mild intention tremor of the arms developed; the sleep and autonomic disturbances worsened. Eight months after onset, the patient had several brief episodes of motor agitation with screaming, dystonic posturing, and rotation of the trunk toward the right. He became more febrile and stuporous but was responsive to intense stimulation. Severe autonomic instability, respiratory insufficiency, brisk tendon reflexes, and a right Babinski's sign were apparent. An infection of the right lung developed that could not be controlled by antibiotics, and the patient died nine months after the ordeal first began.

It was subsequently discovered that two sisters of the patient and many relatives over three generations had died of a similar disease. Pathological studies of the brains of the patient and one of his sisters showed severe neuronal degeneration of the anterior and dorsomedial nuclei of the thalamus. Other thalamic nuclei, the cerebral cortex, and white matter were normal in all the lobes. In particular, the cingulate gyrus, orbital cortex, anterior frontal cortex, amygdala, and hippocampus were unaffected.

In reviewing the literature, Lugaresi and colleagues (1986) point out that autonomic disturbances and memory deficits are considered to be typical features of the medial thalamic syndrome, in which altered states of vigilance, changes of mood, and dementia are also present. Motor dysfunction, such as tremor or other involuntary movement, is more characteristic of the anterolateral thalamic syndrome and is attributed to involvement of cerebro-rubrothalamic pathways. These correlations indicate that the anterior and dorsomedial thalami play an important role in integrating and expressing sleep, autonomic functions, and neuroendocrine circadian rhythms.

Only shortly before this patient's death did stupor, accompanied by relentless dreaming activity and myoclonus, become the dominant feature. Significant cognitive impairment was not observed, except for an isolated long-term verbal memory deficit. Sleep recordings showed that the stuporous, dream-like state was different from hypersomnia. The stupor was characterized by desynchronized activity similar to that of the REM stage, with enacted dreams and an absence of the synchronized sleep pattern typical of non-REM sleep.

Thus, perhaps the subcortical mechanisms we have discussed might be involved in mediating the dream cycle and in maintaining the important biopsychological division between dreams and waking life. When these mechanisms are impaired by brain disease, the behavioral activation ordinarily suppressed during sleep escapes this inhibition, and the person "acts out" the dream.

But what of the dream content itself? How much thought, imagery, and feeling go into the construction of a particular dream at a particular time for a particular person? This, after all, is what Freud developed his dream interpretation method to find out. Can the neuropsychodynamic model illuminate how we actually come to dream *what* we dream about?

CHAPTER 11

The Wounded Muse: Effects of Brain Damage on Dreaming

Having just dealt with the effects of brain disease on dream generation, with how dreams are formed, we now turn to the effects of acquired brain damage on the dream *content* of individuals who, for the most part, were dreaming normally before the injury.

Localizing Dream Content: An Early Study

In the course of a more general investigation of psychological changes associated with posterior parietal lesions, Humphrey and Zangwill (1951) reported on three patients in whom cessation of dreaming occurred as an aftereffect of brain injury. The loss of dreaming appeared to be permanent in two cases and temporary in one. All three patients reported marked deficits of visualization in the waking state, together with some degree of visuospatial loss. The injury in each patient involved the occipitoparietal region of the brain, an area important to higher order visual perception in general. In two cases the injury was on the right side, in one case on the left.

Humphrey and Zangwill (1951) suggested that visual thinking, dreaming, and imagination might be susceptible to organic dissolution in the same manner as the disintegration of symbolic thought in aphasia. But whereas aphasia is specifically associated with lesions of the left hemisphere, disorders of visual imagination appeared to follow lesions on either side (actually, more likely on the right, at least in this small sample) and to be especially marked in cases with occipitoparietal involvement. These authors suggested that dreaming is likely to be affected only in those

142

agnosic states in which there is an appreciable impairment of visual imagery.

Lobotomized Dreaming

Jus and colleagues (1973) studied the effects of prefrontal lobotomy on dream recall in thirteen chronic schizophrenic patients and nonlobotomized schizophrenic controls, utilizing all-night sleep EEG recordings and awakenings during REM sleep. Neither the duration of the REM stages nor the number of actual rapid eye movements themselves differed significantly between lobotomized and nonlobotomized subjects. However, the lobotomized subjects reported a significantly lower incidence of having dreamed, whether or not they could recall the content of those dreams. This was not due merely to poorer overall recall ability after surgery, since the results of waking memory assessment showed no significant differences between the lobotomized and control groups.

In conceptualizing their results, the investigators noted that research on frontal-lesioned animals has shown abnormally rapid decay of delayed conditioned signals (Konorski & Lawicka, 1964). Also, Luria (1960) found that frontally lesioned humans show significant impairment in the speed and efficiency with which they scan a visual array for detail. Milner (1963) has shown that after frontal lobectomy in man, a dissociation occurs between the ability to verbalize the requirements of a concept-formation test and the ability to use this verbalization as an effective guide to action. Psychophysiological studies of patients with frontal lobe damage have demonstrated certain types of complex perceptual and perceptuomotor impairment (Teuber, 1964), and other studies have indicated a derangement of behavioral programming and a failure of memory registration (see Stuss & Benson, 1984, 1986, for more recent reviews). Jus and colleagues (1973) thus hypothesized that the deficit in efficient internal scanning due to frontal lobotomy might have been the cause of the inability of these patients to access and recall their dreams. (A similar frontal lobe-mediated internal scanning deficit has been proposed to explain the retrieval deficit in Korsakoff's syndrome; see Butters, 1979.)

Morpheus's Left Hand: The Cerebral Hemispheres and Dreaming

Recall from Chapter 8 that a number of dream theorists, most prominently Bakan (1977–1978), have emphasized the role of the right cerebral hemisphere in mediating the formation and expression of visually oriented dream content. Greenwood and colleagues (1977) reasoned that if visual dreaming is mediated by the right hemisphere, then even if patients with a severed corpus callosum showed normal REM episodes and presumably normal visual dreams, they might be unable to make a verbal report of the dream's visual elements because the disconnected verbal-articulatory left hemisphere would have no access to the right hemisphere-generated visual dream experience.

To study this, all-night sleep EEGs were recorded from three patients with partial or complete commissurotomies. Upon entering a REM episode, the subjects were awakened and questioned about dream content. The investigators found that all of the subjects were able to recount some visual dreaming, which failed to support the notion of selective right-hemisphere visual dream mediation.

Kerr and Foulkes (1981) report the case of a forty-four-year-old man who was deprived of a good portion of his right temporal lobe cortex due to a combination of cerebrovascular pathology and neurosurgery for epilepsy. Despite demonstrating a superior IQ and essentially normal performance on several types of visuospatial tasks, he seemed singularly impaired in his ability to represent extrapersonal space kinematically, that is, to project an element of personal body interaction into the solution of tasks requiring internal mental representations of manipulative activity. For example, although he could discern figure from ground in an embedded figures test and complete three-dimensional block designs, he did no better than chance when asked to mentally visualize the folding and unfolding of pieces of paper or to rotate figures and objects mentally. His dreams were characterized by a relative absence of imagery, instead being composed of self-involving narratives that were sequential and story-like in form. "The imaging part eludes me," he said of his dreams; the dream setting was typically experienced as "a general just knowing, rather than a sensing," "more abstract in the mapping of something" rather than a "visual seeing" (pp. 605–606). Thus, the production of a dream-like narrative, the basic dream *story*, was relatively preserved in the face of right temporal lobe damage. What was diminished was the sensory embellishment, the visual imagery that for most of us constitutes the rich, symbolically laden manifest content of dreams.

In conceptualizing this case, Kerr and Foulkes (1981) appeal to Foulkes's (1978) earlier theory, according to which the frontal regions of the left hemisphere mediate the running narrative span of the dream, just as they mediate the verbal intentionality underlying the generation of waking narratives. In this model, the visual-imaginal aspect of dreams is a matter of "surface representation" of manifest content, and this may be the component subserved by the right hemisphere. However, the narrative aspect, the integral dream story, is generated or facilitated by the left-hemisphere–frontal system of personal consciousness, the system that allows for the experience and expression of a personal identity and of a sense of the relevance of the dream story to the dreamer's life. The ability to recall (and therefore presumably to generate) dreams at all can thus be virtually obliterated by left-hemisphere or frontal damage.

Given that brain damage that produces symptoms during one's waking life can also affect dreaming while one is asleep, can brain damage that occurs *during* sleep determine or influence the content of ongoing or developing dreams? Such appears to be the case for a thirty-seven-year-old word processor salesman, reported by Harrison (1981), who described a nightmare that began with his being seated at the keyboard of an enormous word processor screen. To his dismay, he could not get the screen to show any words, only carriage return symbols. He awoke at this point to discover that he could not move his right arm normally.

Thinking that he had merely not awakened fully, he tried to lean on his right elbow to hoist himself out of bed, and promptly collapsed to the floor as his weakened arm gave way. The fall woke his wife, but he found he was unable to speak to her. Heaviness of the arm lasted a few hours and his expressive speech and typing difficulties gradually improved over the next several days, although two weeks later he was still making errors at the keyboard. The symptoms gradually abated, and angiography revealed dissection of the left middle cerebral artery, presumed to be the cause of his left-hemisphere stroke. It is not reported whether subsequent dreaming was affected. Similar to the epileptic dreams described in the last chapter, this patient's stroke constituted a neuropathological event that was apparently able to shape and determine the manifest content of a dream *while* he dreamed it.

Seven patients reported loss of dreaming associated with aphasia following acute vascular lesions of the left hemisphere in a study by Epstein and Simmons (1983). The type of aphasia varied, with four subjects having primarily expressive and three having receptive aphasias. Only one of the seven patients had a visual field cut, and a CT scan performed on three of the patients showed the lesion to involve midhemispheric regions, with no direct involvement of visual areas. The authors hypothesize that areas subserving imagery may have been disconnected from those sequencing the imagery, linking the imagery with meaning, or raising the imagery to awareness during sleep.

Fifty-three patients with vascular or neoplastic unilateral brain lesions were involved in a study by Murri and colleagues (1984). A questionnaire used to assess the frequency of morning dream recall showed that this recall was lower in patients with posterior cerebral lesions than in those with anterior lesions or in normal controls. A direct relationship was found between lesions and visuoperceptive deficiencies in fifteen of the posterior-lesioned patients and in only five of the anterior-lesioned patients; this held true for both left and right hemispheres.

Thus, a number of these findings seem to disagree with the hypothesis of such theorists as Bakan (1977–1978), who emphasizes an exclusive, or at least predominant, role for the right hemisphere during dreaming. Yet in the cases just reviewed, the different results related to the left hemisphere, and apparently dependent on the presence or absence of language disturbances, did not appear to be due to the language problems per se but rather to the co-occurring visuoperceptive deficits. Indeed, the loss of dream recall affected those aphasic patients with posterior lesions who also manifested a high degree of visuoperceptive disorders. On the other hand, patients affected by posterior lesions on the left side, without language deficits, maintained their dream recall when visuoperceptive functions had not been altered.

In a subsequent study, Murri and colleagues (1985) examined nineteen hospitalized patients who had vascular or neoplastic lesions localized to either the left or right hemisphere. Dream recall was evaluated by means of a simple diary indicating the presence or absence of remembered dreams each morning. In addition, the investigator periodically woke each patient during REM sleep and asked if he/she had been dreaming. If the answer was yes, the subject was asked to describe the dream. Dream content was evaluated according to a seven-point scale of dream-like fantasy, ranging from 0 (no content reported, feels mind was blank) to 7 (perceptual content hallucinatory, bizarre, dramatic, or unusual).

Results showed that the site of the lesion appeared to be the only relevant factor; patients unable to report dreaming on provoked awakening often had lesions within the temporo-parieto-occipital region. Whether the lesion was located on the left or the right did not appear to be important. The results obtained from the diary and sleep interruption methods were not significantly different. Thus, in the case of unilateral lesions—damage to either hemisphere itself—the subjective, spontaneous dream report is consistent with the REM awakening report, unlike the case with Greenwood and colleagues' (1977) commissurotomy patients, for whom spontaneous dream recall was absent but awakening during REM sleep revealed the presence of dreaming. Apparently, destruction of the relevant dream-contributory areas of either hemisphere itself impairs the very ability to elaborate a normal dream whereas merely disconnecting the two halves of the brain cuts off interhemispheric communication and normal waking recall but may leave the dream itself essentially intact.

Dreams and Waking Imagery: Similarities and Differences

Schanfald and colleagues (1985) studied eight right-handed male patients with cerebrovascular brain damage. Four patients had expressive aphasia and one had receptive aphasia due to left hemisphere damage; three patients had visuospatial disorders due to right-hemisphere damage. The patients were given two assessment interviews measuring narrative abilities for pictorial thematic content. A presleep evaluation, the Picture Story Test, was administered on the first night to evaluate the patients' ability to comprehend and narrate imagistic content. This test consists of six multiscenic pictures of continuing thematic content (somewhat similar to the Wechsler Picture Arrangement subtest cards); the patient is shown one picture at a time and asked to narrate a story about it. Each patient also had a series of sleep EEG recordings, for while he was awakened at the end of each REM period and sporadically during non-REM periods. If he recalled something upon awakening, he was asked to describe it verbally. For patients with language problems, this report also necessitated writing and gesturing, and the patients were also asked to make drawings of their dreams.

From the accounts of dreams given verbally or in drawings, it was obvious that regardless of the type of brain damage and despite the evidence of language disturbances or disturbed visuospatial contructions when awake, the patients were able to generate dream activity and to describe the dreams they had experienced. Interestingly, whereas all patients with language disorders made the same types of aphasic errors on the Picture Story Test and in spoken or written dream narratives, drawing the dream resulted in better dream recall for all subjects. The drawings always included items not mentioned in the verbal description. For patients with right-hemisphere damage, the results of this drawn dream-recall task differed markedly from results of draw-from-memory tasks involving externally presented stimuli while awake. The latter showed gross visuospatial errors while the former were reasonable pictorial representations, similar to drawn copies of externally presented stimuli.

Thus, the results of this study by Schanfald and colleagues suggest that preserved dreaming and memory for dreaming can occur in the presence of severe disturbances in waking visuospatial or language functions. The investigators suggest that the output for stored information may take different routes in the brain during the waking and dreaming states. One aspect of language and narrative functions, then, the generation and recall of a coherent dream, may endure intact despite disturbance in other language and perceptual functions.

Pena-Casanova and colleagues (1985) describe a forty-seven-year-old Spanish patient who suffered a stroke involving the left medial temporo-occipital region. Among other deficits, the patient was unable to name objects, pictures, or faces from a visual inspection of them, had trouble understanding the meaning of concrete words that referred to specific objects, and could not describe the concrete characteristics of an object.

However, his ability to express and comprehend abstract words, concepts, and descriptions was perfectly normal.

For example, he was able to tell that a rose and a carnation both belong to the conceptual class of flowers and that Catalonia roses are offered on Saint George's Day (a Spanish holiday), but it was very difficult for him to describe what a rose or a carnation actually looks like. Only when coming up with the name or description for something involved any sort of internalized visualization of the object did the patient experience difficulty. His problem, in other words, was one of accessing language from visual information, as well as in evoking the image from verbal stimuli. In addition, he reported that since his stroke he had ceased to dream entirely, despite having dreamed virtually every night in the past. Five months later his naming ability had improved somewhat, but he recalled having only one dream during that time.

So far, we have considered case histories and experimental studies involving patients who suffered some acquired injury to a previously intact and healthy brain. However, Botez and colleagues (1985) report a case of what they term "inborn defective revisualization," without other significant neurologic deficits. The subject, a thirty-eight-year-old left-handed Canadian high school teacher and psychotherapist, complained of a lifelong inability to visualize known faces, houses, events, or objects. He stated that he was used to thinking and representing the outside world in verbal symbols. Asked why he waited till age thirty-eight to bring this problem to medical attention, he replied that in his younger days he was able to compensate better for the disability. Also, his wife had often helped him verbally memorize specific events, but since their separation he had been experiencing more difficulties in everyday activities.

The subject related that he had always had extreme difficulty in visualizing the external world. If he closed his eyes for only a few moments, he experienced a total memory blank. He was unable to revisualize places, objects, persons, distances, and dimensions of either living or inanimate things he had seen. For example, he was unable to evaluate mentally the dimensions of an elephant compared to a dog; however, he claimed to "know" the dimensions of both by "learning." He likewise was unable to visualize his own car but could recognize it among others by virtue of idiosyncrasies of detail such as color, shape, and so on. Getting from one place to another in a building or on the street involved verbally memorizing the separate stages of the trip (turn left at the third door; make a right at the bottom of the hill, etc.), since he was unable to form any kind of mental map to aid in these negotiations. Interestingly, he had no trouble getting around Manhattan Island because of the rectangular layout of that part of New York City.

The subject was unable to visualize the faces of his own children or of his ex-wife; he could nevertheless name the color of their eyes, hair, and other facial details. While he could recognize familiar people such as family members from among a crowd, new acquaintances had to be subsequently identified by details of appearance or clothing. He could not use revisualization as an aid to memory but had to rely on verbal prompts and descriptions. He had great difficulty following the action of TV shows and movies. Whenever his current girlfriend left his apartment, he had no kind of visual image of her and therefore failed to experience the relevant sentiments of longing or desire. Finally, he described his dreams as being "vague" and occurring in grey or black. He said he dreamed mainly in voices rather than images, and those faces that did occasionally appear in his dreams did not physically resemble the persons concerned, a condition reminiscent of Freud's concepts of condensation and displacement, as well as of the phenomenon of reduplication, discussed in an earlier chapter.

A nuclear magnetic resonance (NMR) scan showed a flattening or stretching of the posterior-superior third of the corpus callosum but without any recognizable abnormality of the adjacent brain matter. Another NMR scan revealed a dilated right lateral ventricle with underdevelopment of the surrounding brain tissue but no evidence of abnormal intracranial pressure or other brain pathology. There was no way to determine whether the findings represented an atrophic change, developmental defect, or an obstructive abnormality of cerebrospinal fluid flow. Thus, the defect of visualization shown by this patient seemed to be associated with both an underdevelopment of the right hemisphere and an associated maldevelopment of the posterior portion of the corpus callosum, which is responsible for interhemispheric transfer of visual information. The authors point out, however, that even this evidence for malfunctioning of the corpus callosum in their patient was "not impressive."

Epileptic Dreaming Revisited: Functional Neuropsychological Dream Disruption

Brain impairment need not be due only to structural lesions. As we have seen so far throughout this book, paroxysmal disorders can produce transient alterations in brain functioning that may symptomatically resemble the more permanent neurosyndromes resulting from stroke- or trauma-induced brain damage.

Like Epstein (1967), whose work on "epileptic dreams" we discussed earlier, Hoboda (1986) approached the issue of cerebral localization and dreaming by studying the effects of seizure activity on REM sleep; however, he took a more systematic, experimental approach. Whole night sleep recordings were carried out with a group of psychomotor (temporal lobe) epileptics and control groups of patients with other (nonpsychomotor) types of seizures, as well as with normal subjects. A specific relationship was found between right focal temporal lobe activity and REM sleep, and Hoboda speculates that the high vigilance level during REM sleep may lower the threshold to focal epileptogenic activity in the lateral and posterolateral regions of the brain. However, the REM-induced interictal activity in temporal and temporoparietal areas of the right hemisphere may have a positive feedback effect on the REM process that provokes it. This would result in a marked prolongation of the REM phase of sleep, a mechanism perhaps not unlike the phenomenon of kindling, discussed in connection with hysteria in Chapter 5.

Thus, it seems that due to a peculiar form of synchronous discharge of certain groups of epileptic neurons in right temporal and temporo-occipital brain areas, the right hemisphere can be specifically activated during sleep, maintaining the REM phase of sleep for an atypically long period of time. This might also explain the dominant role and functional specialization of the right hemisphere in REM sleep and dreaming that is hypothesized by a number of authors. According to Hoboda (1986), the temporal and temporo-occipital regions of the right hemisphere play an important role both in the intensity of local epileptogenic discharges during REM sleep and in the positive feedback effect of these pathological activities.

But, as should be apparent at this point, each of the neuroanatomical regions and neurophysiological processes we have discussed is unlikely to be the source of human dreaming in and of itself. Let us now examine how the data on the neuropsychology of dreaming can be put together to elaborate a neuropsychodynamic model of the dream-work.

CHAPTER 12

The Neuropsychodynamics of the Dream-Work

Freud's goal was to create a fully integrated model of the mind, encompassing such seemingly diverse phenomena as symptoms, dreams, and everyday slips. This chapter takes what we have learned so far about the neuropsychology of the dream process and attempts to weave it into a broadly comprehensive neuropsychodynamic framework.

The Brain and the Dream-Work: A Neuropsychodynamic Model

If frontal lobe activity can be said to underlie the recursive evaluation and planning of behavior and the left-hemisphere language system to provide a means of self-articulating thoughts, feelings, and goals, then how might these two functional systems collaborate with right-hemisphere image-generation mechanisms in the actual forming of a dream?

In the present conceptualization, a dream is essentially qualitatively similar to other forms of overt and incipient mentation and behavior. As we have seen, the frontal lobes are necessary for the formation of plans of action, for the coherent linking together of sequences of actions directed toward a goal, and for the recursive evaluation of the subcomponents of the action sequence to ensure that the overall behavior remains stable in the face of changing objectives or shifting external demands. Again, this programming and evaluative function operates whether the activity is overt, that is, the person is actually doing something, or incipient, that is, he/she is just planning or thinking about doing something.

151

In *daydreaming*, we retain a certain conscious direction over the thread of the fantasy, although the imagined chain of events may achieve some measure of self-propelled psychical autonomy. This, of course, is what ordinarily makes daydreaming fun; even as our minds are free to wander in fancy, we retain a certain element of control over the direction and content of the reverie. That is because there remains some faculty of self-observation that lets us know that the transpiring events are actually in our imagination, that is, are fantasy rather than reality. In dreams, this superordinate monitoring agency, this observing ego, is suspended, so that the fantasy activities and experiences are perceived for the moment as real.

In the present view, the coherence that a dream possesses, the integrity of the dream narrative, is largely due to the action of the frontal lobes, similar to the integrity of behavior and thought that is similarly structured during waking life. Just as during waking life the verbal autoarticulatory apparatus of the left hemisphere acts in concert with frontal mechanisms to give behavior a sense of ego-autonomous goal-directedness, these mechanisms operate similarly in dreams to construct the dream narrative. Right-hemisphere and posterior brain mechanisms probably contribute the imagery and the emotional range and intensity that flesh out the dream narrative, just as sensitivity to image, feeling, and nuance in waking life gives that life its overall range and richness of experience.

Thus, damage to frontal mechanisms disrupts the programming and recursive self-evaluation of the dream process, just as it does to similar aspects of waking life. The result may be a dream that is all content and little structure, a pastiche of images and words that remains relatively unorganized. And that which is unorganized is difficult to remember and recall, as Jus and colleagues' (1973) frontal lobotomy patients demonstrated.

Damage to left-hemisphere linguistic mechanisms disrupts the auto-articulatory, ego-referent aspect of dreams. The result is that even though a dream structure may be present, it is wrought wholly or largely of images, unaccompanied by linguistic codes for comprehensibility. With right-hemisphere damage, the dream narrative is retained but without the imagistic and affective texture that gives a dream its immediacy and flavor, as in Kerr and Foulkes (1981) and Botez and colleagues' (1985) subjects.

All these mechanisms and processes, then, contribute to the construction of dreams, to the formation of the *dream-work*. Thus, dreaming is not all imagery or all right-hemisphere processing, as some authors have argued. Freud (1900), after all, made the point that "dreams construct a *situation* out of these images" (p. 83). Given these considerations, it should not be surprising that in many cases brain injury causes equivalent derangements in both waking and dreaming life. And when the opposite occurs—when there are dissociations between waking and dream phenomena—such a situation serves to illustrate how the neuroanatomic organization of seemingly unitary functions (such as language or imagery) is really composed of psychological and behavioral subcomponents that neither neuropsychology nor personality theory has yet taken full account of (Miller, 1986a, 1986b, 1990).

More important, from time to time we all have different dreams that seem to replicate the kinds of phenomena seen in different brain-damaged individuals. Sometimes we dream mainly in images, other times largely in words. Some of our dreams have a story line so tight that they seem to have been virtually scripted; other dreams seem aimless and fragmented. Why?

Contrary to the "disconnection hypotheses" of some authors, the present view is that the dream state typically involves an oscillation between periods of reduced functional connection and periods of hyperconnection. In fact, both hypo- and hyperconnection may occur simultaneously in different parts of the neuropsychological apparatus responsible for dreaming. The ability to suspend the reality-oriented faculty during a dream so that the bizarre dream events seem "real" would imply some sort of disconnection from ego-evaluative mechanisms. At the same time, the transmogrifications of thought and image by the dream-work, which involve condensation, displacement, representability, and symbolism—often with unique concatenations of conceptual, imagistic, and emotional material—could only be possible if there were an enhanced interaction between the two hemispheres in the elaboration of the dream-work. In fact, Freud's (1900) account of the dream-work contains a number of references to such psychological dream transformation processes involving thought, imagery, and affect. For example:

> A dream-thought is unusable so long as it is expressed in an abstract form; but when once it has been transformed into pictorial language, contrasts and identifications of the kind which the dream-work requires, and which it creates if they are not already present, can be established more easily than before between the new form of expression and the remainder of the material underlying the dream. This is so because in every language concrete terms, in consequence of the history of their development, are richer in associations than conceptual ones. We may suppose that a good part of the intermediate work done during the formation of a dream, which seeks to reduce the dispersed dream-thoughts to the most succinct and unified expression possible, proceeds along the line of finding appropriate verbal transformations for individual thoughts. Any one thought, whose form of expression happens to be fixed for other reasons, will operate in a determinant and selective

manner on the possible forms of expression allotted to the other thoughts, and it may do so, perhaps, from the very start—as in the case of writing a poem. (p. 375)

How else to account for the common experience whereby the dreamer, upon awakening, "knows" what the dream was about but "just can't put it into words"? Is the now-awake person suffering from a disconnection syndrome? Hardly. My view here is that during sleep, probably in tune with some aspect of the REM cycle, a form of inter- and intrahemispheric experience-generation takes place that is unlike that occurring in normal waking life, because the neuropsychological dynamics are likewise alien to the normal waking brain state. That we can recall and relate most, or at least some, of our dreams is due to the fact that the hypothesized oscillations in functional connectivity during dreaming sleep vary around a midpoint that is close in kind to that of the waking state. But the dreams that occur at the extreme poles of the inter- and intracerebral hypo- and hyperconnection continuum may remain forever in a realm foreign to our waking venue.

The subcortical limbic and brain stem REM-generation mechanisms probably contribute the "drive" to the dream, as well as control and coordinate the muscular and sensory systems that would ordinarily translate a plan or impulse into an overt behavior via frontoreticular and frontostriatal mechanisms. Structures like the locus coeruleus seem to be involved in preventing an incipient dream action from turning into the action itself, that is, keeping dream activity from becoming real activity. That this inhibition can be overridden by brain damage is seen in the cases of acting-out of dreams due to brain stem and thalamic disease (Lugaresi et al., 1986; Schenck et al., 1986).

The locus coeruleus also sends projections to wide areas of the anterior forebrain, including the frontal lobes (Aston-Jones et al., 1984), and may thus play a role in determining the action-appropriateness of behavior in general. In addition, the anterior and dorsomedial thalamic nuclei implicated in sleep and dream disturbance (Lugaresi et al., 1986) possess reciprocal connections with amygdalo-hippocampal structures in the temporal lobes, which mediate emotion and memory (Brodal, 1969; Carpenter, 1976).

Paroxysmal brain phenomena during sleep transiently and dysfunctionally release different kinds of cognitive dream modes—indeed, they may also do this during waking life. The kinds of bizarre body transfigurations in temporal lobe epilepsy and narcolepsy may involve reciprocal disconnection and hyperconnection of sensory and higher-order perceptual brain areas—SSII is one candidate—with vestibular and limbic mechanisms, abetted by the brain stem dream-generators and by the cortical mechanisms shaping the dream's content, the dream-work.

Thus, even as dream life resembles waking life in the overall organization of overt and incipient activity, the subcomponential textural structure of dreams involves unique combinations of neurodynamics, mediated by specialized forms of interhemispheric and other intracerebral communication. In its broad strokes, dreaming is similar to waking life in both phenomenology and physiology; in its fine details, it shows striking variations that account for the status of dreaming as a unique extension of waking experience. A dream, then, seems to involve the incipient but not overt acting out of ecologically relevant experience and projected experience (fantasy), a form of motivated action that is planned and internally rehearsed like other kinds of motivated activity but is inhibited from actual expression in the real world (Miller, 1989). How far is this from suggesting that, essentially, "a dream is the fulfillment of a wish" (Freud, 1900, p. 155)?

Dreams and Madness: The Brain Connection

As we have seen, some authors, like Bakan (1977–1978) and Fischman (1983), draw parallels between schizophrenic states and dream mentation, both of which, they believe, rely upon a right-hemisphere cognitive style predominance. Indeed, disturbances in motivation and planning, in keeping thoughts, feelings, and behaviors consonant with the demands of reality—in the stewardship of wishes, that is—seem to characterize the behavior and experience of many psychotic patients. However, the present view is that the neuropsychological deficit in schizophrenia is no more explicable by a simple right-hemisphere disinhibition hypothesis than is the formation of a dream. In fact, neuropsychological studies of schizophrenia have reported a preponderance of findings implicating frontal lobe and/ or left-hemisphere dysfunction (Flor-Henry, 1978, 1979, 1985; Goldberg, 1985; Marin & Tucker, 1981; Merrin, 1981; Miller, 1984b, 1986c; Seidman, 1983).

Muller (1985) has attempted to explain psychotic symptomatology more explicitly in terms of disordered frontal lobe processing. In normal consciousness and thought, Muller says, the time-delay aspect of frontal lobe function is required to introduce a certain remoteness of output (i.e., behavior) from input (i.e., perception), thus enabling the output to become more deliberate and more determined by internally constructed models of reality. These interim representational models may undergo internal modifications even while they are not in intimate contact with either input or output. In humans, language and language-derived concepts add a new dimension of behavioral control, in effect giving the frontal areas still further "steering" power over behavior. So far, the reader will recognize this description as similar to Freud's concept of the secondary process.

According to Muller, psychosis is a mental state characterized by gross impairment of reality testing, that is, by a deficit in approximating internal models of the world to the real world and its exigencies. Dysfunction of frontal mechanisms impairs reality testing by interfering with the comparison of inputs to their corresponding stored perceptual models. Even though the individual may be sensitive to certain environmental cues, he is unable to modulate and guide his perceptions in a useful way. Thus, says Muller (1985), in psychosis,

> there is a deficiency of the guiding function, a malfunction of the superordinated structures in the psychological sense; this has been summarized in different concepts such as disturbance of identity and loss of ego boundaries, inability to maintain a mental set, difficulty in control and maintenance of a selective processing strategy, etc.; or quite generally, problems in reality testing, the central feature of psychosis. (p. 437)

In my view, then, what links schizophrenia and dreams is not a deficit in any unitary function subserved by a single hemisphere or lobe. Rather, different perturbations in the neuropsychological systems that normally regulate behavior will produce different outcomes, depending on where the pathology lies. And in some cases—most cases, really— it need not be pathology at all that underlies differences in personality and behavior but, rather, unique and stable patterns of neuropsychodynamic functioning that contribute to the development of individual profiles of consciousness, character, and cognitive style (Miller, 1986a, 1986b, 1987, 1988a, 1988b, 1990). This will be considered further in Chapter 18.

Thus, from the standpoint of our neuropsychodynamic model, dreaming offers an example of the brain's use of a functional state shift that allows a regressive, acting-out component to fulfill behavioral wishes—that is, to experience alternate behavioral realities—and at the same time, under optimal conditions, provides for the consolidation of past, present, and imagined future experience so that reality-oriented behavior can occur smoothly in waking life. Dreams, then, really do offer a glimpse into another world, a world in which we have the opportunity to examine alternate realities, achieve some insight into our own behavior, and even, in some cases, be a little enchanted in the process.

PART FOUR

Freudian Slips

The public has no claim to learn any more of my personal affairs—of my struggles, my disappointments and my successes. I have in any case been more open and frank in some of my writings (such as *The Interpretation of Dreams* and *The Psychopathology of Everyday Life*) than people usually are who describe their lives for their contemporaries or for posterity. I have had small thanks for it, and from my experience I cannot recommend anyone to follow my example.

—SIGMUND FREUD,
An Autobiographical Study

CHAPTER 13

The Languages of the Brain and the Origin of the Parapraxis

Before there was a "Freudian slip," there was a Freudian brain. Freud's 1891 monograph, *On Aphasia: A Critical Study*, has not received the attention it deserves among scholars of either neuropsychology or psychoanalysis. This is owing largely to the fact that, having been relegated to the status of a "prepsychoanalytic" tract, it failed to make it into the *Standard Edition* of Freud's collected works. (An equally illuminating early work on childhood cerebral palsy [Freud & Rie, 1891] shares a similar fate and is even more obscure to historians of psychoanalysis.)

The importance of *On Aphasia* for the later development of psychoanalysis has been overshadowed—undeservedly in my opinion—by the now-famous *Project for a Scientific Psychology*, in which Freud (1895) sketched out a protoneurophysiological model that was apparently intended solely for the eyes of his friend Wilhelm Fliess (who was associated with one of Freud's early hysteria cases, as we saw in a previous chapter, and was his closest confidant during the early years of his theory building). The *Project*, which lay undiscovered until the 1950s (the title was added posthumously by the editors), did however make its way into the *Standard Edition*, and for that reason it has been hailed over the ensuing decades as a kind of neurophysiological vindication of psychoanalysis, as well as the source of many of the ideas that have become canon in the Freudian metapsychology (see Holt, 1965, 1985, 1989, for more in-depth reviews of this and other aspects of psychoanalytic metapsychology).

On Aphasia, in addition to anticipating many of the future concepts of psychoanalysis in general, is directly related to Freud's later preoccupation with parapraxes. In both *On Aphasia* and *The Psychopathology of Everyday Life*, Freud made the explicit effort to bridge the pathological and the

159

normal—in neurology in the one case, psychology in the other. Indeed, *The Psychopathology of Everyday Life* resonates so strongly with the insights first articulated in *On Aphasia* that there probably would have been no psychoanalytic theory of the parapraxis—no Freudian slip—had there not first been a Freudian theory of aphasiology, one of the foundations of Freud's brain.

The concept of cerebral localization of function, a source of serious scientific study at the beginning of the nineteenth century that was subsequently huckstered by the phrenologists and later adopted back into the fold of established neuroscience, had once again achieved prominence by the time Freud was engaged in his neurological studies. Even so, the idea that complex psychological functions like perception and language could be mapped out point-for-point in the cerebral cortex was beginning to come under criticism in laboratories and clinics throughout the world. But in the German-speaking scientific community, with its passion for orderly preciseness, more and more complicated functional "brain maps" continued to be elaborated in order to encompass the increasing number of contradictions to the previous neater and simpler models.

The predominant view at the time held that language was organized as a network of "speech centers," each involving a separate linguistic aspect or quality—speaking, comprehension, reading, writing—and all linked by a vast crisscrossing meshwork of connecting fibers, much like some sprawling cerebral railway system. (Railroads no doubt provided a convenient concrete contemporary metaphor for these abstract scientific conceptualizations of the brain; later, the telephone, the computer, and then the hologram were to furnish, in their turn, the models on which neuroscientists pegged their theories.)

We consider the individual types of aphasias in more detail in Chapter 16. For now, we note that Freud, following John Hughlings Jackson (1864) and the British school of neurology, was the first in the German-speaking scientific world to subject the contemporary connectionistic theories of language localization to critical analysis. Here, in the brain sciences, Freud was already finding parallels between the pathological and the normal, the unusual and the everyday.

Freud (1891) begins *On Aphasia* by pointing out that the *paraphasias*, that is, language distortions and substitutions observed in patients with organic language disorders, do not differ in principle from the temporarily embarrassing distortions of words or use of phrases out of context that otherwise healthy people fall prey to when fatigued, nervous, or distracted. Thus, rather than reflecting a focal *lesion* in one or another "speech center," Freud says, why not regard paraphasia in the widest sense, as a more general disruption of function, a sign of overall reduced efficiency in the speech apparatus as a whole. This conceptualization, Freud points out, does not exclude the explanation of focal organic damage for paraphasias in their most typical or extreme form but does remove the need for hypothesizing a specific brain lesion for each case of language disturbance.

The physical destruction of one of these brain centers might of course produce an irreplaceable loss of function. However, if only a particular pathway between one center and another is interrupted, it ought to be possible to stimulate the intact center through some other, undamaged, fiber tract. That is, rather than having one-to-one connections, the brain is organized, Freud argues, so that multiple paths to a single goal and multiple goals of a single path exist; essentially, this is the principle of divergence and convergence, which two years later was to form the basis of Freud's (1893) conceptualization of hysteria and which, as we have seen, would also work its way into his subsequent dream theory. Thus, what appears clinically to reflect the wholesale destruction of an anatomical center might just as well represent the simultaneous destruction of several fiber paths to and from that center. This removes the uncomfortably phrenological necessity of positing a separate center for each individual function.

At this point in the 1891 monograph, Freud offers a succinct definition of *paraphasia*: a speech disorder in which the appropriate word is replaced by a less appropriate one that still, however, retains a certain relationship to the correct word. Freud then describes the most common forms of this language disorder, using a classification that comes quite close to that used today. In one type of paraphasia, says Freud, words that have a similar content or are linked frequently in speech are used in place of one another—for example, *"pen"* instead of *"pencil,"* *"Potsdam"* instead of *"Berlin"*; today's neuropsychologists call this *semantic paraphasia*. A different type of paraphasia—*literal*, or *phonemic*, *paraphasia* in modern terminology—involves words of a similar sound being mistakenly used for one another, such as *"Butter"* for *"Mutter"* (the capitalization of nouns in Freud's examples is Germanic) or *"Campher"* for *"Pamphlet."* In addition, if the patient makes mistakes in articulation, single letters are replaced by others, although modern aphasiologists would question whether this constitutes a true language disorder or a more basic motor disturbance of speech vocalization.

Another kind of paraphasia occurs when two intended words are fused into one, such as *"Vutter"* from the German *"Mutter"* (mother) and *"Vater"* (father). Still another involves the replacement of a specific word by a very general one or by a verb, as when we momentarily forget or cannot think of the correct word; for example, forgetting *"clock,"* we say something like "Bring me that . . . thing, that . . . timer."

However, beyond simple paraphasias, there occur the *sensory aphasias* (what today we would call *receptive*, or *Wernicke's*, *aphasia*). Here, speech may be characterized by an endless sequence of senseless syllables, or gibberish—what British neurologists in Freud's day were calling *jargon aphasia*. In other cases we see a poverty of content words, with a corresponding abundance of particles, interjections, and other grammatical parts of speech, along with frequent repetition of nouns and verbs; this description sounds more like the classic *Broca's aphasia*. For Wernicke's part, sensory aphasia consisted of an intact vocabulary with accompanying paraphasia. Freud's view in *On Aphasia* is that sensory aphasia may be attributable to "impoverishment of words with an abundance of speech impulses" (1891, p. 33).

Considerations like these led Freud to regard speech disorders not as representing lesions in specific brain centers or pathways but as generalized changes in the functional state of the brain as a whole. That is, damage to a particular part of the brain's language system does not just leave a "hole" or "gap" in the speech apparatus. Rather, it affects the sum total (today we might say the "gestalt") of the functioning of that speech apparatus as a whole. In fact, says Freud (1891), a great number of organic lesions in neurologic syndromes in general probably manifest themselves in the form of these kinds of diffuse disturbances of function, rather than as a punctate obliteration of isolated mental faculties:

> For decades we have been endeavoring to advance our knowledge of the localization of functions by the study of clinical symptoms; we have got into the habit of expecting a lesion to destroy a number of units of the nervous system completely and to leave the rest completely intact, because only thus, we believe, can clinical experience be made to fit our preconceptions. Yet only few lesions comply with these postulates. Most lesions are not directly destructive and they have a disturbing effect on a much larger number of nervous units than those immediately involved. (p. 30)

Thus, brain damage in the naturally occurring state rarely follows precise anatomical demarcations. Rather, an area of more or less total destruction will usually be surrounded by regions of lesser damage, which in turn are bordered by areas in which the disturbance may only be in function, without visible evidence of actual changes in structure—a conceptualization, as we have seen, that Freud would later apply to hysteria.

Actually, says Freud in *On Aphasia*, there are several ways that a partly destructive lesion could impact on language functioning. Some parts of the speech apparatus could be put out of action by the lesion while the intact parts continue to function as usual. Alternatively, the speech apparatus could react to the lesion as a unitary whole, in which case there is no focal loss in any particular function but a lowering of functioning of the language system overall. Thus, the response to a partial lesion may resemble the disturbance in speech function caused by non-structural impairment—a point vital for understanding Freud's later conceptualization of the parapraxis.

For example, the motor regions of the brain that control the muscles of the upper limbs show both kinds of the aforementioned reactions. A small, focally destructive lesion in the precentral gyrus, the "motor strip," may in some cases cause an isolated paralysis of the thumb muscles. More commonly, however, damage in this area results in a slight weakness of the whole arm, since the motor cortex's "thumb area" is unlikely to be completely destroyed by the pathological process and the surrounding areas may be affected to variable degrees.

This latter form of reaction, that is, a disturbance in overall functioning, says Freud, is what seems also to characterize damage to the speech apparatus due to incomplete lesions. A partial loss, then, can always be shown to be the expression of a general lowering of the functional activity of that center. Thus, focal damage to Broca's area may produce a severe (but probably not total) disorder of expressive speech but may also be associated with other, milder, disturbances of language processing as a whole.

In a passage that reflects the influence of John Hughlings Jackson's ideas of neurophylogenetic "regression" in brain damage, Freud asserts that the aphasias essentially reproduce a state that existed in the course of the normal developmental process of learning to speak. In learning to read, children make use of the process of associating the word image with all the other images of the thing or concept denoted by that word. Learning to write involves the additional integration of motor–kinesthetic images with the visual word images. The difference between this sequence of language development and the language dissolution that occurs with brain damage is that when learning, the individual is restricted by the natural timing of the neurodevelopmental process, that is, by the hierarchy of development of the brain centers and systems that start functioning at different times—the sensory–auditory first, then the motor, later the visual, and lastly the graphic (writing). In the case of pathology, however, the center that has suffered least from the brain injury is the one that seems to be called upon to compensate for the damaged component.

In the case of partial lesions to the speech apparatus, Freud continues, we do not typically see an unruffled canvas of intact language functioning pierced in one place by a precisely delineated lacuna of focal functional impairment. Rather, in addition to whatever language function may be most affected, there is also a diminution of the person's linguistic capacity overall; that is, even the speech centers that have not been injured directly react as wholes, with greater or lesser degrees of alteration of function, to partial lesions.

Following Bastian (1869), Freud hypothesizes that as a result of disease or injury, a brain center may either be (1) no longer excitable, (2) excitable only by sensory stimulation, or (3) excitable in association with another center. In any case of damage, moreover, fiber tracts to and from the affected center, as well as neurons of the center itself, will be affected. Together, this relatively complex pattern of brain damage will determine the specific clinical manifestations of a given patient's speech disorder.

This leads Freud to reject the theory of homotopic (point-for-point) projection of body parts or other body functions onto the cerebral cortex; Freud adopts, in other words, what we would today call a "nonlocalizationist" position. For one thing, again invoking Jackson, Freud suggests that subcortical brain regions may participate along with cortical centers in the determination of complex forms of behavior such as speech. The kind of *projection* whereby the periphery is topographically laid out in the central nervous system may accurately describe how the body surface is coded in the spinal cord, but higher up in the nervous system things become more complexly organized. By the time we have reached the cerebral cortex, we are talking not of point-by-point projection but about a more complex and differentiated *representation* of function. This conception, as we saw in Chapter 4, would appear a couple of years later in Freud's (1893) *Comparative Study* of organic and hysterical conversion symptoms.

In the case of language, Freud goes on to say, the relationship between the representation of functions in the cortex and their projection onto the somatic periphery is analogous to the relationship between a poem and the letters of the alphabet: it is the manifold associations of the individual elements whereby some may be represented several times, others not at all, that determines the finished product; recall Freud's poem analogies in his discussions of hysteria and dreams. Such range, refinement, and breadth of functioning in thought, speech, or action cannot, says Freud (1891), be encompassed by a strict localizationistic model.

> Considering the tendency of earlier medical periods to localize whole mental faculties, such as are defined in psychological terminology, in certain areas of the brain, it was bound to appear as a great advance when Wernicke declared that only the simplest psychic elements, i.e. the various sensory perceptions, could be localized in the cortex, the areas concerned being those of the central terminations of the sensory nerves. But does not one in principle make the same mistake, irrespective of whether one tries to localize a complicated concept, a whole mental faculty or a psychic element? Is it justified to immerse a nerve fiber, which over the whole length of its course has been only a physiological structure subject to physiological modifications, with its end in the psyche and to furnish that end with an idea or memory? (pp. 54–55)

All the more strange that four years later Freud would seemingly turn around and embrace precisely this kind of neuromythological model by stuffing whole ideas and wishes into individual neurons and fibers in his famous *Project*—if, indeed, he really meant for the model to be taken literally, as opposed to having written it, a provisional and discarded bridge to further psychological theory building, for Fliess's eyes only.

Freud now hits upon what emerges as the salient concept in *On Aphasia*, a concept that could indeed serve as a guiding principle for neuropsychodynamic theory:

> The relationship between the chain of physiological events in the nervous system and mental processes is probably not one of cause and effect. The former do not cease when the latter set in; they tend to continue, but, from a certain moment, a mental phenomenon corresponds to each part of the chain, or to several parts. The psychic is therefore a process parallel to the physiological, a "dependent concomitant." (p. 55)

Explicit credit is given to John Hughlings Jackson for providing the foundation on which Freud has built his present arguments refuting the localizationist theory of the aphasias. The British neurologist (e.g., see Jackson, 1932) noted the common cases of motor aphasia in which speech may be virtually eliminated, except for simple, common phrases such as "yes" or "no," and, frequently, curses (the polyglot Freud cites "*sacré nom de dieu*" and "*Goddam*" as examples). Jackson pointed out that, even in normal persons, such expletives belong to the emotional, rather than the intellectual, sphere of language, a neurological dissociation that, as we have seen, would later become a conceptual one in Freud's theory of the dream-work.

But in other cases, Freud notes, the recurrent utterance is not a curse or other automatic ejaculation but a phrase of special significance to the person. From a strict localizationist point of view, it would be quite amazing if the pathological process (stroke, brain tumor, head trauma) were clever enough to spare only those neurons responsible for that particular utterance. Rather, asserts Freud, plausible explanations are possible only within the context of a functional approach. For example, a man who could say only "I want protection" owed his aphasia to a fight in which he had been knocked unconscious by a blow to the head. Another patient, who could utter only "list complete," was a clerk who had suffered a stroke right after he had laboriously completed a catalog for his merchandising firm. For Freud, such instances suggest that these utterances are the last words produced by the speech apparatus before injury or at a time when there might already have existed an awareness of the impending disability, as in a progressive tumor or degenerative process. He explains the persistence of these last utterances by their intensity, that is, they happen at a moment of great inner excitement, as in the persistence of certain hysterical symptoms because of their particular emotional–symbolic salience.

As a historical aside, we may wonder if Freud was implicitly drawing an analogy to the formation of some kinds of so-called "phantom limbs" (a term coined by Mitchell, 1872) whereby the painful position of the limb just prior to its traumatic amputation (as from a battlefield wound or industrial accident—all too common in that era) seems to be replicated in the subjective position and sensation of the now-missing appendage. Here the patient may, for example, insist that he "feels" the absent limb twisted in the gears of a machine, even though he fully realizes that it is gone.

Drawing on the existing knowledge of his day and anticipating some of the concepts of modern neuropsychology, Freud (1891) points out that all of the sensory and motor cortical areas are bilateral while the association area of speech is organized in one hemisphere only:

> Destruction of one visual cortical area, for example, will not interfere with the utilization of visual stimuli for speech, i.e. with reading, because the speech area retains its connections with the contralateral visual cortex which, in this particular case, is provided by crossed white fibers. If however, the lesion moves to the boundary of the visual receptive area, alexia ensues, probably because the connection not only with the homolateral, but also with the contralateral visual area has been severed. We therefore have to add to our theory: the appearance of centers is also created by the fact that the fibers from the cortical receptive fields of the other hemisphere enter at the same place, i.e. on the periphery of the speech area where, in case of lesion, the connection with the homolateral receptive areas is also affected. (p. 65)

This leads Freud to speculate that hemisphericity might, after all, rescue some aspects of the theory of "brain centers," insofar as these centers may be conceived to consist of flexibly organized systems, rather than static, punctate loci:

> The assumption, by the way, that the speech region is connected with cortical areas of both hemispheres is not new but has been taken over from the theory of the centers. The precise anatomy of these crossed connections has not yet been established, but when it is known, it might explain some peculiarities in the localization and extent of the so-called centers, as well as some of the individual features of the speech disorders. (p. 66)

Freud then asserts (anticipating Vygotsky [1962] and Luria [1980] in this respect) that from the psychological point of view, the *word* is the functional unit of speech; it is a complex concept comprised of auditory, visual, and kinesthetic elements. The word, says Freud, is built up from various impressions, corresponding to an intricate process of associations entered into by elements of visual, acoustic, and kinesthetic origins. However, the word acquires its significance through its association with the "idea (concept) of the object," at least if we restrict our consideration to nouns. This idea, or concept, of the object is itself another complex set of associations composed of the most varied visual, auditory, tactile, kinesthetic, and other impressions.

It may come as a surprise to many of today's neurologists and neuropsychologists to realize that a term they use in common professional parlance was actually coined by Freud. For a disturbance in the recognition of objects, which Finkelnburg (1870) had called "asymbolia," Freud coined and defined the term *agnosia*: an impairment in the higher-order recognition of objects not due to a deficit in the sensory pathway per se; the term and its meaning have remained unchanged to this day. For example, in a visual agnosia, optical acuity and visual fields might be intact but the individual is unable to recognize an object (e.g., a cup) for what it is. He/she may describe it accurately (white, round, etc.) but cannot identify it as a conceptual *thing* with a name and a function. The symbolic aspect of the item, that is, its inclusion in a conceptual class of such items (hence, "asymbolia") and the existence of a particular name to symbolically denote kindred members of that class or category, cannot be appreciated through the otherwise intact sensory channel.

If the agnosia is in fact limited to one sensory modality (e.g., vision), use of another modality may help: the person who cannot recognize the cup upon seeing it may identify it correctly if he picks it up and handles it. In other cases, the agnosia seems to cut across sensory modalities and be more generalized; recognition is not possible through any sensory channel. Agnosias that occur in cases of bilateral and extensive cortical damage, says Freud, may also entail a disturbance of speech, since the impetus for spontaneous speech normally arises from perceptual associations of one kind or another. Such syndromes would constitute a separate class of organic language disorders, which Freud calls the *agnostic aphasias*.

Freud (1891) again appeals to Jackson's doctrine that the modes of reaction seen in organic language disturbances represent instances of *functional retrogression* of a highly organized apparatus and therefore correspond to earlier states of functional development:

> This means that under all circumstances an arrangement of associations which, having been acquired later, belongs to a higher level of func-

tioning, will be lost, while an earlier and simpler one will be preserved. (p. 87)

It is from this perspective, says Freud, that a great number of aphasic phenomena can be explained.

But then there is the role of individual experience. Even a rare product of speech that would ordinarily be the first to be lost may turn out to be highly resistant to the pathological process if it had acquired great force or resilience by virtue of intense association with other brain-based ideas, in other words, if it had become *important* to the person. Thus Freud affirms his belief in the impact of individual experience on preexisting innate developmental cycles. Also, Freud notes, by dint of such associative links, a series of words is usually better preserved than single ones and words remain more easily available the more widespread their associations, an observation anticipating the ideoassociational basis for his later theory of hysteria, dreams, and the unconscious, as well as for the method of exploration, free association, developed to study them.

This brings Freud to the question of *transcortical motor aphasia*, where speech is intact, as evidenced by preserved—even echolalic—repetition of phrases, but the ability to use the speech process for productive self-expression is lost. This kind of speech disorder was difficult for some of Freud's contemporaries to explain, especially those who adhered to a strict localizationistic-connectionistic framework. Here, says Freud, we have an instance of the motor element still being capable of stimulation by peripheral association but failing to respond to volitional prodding. In this case, functional factors seem to be capable of producing a dissociation of volition from peripheral stimulation.

However, even though, theoretically, any kind of association may occur among the various elements of speech function, clinical experience shows that certain kinds of associations have preference over the rest. And the most important kind of associations, says Freud, are still the developmental associations, that is, those that have played a leading part in the learning of speech.

In the case of brain damage or disease, there may be a dampening of function in the associative speech network as a whole while the preeminence of the first-used (i.e., first-developed) lines of associations is reestablished. That is—and this is the important point—illness or injury may cause a regression and dissolution of individual differences built upon ontogenetic development. Freud once again enlists Hughlings Jackson: "Different amounts of nervous arrangements in different positions are destroyed with different rapidity in different persons" (quoted in Freud, 1891, p. 100).

Freud sums up as follows:

In considering the effects of lesions on this [speech] apparatus, we found that they could result in three types of aphasia: 1) purely verbal, 2) asymbolic and 3) agnostic aphasia. . . . From the psychological point of view we recognized the word as a complex of concepts (impressions, images) which through its sensory part (its auditory component) is connected with the complex of object associations. We defined verbal aphasia as a disturbance within the word complex, asymbolic aphasia as a separation of the latter from the object associations, and agnostic aphasia as a purely functional disorder of the speech apparatus. (pp. 103–104)

Freud here is modestly restricting his conclusions to the sphere of neurologic language disorders. But as we will now see, the insights first developed by his explorations into the neuropsychology of aphasia would subsequently be applied to the broader area of what he called "the psychopathology of everyday life"—a journey from Freud's brain to the Freudian slip.

CHAPTER 14

"The Psychopathology of Everyday Life"

In the editor's introduction to *The Psychopathology of Everyday Life*, which originally appeared in 1901, reference is made to the first mention by Freud of a *parapraxis* in a letter of August 26, 1898, to Wilhelm Fliess. *Parapraxis* in German is *Fehlleistung*, which literally means "faulty function." Before Freud wrote this tract, the editor points out, the general concept seems not to have existed in psychology, and a new English word had to be invented for it. As we have seen, this is not the only Freudian neologism to have become a regular part of clinical terminology.

The editor goes on to make a point of the "special affection" with with Freud regarded parapraxes, attributable to the fact that they, along with dreams, were what enabled him to extend to normal mental life the discoveries he had first made in connection with hysteria and the neuroses. As this section of the present book will show, it is probably more than mere affection that drove Freud to elaborate his theory of "the psychopathology of everyday life." Rather, drawing together the observations of clinical disorders, dreams, and everyday mental phenomena was an essential and indispensable task for the development of the comprehensive Freudian epistemology. And such a task is also vital for the present neuropsychodynamic model.

Freud (1901) begins his account by discussing the forgetting of proper names, and the chapter opens with an example from Freud's own experience:

> The name that I tried without success to recall in the example I chose for analysis in 1898 was that of the artist who painted the magnificent frescoes of the "Four Last Things" in Orvieto cathedral. Instead of the name I was looking for—*Signorelli*—the names of two other

170

painters—*Botticelli* and *Boltraffio*—thrust themselves on me, though they were immediately and decisively rejected by my judgement as incorrect. When I learnt the correct name from someone else, I recognized it at once and without hesitation. The investigation into the influences and the associative paths by which the reproducing of the name had been displaced in this way from *Signorelli* to *Botticelli* and *Boltraffio* led to the following results. (p. 2)

Whereupon Freud takes us through his characteristically exhaustive self-analytic processes to arrive finally at what appears to be a solution to the puzzle:

I wanted therefore to forget something; I had *repressed* something. What I wanted to forget was not, it is true, the name of the artist at Orvieto but something else—a something, however, which contrived to place itself in an associative connection with its name, so that my act of will missed its target and I forgot *the one thing against my will*, while I wanted to forget *the other thing intentionally*. The disinclination to remember was aimed against one content; the inability to remember emerged in another. It would obviously be a simpler case if disinclination and inability to remember related to the same content. Moreover, the substitute names no longer strike me as so entirely unjustified as they did before the matter was elucidated: by a sort of compromise they remind me just as much of what I wanted to forget as of what I wanted to remember; and they show me that my intention to forget something was neither a complete success nor a complete failure. (p. 4)

Freud is now prepared to delineate the three conditions he regards as necessary for forgetting a name, particularly when accompanied by paramnesia, or "false recollection": first, there must exist a "certain disposition" for forgetting the name; second, a process of what Freud cryptically refers to as "suppression" must be carried out shortly before; and third, there must exist the possibility of establishing an external associative link between the name and the previously suppressed element by dint of some similarity of sound or content. In addition, two factors seem to be decisive in bringing the erroneous, paramnesic, "substitute names" to consciousness: first, the effort of attention and, second, an "inner condition" that attaches to the psychical material.

Freud next considers the forgetting of foreign words and notes that while we rarely forget the current vocabulary of our own language in normal usage, with foreign words the susceptibility to forgetting is notorious, affected by such factors as our level of command of the foreign language, our general health, and our state of alertness or fatigue. But there is another mechanism of forgetting, says Freud—the disturbance of a thought by an internal contradiction that arises from the repressed, a process Freud promises will turn up repeatedly as an explanation over the ensuing course of his book.

Freud then takes up the forgetting of names and sets of words. Forgetting names and phrases, says Freud, occurs when the material we forget or blurt out in distorted form has been brought by some associative link into connection with an unconscious thought-content. By virtue of this entrapment by a repressed, unpleasant association, the otherwise "innocent" word or phrase is dragged under the surface of consciousness and momentarily forgotten or transformed.

Forgetting people's names, Freud tells us, is a kind of parapraxis for which he is personally able to supply many examples, since he himself falls prey to it often—but not necessarily for psychogenic reasons. Thus, Freud, many of whose insights have emerged from the relentless examination of his own psyche, here uses self-observation of a somewhat different sort, of the processes of his own brain—Freud's brain—to elaborate yet another grand principle of mental life:

> The mild attacks of migraine from which I still suffer usually announce themselves hours in advance by my forgetting names, and at the height of these attacks, during which I am not forced to abandon my work, it frequently happens that all proper names go out of my head. Now it is precisely cases like mine which could furnish the grounds for an objection on principle to our analytic efforts. Should it not necessarily be concluded from such observations that the cause of forgetfulness, and in particular of the forgetting of names, lies in circulatory and general functional disturbances of the cerebrum, and should we not therefore spare ourselves the search for psychological explanations of these phenomena? Not at all, in my view; that would be to confuse the mechanism of a process, which is the same kind in all cases, with the factors favoring the process, which are variable and not necessarily essential. (p. 21)

In other words, Freud explains, an unknown but powerful neuro-psychical force, abetted by the circulatory disturbances of migraine, robs him of his access to the proper names in his memory store; this force can in other cases bring about the same failure of memory, even at times of perfect health and unimpaired neural efficiency. Here is a clear expression in neuropsychodynamic terms of the principle of "dependent concomitants" first articulated by Freud in *On Aphasia*.

A case added to the text in 1910, and anecdotally attributed to Ferenczi, concerns a woman who had lost her husband when she was thirty-nine and had no prospect of marrying again. She developed great difficulty in recalling anything having to do with the words "youth" and "age." What is striking about this case, says Freud, is that the ideas camouflaging the missing words were associated entirely with its content and that associations with its sound were absent—a purely semantic paramnesia, as we might call it today, rather than a phonemic one. In other cases, a pair of words that are similar in sound can have the same effect as a single word that has two meanings, recalling the process of condensation that occurs in dreams.

The temporary forgetting of names, Freud points out, is the most frequently observed of all the parapraxes; perhaps Freud was drawing a parallel to the fact that anomia—loss of ability to recall the names of objects or people—is the most common kind of aphasic disorder. In ordinary mental life, proper names may be temporarily forgotten when the intended reproduction of the name is interfered with by an alien train of thought that at the time remains unconscious but that has developed some association or connection with the name.

Freud then turns his attention to memory and memory slips, beginning with the question of childhood memories and so-called *screen memories*. The ordinary, "innocent" memories of childhood that we readily recall actually owe their existence to the process of displacement, whereby they have come to substitute for other, "true," memories that have real psychodynamic significance. The true, significant memories, however, have been repressed and replaced by these screen memories.

Freud describes several ways in which a screen memory might operate. First, the true memory may be replaced by a screen memory from an earlier period of time; this Freud terms a *retroactive*, or *retrogressive*, screen memory. Or the opposite might occur: a neutral screen memory of more recent origin replaces the true memory of an event that actually took place further back in time. Freud refers to these screen memories as having been *pushed ahead* or *displaced foward*. Yet another possibility is that the screen memory is drawn from the same time period as the true memory; these Freud calls *contemporary*, or *contiguous*, screen memories.

Thus, nothing is really forgotten, in the sense of a memory trace just fading away. Failure to recall, in the Freudian scheme, is due to active interdiction by a related but not quite equivalent memory of the original "true" memory, which for psychodynamic reasons remains unconscious. Given this, says Freud, it may well be that the forgetting of childhood events can supply us with the key to understanding those amnesias that lie at the basis of the formation of all neurotic symptoms.

Freud then discusses the various preferred types of recall that different people might have. Some remember mainly in visual images, others rely on a more literal, verbal retrospection, and the recall of still others seems to depend on action rather than reflection; Freud cites Charcot's (1889) classification of people into *audifs, moteurs* and *visuels*. However, in dreams, says Freud, we all become *visuels*. Similarly, childhood memories are typically of the visual type, owing to the young child's insufficiently developed language abilities. Thus, in our recollection of the earliest childhood memories, we possess not the genuine memory trace but a later, psychodynamically altered and perhaps verbally embellished revision of it—again, note the similarity to the actions of the dream-work. These childhood memories, then, come in general to acquire the significance of screen memories and in so doing, Freud points out, offer an analogy with the kind of selectively self-serving collective memory that a nation preserves in the form of its legends and myths.

Next, Freud tackles what has come to be regarded as the quintessence of parapraxia: slips of the tongue, or what most people commonly mean when they speak of having made a "Freudian slip." Here, Freud makes the analogy with organic paraphasic language disorders explicit, although the analogy would likely be lost on readers unacquainted with the *On Aphasia* monograph (which is no doubt why the editor of the current edition of *The Psychopathology of Everyday Life* takes such pains to point out the connection in a special footnote). Freud describes the combination of external and internal influences that can produce this class of parapraxis. For one thing, a slip of the tongue can be caused by the influence of another component of the same speech, for example, an anticipatory sound or a perseveration; in other words, the parapraxis can be due to the influence of aspects of the linguistic surface structure of uttered speech. Alternatively, it can result from another formulation of the actual ideas that are contained within the sentence or context that the speaker intends to say; in this case, the parapraxis is more of an ideational than a phonemic or syntactical interference, but it is still very much "on the surface" of speech.

However, it is the "deeper" causes of verbal slips, such as those occurring in the Signorelli case, that most interest Freud. These Freud refers to as influences "outside" the word, sentence, or context, influences that arise from the symbolic associations between repressed ideas and the surface structure of the utterance in progress. In this sense, says Freud, the formation of substitutions and contaminations that occur in slips of the tongue represents a "short form" of the work of condensation that takes its most extensive and elaborate form in dreams.

Freud here takes his cue from the views of Wundt (1900), who noted in his extensive work on speech development that certain characteristic psychical influences seem to typify verbal slips. For one thing, they seem to be *positively* determined in the form of the uninhibited stream of sound associations and word associations evoked by the spoken sounds. In addition, Wundt points out, there is a *negative* factor in the form of the suppression or relaxation of the inhibitory effects of the will on this associative speech network and of the attentional processes, which also represent an active function of the will.

Freud concurs emphatically with Wundt's (1900) views in this area, in fact, if anything, stressing even more than Wundt himself that the positive influences on verbal slips in the form of the uninhibited stream of associations and the negative factor, that is, the relaxation of the inhibiting attention, invariably act in concert to achieve their effect, so that the two factors become merely different ways of regarding the same process. What happens, says Freud, is that the uninhibited stream of associations comes into action as a result of the relaxation of inhibiting attention.

An intriguing observation appears in the 1910 and 1912 editions only: it commonly happens, says Freud—again, seeming to reflect his special attraction to polylingual phenomena—that someone not speaking in his native language will exploit, albeit unconsciously, his clumsiness in the second language for the purpose of making highly significant slips of the tongue that would not occur in the more familiar mother tongue. His poorer proficiency in the second language constitutes the "excuse" for letting the repressed material "slip out." (Recall the polylingual expressions of hysteria that occurred in the case of Anna O.)

The practical, clinical side of slips of the tongue, says Freud, comes in the course of psychoanalytic therapy when such a slip on the patient's part provides the therapist with ammunition in disputes regarding the aptness of psychodynamic interpretations deemed valid by the therapist yet protested against by the patient. Here, the content of the slip reveals the motive that the patient resists becoming conscious of. More broadly, Freud—ever fascinated with language in all its aspects—regards ambivalence in verbal expression as a sure sign of commensurate wishiwashiness in conviction.

> Even in forming an appreciation of an author's style, we are permitted and accustomed to apply the same elucidatory principle which we cannot dispense with in tracing the origins of individual mistakes in speech. A clear and unambiguous manner of writing shows us that here the author is at one with himself; where we find a forced and involved expression which (to use an apt phrase) is aimed at more than one target, we may recognize the intervention of an insufficiently worked-out, complicating thought, or we may hear the stifled voice of the author's self-criticism. (p. 101)

Freud now considers what he calls "misreadings" and slips of the pen, errors involving reading and writing that probably first piqued Freud's interest during his early studies of organic language disorders. In one kind of misreading, it is the predisposed mental set of the reader, not the text being read, that primarily influences the psychological alteration of the text, causing the reader to read into the text something with which he/she is preoccupied—we have all had this kind of experience. The only contribution toward a misreading that the text itself need make lies in some feature of the verbal image that the reader can easily alter. Accordingly, this kind of misreading is more common in cases where the reader's vision is impaired, as, for example, in migraine and other transient disturbances of the sensorium, or when the page is merely glanced at, these being examples of "facilitating factors." Here, as in the case of speech, Freud admits to the possibility of some forms of parapraxis being determined primarily by "surface" aspects of the material.

The other kind of misreading depends to a much greater extent on the actual content of the text itself; here, in fact, the text must be understood correctly at some level for the parapraxic process to operate. This is because the reading material contains some information, allusion, or implication that arouses the reader's defenses and that is therefore unconsciously revised by a misreading that fits in with a repudiation of a disturbing impulse or with the fulfillment of a wish. That is why, in such cases, we can assume that the text was initially understood correctly and, at some level below consciousness, processed and prejudged by the reader before it underwent psychical revision.

Slips of the pen include perseverations, or redundant repetitions, in writing and copying. Here, if the writer repeats a word he has already written, this is probably an indication that it was difficult for him to let the subject go, that in fact he could have said more on that point but had omitted to do so for one reason or another. Perseveration in copying another's writing appears to represent an emphatic endorsement of the tract being reproduced, a substitute for saying, "I, too."

Freud next notes that when asked to read a passage aloud, our attention typically wanders from the text and turns to our own thoughts. The result is often that while a listener is treated to a nearly flawless recitation of the tract, the reader himself can scarcely recall the content of what he has just read aloud. That is, says Freud, the reader has been reading *automatically*, and this is merely one example of a whole class of activities that we do unthinkingly, or with hardly any conscious attention; (here Freud may have been recalling the phenomenon of transcortical aphasia, which typically involves intact repetition without comprehension). From this kind of observation Freud reasons that slips in speaking, reading, and writing cannot stem merely from lapses in voluntary attention, as Wundt (1900) seems to suggest. Rather, attention is *captured* and actively diverted from the task by an intrapsychic unconscious agency of the psyche.

Freud now returns to memory and to the forgetting of impressions and intentions, to what might be called "memory slips," memory being for Freud one of the most poorly understood phenomena that psychology has to grapple with:

> If anyone should feel inclined to overestimate the state of our present knowledge of mental life, a reminder of the function of memory is all that would be needed to force him to be more modest. No psychological theory has yet succeeded in giving a connected account of the fundamental phenomenon of remembering and forgetting; in fact, the complete analysis of what can actually be observed has so far scarcely begun. Today, forgetting has perhaps become more of a puzzle than remembering, ever since we have learnt from the study of dreams and pathological phenomena that even something we thought had been forgotten long ago may suddenly re-emerge in consciousness. (p. 134)

With regard to what he calls the "forgetting of impressions and knowledge," Freud emphasizes a point that has become virtually axiomatic in psychodynamic theory: disturbing memories succumb especially easily to motivated forgetting. At least one practical application of this is in the area of forensic psychology, and Freud urges caution in assuming that the process of putting a witness under oath automatically ensures that an accurate rendering of events will ensue. Rather, what typically emerges is an account comprised of part fact, part ordinary jumbling of events, and part unconsciously determined transfigurations of recall.

Once more setting his sights on the broader picture, Freud points out that this kind of selective remembering and forgetting applies also to the legends and traditions of various cultures or nationalities; that is, whatever is distressing to the national tradition is conveniently erased from memory or altered while more favorable aspects are recalled and even embellished in the cultural history.

However, beyond merely forgetting events we have passively observed or had happen to us, we may on occasion forget to do something that we consciously had planned or intended to do. In such cases, says Freud, it is difficult to explain this kind forgetting as a simple lapse in attention.

> No group of phenomena is better qualified than the forgetting of intentions for demonstrating the thesis that, in itself, lack of attention does not suffice to explain parapraxes. An intention is an impulse to perform an action: an impulse which has already found approval but whose execution is postponed to a suitable occasion. Now it can happen that during the interval thus created a change of such a kind occurs in the motives involved that the intention is not carried out;

but in that case it is not forgotten: it is re-examined and cancelled. (p. 151)

There are some people, notes Freud, who are known for being generally forgetful "by nature" and who are therefore excused their lapses in much the same way as are nearsighted people who squintingly bypass their acquaintances on the street. These habitually forgetful types fail to recall their small promises and commitments and generally show themselves to be ureliable in everyday matters. Moreover, they seem to expect that other people not take these minor offenses amiss; there's "nothing personal" in them, the forgetful one insists, and they are not to be regarded as willful acts of duplicity or spite. Rather, just as we good-naturedly dismiss another person's poor vision, hearing impairment, limping gait, mental dullness, and so on, these people's forgetfulness or absentmindedness, though occasionally annoying, represents, they would have us believe, a harmless constitutional idiosyncrasy to be gently disregarded. This is a view for which Freud has little sympathy:

> I am not one of these people myself, and have had no opportunity of analyzing the actions of a person of this kind, so that, by examining the choice of occasions for forgetting I might discover its motivation. I cannot, however, help suspecting on the basis of analogy that in these cases the motive is an unusually large amount of unavowed contempt for other people which exploits the constitutional factor for its own ends. (p. 157)

Following this, Freud discusses "bungled actions," which are distinguished from "symptomatic and chance actions," discussed in a subsequent section of his book, in that the former involve a "normal" intention but disturbed execution—that is, a wrong result—while in the latter there is no ostensible purpose for the action in the first place—the whole behavior itself seems inappropriate or pointless. However, says Freud, in practice no sharp demarcation can be drawn between these two types of action slips.

One of the functions of a bungled action is to psychodynamically represent a self-reproach: the present mistake seeks to replicate an error that has been committed in a different time and place.

> It is in fact my belief that we must accept this judgement for a whole series of seemingly accidental clumsy movements. It is true that they make a show of something violent and sweeping, like a spastic-ataxic movement, but they prove to be governed by an intention and achieve their aim with a certainty which cannot in general be credited to our conscious voluntary movements. Moreover, they have both features—

their violence and their unerring aim—in common with the motor manifestations of the hysterical neurosis, and partly, too, with the motor performance of somnambulism. This fact indicates that both in these cases and in the movements under consideration, the same unknown modification of the innervatory process is present. (p. 168)

Freud points out that individual clumsy actions do not by any means always have the same meaning but serve as a method of representing one purpose or another, according to circumstances. And in some cases, sniffs Freud with bourgeoise hauteur, clumsiness may even represent the manifestations of class-conscious resentment.

When servants drop fragile articles and so destroy them, our first thought is certainly not of a psychological explanation, yet it is not unlikely that here, too, obscure motives play their part. Nothing is more foreign to uneducated people than an appreciation of art and works of art. Our servants are dominated by a mute hostility towards the manifestations of art, especially when the objects (whose value they do not understand) become a source of work for them. On the other hand, people of the same education and origin often show great dexterity and reliability in handling delicate objects in scientific institutions, once they have begun to identify themselves with their chief and to consider themselves an essential part of the staff. (pp. 173–174)

Aside from the relatively harmless, even amusing, bungled behaviors that plague us in daily life, parapraxes of action can have a dire side as well, as when they contribute to the occurrence of serious accidents and injuries. When such "accidents" occur, says Freud, they usually can be shown to have their origin in an impulse to self-punishment, which for most people finds expression in simple self-reproach or the formation of neurotic symptoms. In extreme cases, however, the intrapunitive impulse takes ingenious advantage of a chance situation or lends assistance to that situation until the desired injurious effect is brought about. Such occurrences often betray the unconscious intention by a striking composure that many of these individuals retain in what is ostensibly a serious accident. Indeed—although Freud himself omits to point this out here—this seems quite similar to *la belle indifférence* that frequently accompanies comparably serious hysterical impairments of function.

Since even a *conscious* intention of committing suicide or some form of serious self-harm chooses its time, means, and opportunity, it is all the more understandable that an *unconscious* intention should wait for such an appropriate facilitatory occasion. And if such a "furious raging," as Freud puts it, against one's own integrity and one's own life can be hidden in this way behind apparently accidental clumsiness and motor inefficiency, it is a small step to apply such an interpretation to many of the "mistakes" that seriously endanger the lives and health of *other* people; in our own time, the example of auto accidents springs to mind.

Freud now considers symptomatic and chance actions, distinguished from the aforementioned bungled actions. In contrast to the latter, where at least the original intention of the act has some ostensible purpose, "symptomatic acts"—the term Freud prefers for them—seem to occur for no discernible reason, "just to have something to do," as we might say. They are typically unobtrusive, their effects relatively minor. But symptomatic acts give expression to something that the actor himself does not suspect in them and that he does not as a rule intend to impart to other people but to keep to himself. They thus reveal "secrets." For the psychotherapist, they often provide valuable clinical clues, whereas to the astute observer of human nature, Freud notes, they often betray much more than the subjects concerned would care to have revealed.

Good examples of this are the types of symptomatic acts that occur in matrimonial matters, which, Freud exclaims, are often of such significance as to function as veritable omens:

> I was once the guest of a young married couple and heard the young woman laughingly describe her latest experience. The day after her return from the honeymoon she had called for her unmarried sister to go shopping with her as she used to do, while her husband went to his business. Suddenly she noticed a gentleman on the other side of the street, and nudging her sister had cried: "Look, there goes Herr L." She had forgotten that this gentleman had been her husband for some weeks. I felt a cold chill as I heard the story, but I did not dare to draw the inference. The little incident only occurred to my mind some years later when the marriage had come to a most unhappy end. (p. 203)

Carelessly losing objects of value serves to express a variety of impulses: the "carelessness" may either be acting as a symbolic representation of a repressed thought—that is, it may be repeating a warning that one would be glad enough to ignore—or, more commonly, it may be offering a sacrifice to the obscure powers of destiny to whom, Freud reminds us, homage is still paid in this supposedly modern age.

Freud is next concerned with the subject of errors, addressing first those errors in memory that he distinguishes from forgetting accompanied by paramnesia. In the latter (as occurs, for example, in an organic Korsakoff's syndrome) there may be no awareness on the part of the subject that he/she is remembering incorrectly; we would say the patient lacks awareness of, or insight into, his deficit. But in the parapraxic memory error, we realize, often painfully, that we are remembering wrongly. We grope helplessly for the lost item as it scurryingly evades our mental grasp, perhaps throwing out decoys that we recognize as erroneous but that we can do little about except frustratedly cast them aside and continue our search.

Remembering incorrectly can have two separate causes. The first is simply genuine ignorance; even Freud acknowledges that sometimes people can make an honest mistake, as, for example, when he himself confused two historical sites simply because, he dryly informs us, they had the same name. But for most people at most times, the parapraxic memory errors of real interest typically derive from another source: "Where an error makes its appearance, a repression lies behind it" (p. 218).

Of all the parapraxes, errors seem to have the least rigid mechanism. That is, while the occurrence of an error indicates the presence of some psychic conflictual disturbance, the particular form that the error takes is not necessarily determined by the content or quality of the repressed disturbing idea. In fact,

> the same is true of many simple cases of slips of the tongue or pen. Every time we make a speaking or writing slip, we may infer that a disturbance has occurred outside our intention; but it must be acknowledged that slips of the tongue or pen often obey the laws of resemblance, of indolence or of the tendency to haste, without the content of the disturbing element necessarily making any unique contribution of its own character to the resulting mistake in speech or writing. It is the compliance of the linguistic material which alone makes the determining of the mistakes possible, and at the same time sets the limits up to which the determining can go. (Freud, 1901, pp. 221–222)

Freud seems to be saying that—unlike the case with hysterical conversion phenomena, where the actual nature of the symptom (blindness, paralysis, loss of memory) is often precisely determined by its symbolic relationship to the instigating intrapsychic conflict—in many parapraxic manifestations the conflict may initiate the process but its form is influenced more by the ordinary psychological rules of association.

Exactly how a repressed wish can be satisfied by means of an error is described in an example provided by Maeder (1908), which Freud cites in one of the later editions of *The Psychopathology of Everyday Life*.

> A colleague who had a day free from duties wanted to enjoy it without any interruption; but he was due to pay a visit in Lucerne to which he did not look forward. After long deliberation he decided to go there all the same. He passed the time on the journey from Zurich to Arth-Goldau in reading the daily papers. At the latter station he changed

trains and continued reading. He traveled on till the ticket-inspector informed him that he was on the wrong train—the one traveling back from Goldau to Zurich, though he had a ticket for Lucerne. (Freud, 1901, p. 226)

Since Freud was so fond of train anecdotes, I cannot resist drawing a comparison between the tale related above and one that appeared in an episode of the American television comedy series *The Honeymooners*— mainly because it illustrates the timelessness and transcultural appeal of stories that speak to our recognized human tendency to fool ourselves, to commit Freudian slips.

In the episode, Ralph and Norton are excited about going to the annual convention of the Raccoon Lodge in Minneapolis, where they expect to have a riotous good time with the boys, without impediment of wives. However, when it appears that Ralph will be unable to secure the money for the trip without importuning his wife, Alice, he makes a virtue of necessity by gallantly inviting her and her friend Trixie (Norton's wife) along. He does this at the considerable risk of humiliation at the convention, where his lodge brothers will no doubt tease him relentlessly for such apparent uxoriousness—not to mention the general dampening effect on unbridled fun and games that such spousal accompaniment portends. But Ralph really wants to go. He swallows his pride and makes the grand gesture of inviting Alice, whereupon she informs him that she already decided to make a gift of the money for him to go to the convention without her—but now, of course, she will gladly accept his invitation.

Ralph, devastated at having blown his chance at an unfettered vacation, nonetheless collects his wits and decides to make the best of the situation. The traveling plans are for Ralph and Norton to meet Alice and Trixie at the railway station in New York and for all to board the Minneapolis-bound train together for the trip to the convention. When the two men arrive at the train, the wives are nowhere to be found. As time to departure runs out and the train begins to move, Ralph and Norton exult in the fact that the wives have missed the train, giving them at least one whole free day at the convention without them. As they settle in for the trip, one cockamamie mishap after another strains the relationship between the two pals until, on the verge of blows, they are approached by a conductor who demands an explanation for the disturbance. Ralph then fumes about having to be locked up with Norton all the way to Minneapolis, whereupon the conductor informs the two that the train they're on is going in the opposite direction, to Norfolk, Virginia.

We may ask, Did reluctance to attend the Raccoon convention with their wives unconsciously impel the two lodge brothers, like Maeder's

(1908) colleague, to board a train in the wrong direction and thus physically distance themselves from the situation as a concrete analogue to the wished-for psychical distancing?

Aside from its clinical applications and general human interest value, notes Freud (1901), the phenomenon of parapraxic errors also has broader implications for the science of epistemology and the conduct of empirical research:

> It may perhaps be thought that the class of errors whose explanation I have given here is not very numerous or particularly significant. But I leave it open for question whether there is not some ground for extending the same line of approach to our assessment of the far more important *errors of judgement* made by human beings in their lives and in scientific work. Only for the rarest and best adjusted mind does it seem possible to preserve the picture of external reality, as it is perceived, against the distortion to which it is normally subjected in its passage through the psychical individuality of the percipient. (pp. 228–229)

In a chapter that first appeared in the 1907 edition of *The Psychopathology of Everyday Life*, Freud deals with "combined parapraxes," that is, combinations of an act of forgetting and an error. Freud says that he does not mean to imply that cases of such combined parapraxes can teach us anything new that could not already be observed in the simpler instances. However, the fact that a parapraxis can change in form but still retain the integrity of its outcome gives a vivd impression of a will striving for a definite aim and thus contradicts the notion that a parapraxis is a matter of mere chance and in need of no interpretation. We may also be struck, says Freud, by the fact that in these cases a conscious intention should fail so completely to prevent the success of the parapraxis, that is, that our conscious "free will" should be powerless to thwart or alter the unconsciously determined parapraxic event.

Two examples illustrate this. The first comes from a reader of Freud's who was so obviously impressed by an earlier edition of *The Psychopathology of Everyday Life* that he was moved to send Freud the following story:

> "Some years ago I allowed myself to be elected to the committee of a certain literary society, as I thought that the organization might one day be able to have my play produced; and I took a regular part, though without being much interested, in the meetings, which were held every Friday. Then, a few months ago, I was given the promise of a production at the theatre at F.; and since then I have regularly *forgotten* the meetings of the society. When I read your book on the subject I felt ashamed of my forgetfulness. I reproached myself with the thought that it was shabby behavior on my part to stay away now that I no

longer needed these people, and resolved on no account to forget the next Friday. I kept on reminding myself of this resolution until I carried it into effect and stood at the door of the room where the meetings were held. To my astonishment it was locked; the meeting was over. I had in fact made a mistake over the day; it was now Saturday!" (cited in Freud, 1901, p. 230)

A second example combines a symptomatic act with a case of mislaying:

A lady traveled to Rome with her brother-in-law, who is a famous artist. The visitor was received with great honor by the German community in Rome, and among other presents he was given an antique gold medal. The lady was vexed that her brother-in-law did not appreciate the lovely object sufficiently. When she returned home (her place in Rome having been taken by her sister) she discovered while unpacking that she had brought the medal with her—how, she did not know. She at once sent a letter with the news to her brother-in-law, and announced that she would send the article she had walked off with back to Rome next day. But next day the medal had been so cleverly mislaid that it could not be found and sent off; and it was at this point that the meaning of her "absent-mindedness" dawned on the lady: she wanted to keep the object for herself. (Freud, 1901, p. 231)

Freud's correspondent failed, in spite of his "good intentions," to attend the meeting of the literary society, and the lady found it impossible to part with the medal. The unknown factor that opposed these intentions found another outlet after the first path had been barred to it. For what was required to overcome the unconscious motive was something other than a conscious counterintention; no increased "force of will" could deflect the psychodynamically motivating impetus that guided thought and behavior toward the unconscious goal. Rather, says Freud, what was called for was a piece of psychical work that could make what was unknown known to consciousness, analogous to the psychoanalytic work necessary to uncover the roots of pathological symptoms.

In the last chapter of the book, Freud devotes considerable space to addressing the issue of determinism and the belief in chance and superstition, developing what might be regarded as the first true psychoanalytic epistemology. He begins by summarizing the main conclusions that emerge from the previous chapters: many seemingly inexplicable mental and behavioral phenomena, if viewed through the analytic lens, prove to be determined by valid motives, albeit unknown to consciousness. But in order to qualify as a bona fide parapraxis, a given event of this type must fulfill certain qualifications. First, it must not exceed what we would reasonably regard as "within the limits of the normal"; that is, it must not be a severe neurotic, hysterical, or other pathological symptom. Second, the disturbance must be momentary, or at least temporary, not a stable, long-lasting, or habitual feature of behavior. Third, the same function must have been performed correctly before, or we must at all times believe ourselves capable of carrying it out correctly. Fourth, if we are corrected by someone else, we must at once be able to recognize the validity of the correction and the fact that our own thought or action has been in error; that is, there is little or no "resistance," as there is in the case of pathological symptoms. Finally, even if we are at some level dimly aware of the parapraxis while it is occurring, we must not perceive in ourselves any particular motive for it. Instead, we are tempted to explain it away by lack of attention, a chance event, a "fluke," and so on.

Turning to the issue of motives, Freud notes that many people contest the idea of psychic determinism by appealing to a special feeling of conviction that there "must" be free will and that their actions—most of them, anyway—are determined by a rational, deliberative, internal decision-making process that is in some sense self-directed. But Freud observes that this deliberative, volitional explanation for our actions does not appear to be commonly invoked when great, important, or noble decisions are made. Rather, in such cases the doer may appeal to a compelling inner psychical motive force; "Here I stand, I can do no other," quotes Freud, and present-day watchers of TV evening news programs can recall similar accounts of daring rescues by courageous bystanders: "I don't know what came over me, I just *had* to do it." On the other hand, it is precisely with regard to relatively unimportant matters that we would like to claim that we could just as well have acted this way or that of our own free accord.

Freud has no real interest in debating these popular claims to a feeling of conviction of free will. But, he points out, if we are willing to acknowledge any distinction at all between conscious and unconscious motivation—that, at least, not *all* of our decisions and actions are rationally and volitionally determined *all* of the time—then we must concede that what is *not* determined by our conscious free will must receive its motivation from somewhere else, leaving room for a certain degree of psychic determination.

Freud next addresses the phenomenon of *déjà vu*, the feeling one has while visiting a place for the first time that he/she "has been there before." We considered déjà vu in previous chapters in the context of dreams and temporal lobe epilepsy, but it has occurred in waking consciousness to almost everybody at one time or another; in such isolated instances it has no necessary implication for neuropathology or psychopathology. It is wrong, Freud says, to regard the feeling of having experienced something before as merely an illusion. It is, rather, that at such moments something really is touched upon that we have already experienced once before, only we cannot consciously remember it because it has never *been* conscious. In other words, the feeling of déjà vu corresponds to the recollection of an unconscious fantasy.

In a footnote added to the 1924 edition of *The Psychopathology of Everyday Life*, Freud refers to a short paper he wrote in 1913 describing another phenomenon that is very similar to déjà vu, called *déjà raconté*, the false conviction of having already previously reported a particular memory of special interest when it arises in the course of psychoanalytic treatment. The doctor in such cases is sure that this subject matter has never been raised before and is, as a rule, able to convince the patient of his/her error. The explanation for this kind of parapraxis is probably that the patient has felt an urge to communicate this information and intended to do so but for one reason or another has never gotten around to it; he/she now takes the memory of the intention as a substitute for the actual carrying out of the intention.

Freud then reiterates his most important point (illustrated previously by the migraine example): brain mechanisms may interact with psychodynamic forces to produce the particular manifestations of symptoms or parapraxes. Repressed material, says Freud, exploits whatever innervatory processes may be operative in a given person's brain, processes that are either a characteristic feature of that person or are influenced by events of the moment (such as migraine, epilepsy, fatigue, and so on). For example, in the case of verbal parapraxes, the data and theory of philosophers and philologists alike can be used to explore the structural and functional relations that serve such unconscious motives.

> If we distinguish, among the determinants of parapraxes and symptomatic acts, between the unconscious motive on the one hand and the physiological and psychological relations that come to meet it on the other, it remains an open question whether there are, within the range of normality, yet other factors that can—like the unconscious motive, and in place of it—create parapraxes and symptomatic acts along the lines of these relations. It is not my task to answer this question. (pp. 270–271)

. . . Well, not anymore, anyway. As his various biographers and historians never tire of telling us, Freud by this time had forsaken neurology and neurophysiology in favor of the *psycho*dynamic. But, as we have observed repeatedly, the early model of Freud's brain remains indelibly and lastingly etched on the edifice of psychoanalytic theory.

The immutability of unconscious memories is one of the fundamental tenets of psychoanalysis and forms the theoretical basis for the efficacy not just of analysis but of all the varieties of "uncovering" therapies. It is therefore of interest that one of the strongest expressions of this theory appears in a footnote added to the 1907 edition of *The Psychopathology of Everyday Life*, where Freud addresses more specifically the issue of forgetting, implicitly tying it in with his earlier insights regarding the dream process.

Mnemic material, says Freud, is subject in general to two influences, namely, condensation and distortion. *Condensation* affects mainly memory traces that have for the most part grown weak or indifferent and are thus susceptible to this kind of confabulatory blending together. More resistant memory traces are dealt with by the process of *distortion*, which also affects the weaker memory traces as well. The important point is that memory traces do not simply dissipate over time; their alteration in the various forms of our conscious recollection is an active process that has its basis in active psychodynamic forces. Repressed memory traces remain entirely intact, even after the longest intervals, because

> the unconscious is quite timeless. The most important as well as the strangest characteristic of psychical fixation is that all impressions are preserved, not only in the same form in which they were first received, but also in all the forms which they have adopted in their further developments. This is a state of affairs which cannot be illustrated by comparison with another sphere. Theoretically, every earlier state of the mnemic content could thus be restored to memory again, even if its elements have long ago exchanged all their original connections for more recent ones. (p. 275)

Finally, Freud makes the link between parapraxes, dreams, and neurotic symptoms explicit. In both dreams and parapraxes, we find such phenomena as condensation and other "compromise-formations." The psychodynamics are the same: by unfamiliar paths and by way of external associations, unconscious thoughts find expression as modifications of other thoughts. The incongruities, absurdities, and errors of the dream content, which result in the dream being scarcely recognized as the product of psychical activity, originate in the same way. In dreams, as with both neuroses and parapraxes, the appearance of an incorrect function is explained by the peculiar mutual interference between two or more correct functions:

> If we compare [parapraxes] to the products of psychoneuroses, to neurotic symptoms, two frequently repeated statements—namely, the borderline between the normal and the abnormal in nervous matters is a fluid one, and that we are all a little neurotic—acquire meaning and support. Without any medical experience we can construct various types of nervous illnesses of this kind which are merely hinted at—*formes frustes* of the neuroses: cases in which the symptoms are few, or occur rarely or not severely—in other words, cases whose comparative mildness

is located in the number, intensity and duration of their pathological manifestations. (pp. 278–279)

What, after all, distinguishes a neurotic symptom from a parapraxis? Only the depth and range of circumstances that the disturbance affects. Parapraxes are characterized by the fact that the slips are located in the "least important," that is, everyday, psychical and behavioral activities. However, when the manifestations make their appearance in the "most important" functions—that is, are able to disturb health, sex, work, social life, and so on—this, says Freud, is the mark of neurosis, not parapraxis.

But there is one thing which the severest and the mildest cases have in common, and which is equally found in parapraxes and chance actions: *the phenomena can be traced back to incompletely suppressed psychical material, which, although pushed away by consciousness, has nevertheless not been robbed of all capacity for expressing itself.* (p. 279)

It is to the mechanisms of such expression that we now turn to see how we might pick up where Freud left off and explore the neuropsychodynamic basis for some kinds of parapraxes—to begin the work of elaborating a *neuro*psychopathology of everyday life.

CHAPTER 15

The Neuropsychopathology of Everyday Life I: Action Slips

To move a limb is no simple thing. Particular arrays of motor neurons in the spinal cord must fire at certain rates to effect the contraction of specific muscles. Complex sensorimotor feedback mechanisms within the spinal cord itself regulate the timing and coordination of these neuromuscular relationships. The spinal system is, in turn, acted upon from above by descending fibers carrying regulatory information from brain stem, cerebellum, basal ganglia, thalamus, and cortical structures, all coordinated in interlocking and overlapping feedback loops. Just as the spinal mechanisms are influenced by these systems from above, the initial signal to move, generated by the primary motor cortex, is affected by many of the same structures in different ways from below. Thus, the ongoing cortical signal continuously receives feedback data from the muscles themselves, from other brain loops in the motor system, and from the sensory effects of the movements. In this way, a particular motor act—scratching your nose, for example—is essentially "sculpted," as Sir John Eccles (1973) liked to put it, from the vast repertoire of possible combinations of muscle movements.

But beyond its ability to produce the contraction of muscles, the brain must coordinate and direct those movements toward some purpose, some behavioral goal, and this is a task that is carried out by areas outside the primary motor strip. Before there was a "parapraxis" there was the concept of *praxis*, the ability to perform a motor act in a normal and functional manner. The loss of this ability was duly termed *apraxia* by neurologists; by Freud's time, several clinical forms of apraxia had already been delineated in the German literature by Gogol (1874) and later by

189

Liepmann (1900), who provided probably the most comprehensive description up to that time.

Collectively, the apraxias refer to a group of disorders that interfere with the ability to perform a complex motor act in a skillful and task-appropriate way, that is, to coordinate a series of movements into a fluid and efficient sequence in order to accomplish some immediate goal—to turn a flurry of muscle twitches into a coherent *act*. In an apraxia, the ability to perform the individual muscular contractions is preserved but the ability to combine them into an act is impaired.

For example, in *ideomotor apraxia*, the ability to place a key into a lock may be impaired: the person twists his/her hand this way and that, unable to perform the right moves even though motor strength is intact. In *ideational apraxia*, individual acts may be preserved, but complex sequences of acts—which amount to behaviors—are affected. For example, a typical ideational apraxic patient who wants a smoke might put the matchbook in his mouth and attempt to strike the cigarette pack with the unlit cigarette, then might try putting the cigarette in his mouth correctly but striking the pack to the matchbook, and so on. The intention is there, the motor strength is there, but what is disrupted is the intermediate step of translating the will to act into the precise sequence of timed movements that would effect the goal. (One wonders if Freud had these two apraxias in mind when he formulated the distinction between "bungled" and "symptomatic" parapraxes.) Other, more complex and bizarre, syndromes will be discussed in the following paragraphs.

But even beyond these kinds of apraxias, which tend to be seen with damage to the left posterior parietal lobe, there is the question of where the impulse to act arises in the first place—the question, that is, of *volition*. Such a complex function is far less easy to localize in any one structure or region of the brain. But, as we shall see, both the neuropsychology of the apraxias and the psychodynamics of action parapraxes point straight to the heart of what it means to *will* an act.

Disorders of Action and Volition

Ferro and Kertesz (1984) report the case of a sixty-one-year-old right-handed hypertensive and diabetic man who was hospitalized because of the sudden onset of left-sided weakness and moderate hemiparesis. CT scan showed a small lesion in the posterior branch of the right internal capsule, the white matter bundle where fibers to and from the cortex of each hemisphere converge in a sort of major "trunk line" that links up with subcortical structures and pathways. The effect of the damage in this case was a peculiar form of neglect syndrome in which any kind of spontaneous activity in the affected hemispace was precluded.

For example, the patient would not reach for items placed on his left side, although right-sided items were retrieved without difficulty. The hemineglect also disturbed reading and writing and was especially noted on drawing and other visuospatial tasks. The deficit was restricted to tasks requiring spontaneous motor performance under visual control in the contralateral hemispace. External verbal cues improved exploratory behavior; that is, when the patient's actions were guided by speech from the examiner, his performance improved.

In conceptualizing their case, Ferro and Kertesz (1984) cite Heilman and Valenstein's (1979) proposal that hemispatial neglect is secondary to a hypokinesia, or diminution of activity, for any act that must be performed in the neglected hemispatial field. The performance of Ferro and Kertesz's patient on line bisection was worse when the lines were placed in the left hemispace. Hemispatial akinesia was present mostly when the motor exploratory activity was carried out under visual control. When direct visual control was removed and the patient used an internal representation of space, neglect was no longer present, particularly on tasks where verbal instructions specified that the patient should describe or explore the left and right parts of the presented stimuli. The fact that verbal cues could act as "external volition" and improve exploratory behavior suggests that the hemispatial akinesia in this case was due to an "intentional disorder," a defect of the will to explore the contralateral half-space, and not to a loss of the motor programs themselves that are responsible for the distribution of movements within extrapersonal space.

Neuroanatomically, the investigators believe that the internal capsule lesion probably deprived the posterior parietal cortex of visual information from ipsilateral visual association areas (by damaging the optic radiations), as well as from the pulvinar, a nucleus of the thalamus involved with higher-order perception. On the basis of experimental findings with monkeys, Mountcastle and colleagues (1975) proposed that the posteroparietal association cortex controls operations within extrapersonal space and that the main visual input to the posteroparietal lobule comes from the thalamic pulvinar. Thus, a pulvinar–parietal disconnection was probably the anatomic basis for hemispatial neglect in this patient. The compensating effect of verbal cues suggests that the left hemisphere is able to activate the right parietal lobe and the motor exploratory programs toward the contralateral half-space through intact interhemispheric connections. And preservation of the parietal lobe itself explains why this patient could describe accurately the left half of recollected images.

Most of us have seen one version or another of the old grade-B horror movie where the character's own hand (perhaps transplanted from the cadaver of some notorious psycho-killer) appears to take on a life of its own, commits mayhem "against the will" of its owner, and even, in some versions, begins to strangle the owner himself. Such cinematic fantasies have, in fact, some basis in reality. The concept of the *alien hand* was introduced by Brion and Jedynak (1972) on the basis of their observations of three patients with tumors of the corpus callosum. In reviewing the syndrome following cerebral commissurotomy, Bogen (1979) described the alien hand sign as a circumstance in which one of the patient's hands behaves in a way that the patient finds foreign, alien, or at least uncooperative—that is, in a way that is "against the will" of its owner.

Goldberg and colleagues (1981) described a case in which the alien hand sign on the right side occurred as a result of a stroke involving the left medial frontal cortex. The patient was a sixty-three-year old right-handed woman who was first observed to have difficulty speaking and a weakness in her right leg. She appeared alert but would not initiate conversation. CT scan and a subsequent isotope scan demonstrated a lesion in the left medial frontal cortex.

Several unusual types of motor behaviors were observed in the patient's right hand, including a strong grasp reflex that indicated a disturbance in the higher-order cortical inhibition of automatic grasping that occurs when an object is placed in the hand (infants show automatic grasping as a natural neurodevelopmental feature). In addition, the patient would reach out spontaneously with the right hand, grab something, and then would not be able to let go. She was unable to inhibit this behavior, although she was quite aware of it and was obviously frustrated by her inability to prevent it. She tended to restrain the movement of the right arm by holding it by her side with the more "obedient" left arm.

At times, the right arm was noted to interfere with tasks being performed by the left arm. This so-called *intermanual conflict* was observed at one point when the patient's right hand sprang up to keep her glasses on her face after her left hand had begun to remove them. She was aware of these conflicting actions but was, again, frustrated by being unable to prevent them consciously, volitionally. Finally, motor perseveration was evident: the patient would begin to perform a task with her right arm, which would then repeat the activity uncontrollably, interrupting the completion of the task. The left arm would thereupon interrupt the perseveration by restraining the right arm and then complete the task. This was noted, for example, on several occasions when the patient was attempting to apply the brakes on her wheelchair.

Later, she slowly improved her ability to inhibit the unwanted behavior of the right arm through concentrated effort—by "force of will." When these unwanted activities of the right arm began to interfere with performance on tasks, they could be interrupted by the examiner through the issuance of a simple motor command, such as "Place your right arm across your lap." The patient would then be able to obey this directive and, in the process, override the aberrant motor behavior, a result reminiscent of the removal or alteration of hysterical symptoms by hypnotic suggestion.

In the fifth week after her stroke the patient began to walk alone. Her right arm, however, still tended to spontaneously reach out and grasp objects that she passed, such as door knobs, thus interfering greatly with her ambulation. This was minimized by having her repetitively tap on her thigh with her right hand as she walked or by having her walk with a cane held in her right hand. By thus keeping the capricious right limb "busy," she was able to keep it out of mischief (cf. the proverb "For Satan finds some mischief still / For idle hands to do").

In conceptualizing their case, Goldberg and colleagues (1981) begin by noting that their patient displayed a strong grasp reflex in her right hand. She showed motor perseveration, that is, inappropriate repetition of a simple movement of the right hand and arm, which was usually triggered by an attempt at voluntary activity. She additionally exhibited a speech disorder consisting of a lack of spontaneous speech output with preserved ability to repeat, a pattern typically designated as transcortical motor aphasia, the kind of language disturbance that was of such interest to Freud (1891).

In this patient, then, apparently purposeful, goal-directed movements appeared to be occurring in the right arm independent of conscious volitional control. There was also evidence of conflict between the motor behaviors of the two arms, with the right arm being the identified offender and the left arm the "corrector"; that is, the patient was able to adaptively control the unwanted activity by restraining the right arm physically with the left.

The authors point out that there are two fundamental zones of the medial surface of the frontal lobes, damage to which may be implicated in the appearance of this kind of psychomotor disturbance, as well as in the speech disorder. These are the *supplementary motor area* (SMA) and the *cingulate cortex*, which are reciprocally connected (Damasio & Van Hoesen, 1980). Electrical stimulation in conscious human subjects seems to elicit similar forms of behavior from both the SMA and the anterior cingulate cortex. Penfield and Jasper (1954) reported that stimulation of the SMA produced vocalizations, speech arrest, complex coordinated or repetitive movements that usually appeared in the contralateral arm, and arrest or slowing of voluntary action, following which the patient usually appeared puzzled by his inability to execute the action he/she intended. Talairach and colleagues (1973) found that continuous electrical stimulation of the anterior cingulate cortex in epileptic patients produced complex, highly integrated forms of motor activity that resulted from a compounding of various simple "primitive" movements and that appeared most often in the contralateral arm.

Goldberg and colleagues (1981) cite Damasio and Van Hoesen's (1980) description of four patients with lesions involving the left SMA. These patients were noted initially to have a global akinesia that eventually became circumscribed to the right side of the body. Damasio and Van Hoesen concluded that damage to the SMA decreased the "drive" to execute both spontaneous and volitional movement.

Regional cerebral blood flow (rCBF) studies in man have demonstrated bilateral activation of the SMA in association with various complex movements of the extremities, as well as with speech. On the basis of these rCBF studies, as well as additional evidence in man and animals, Orgogozo and Larsen (1979) have suggested that the SMA may act in a "supramotor" capacity in the cortical organization of voluntary movements. They postulate that the SMA may contribute to the establishment of new motor programs and to the executory control of established subroutines according to external and internal inputs. The anatomical and physiological data suggest that the SMA could be the system where external inputs and commands are matched with internal needs and drives, thus enabling the formulation of a strategy of voluntary movement.

Goldberg and colleagues (1981) thus interpret the alien hand sign and the accompanying dissociative psychomotor disturbances, as well as the speech disorder associated with left medial frontal cortex damage, as expressions of faulty initiation, execution, and inhibition of preexisting, essentially intact motor subroutines. These program controls may no longer be coupled normally to external and, particularly, to internal inputs. The appearance of these dissociative phenomena may thus be related to damage to the SMA, its connecting fibers, or to associated structures located on the medial frontal surface of the hemisphere contralateral to the involved extremity. The action subroutines, though intact, cannot be activated by the cerebral substrate of intentionality, of "will." Yet if this disconnection does not also involve the pathways from external input, then the "will" of some outside agent—for example, the examiner's command—could induce the action.

Could the mechanism of "suggestion"—hypnotic or otherwise—as understood in psychoanalysis, depend on some kind of temporary neuropsychodynamic suspension of this internal-directedness aspect of volitional movement in favor of responsiveness to an outside agent? Further, recalling our earlier description of frontal lobe functions in general, if SMA disinhibition can produce an "alien hand," could more extensive or generalized frontal impairment be responsible for a kind of generalized "alien behavior" that characterologically impulsive, noninsightful people seem to display? This, of course, moves us from action into the realm of personality, which I have considered more extensively elsewhere (Miller, 1990) and which will be elaborated upon further in Chapter 18 of the present book.

Watson and colleagues (1986) report the case of a sixty-five-year-old right-handed man who experienced sudden leg weakness and difficulty using his right hand. During this episode he was able to understand what was said by others around him but remained mute himself. What language he did express was uttered in short, clipped phrases, with greatly diminished grammatical complexity. He also showed an apraxia of both arms, with the left more affected than the right. He was most impaired in pantomiming actions to command; his performance often improved if he could imitate the action done first by someone else and usually improved further with the use of the actual object. Although many aspects of the pantomimes were incorrect, the postures and positionings of the arms contained a sufficient number of correct elements to tell that the patient was attempting to make the requested movement. He was slow in initiating pantomimes, and after finally doing so, he incorrectly performed the individual movements, with errors in both spacing and timing. He could not correctly position the digits of his hand in space for performing skilled manual acts, and the sequencing of the movements of individual digits was also abnormal.

In some respects, this patient's errors were like those seen in patients who have ideomotor apraxia from left parietal lobe lesions. However, unlike many patients with parietal lesions, who may lack full awareness of their disability and seem confused by their inability to carry out the actions, the patient in Watson and colleagues' case *knew* that he was not performing the movement correctly; recall that such self-awareness of error was one of Freud's (1901) criteria for distingushing a parapraxis from a symptom. The patient would often look at his hand in dismay while trying to position it correctly. For example, while observing his hand incorrectly pantomiming the use of scissors, he became frustrated and finally said, "If you would give me the scissors, I could show you how to do this" (Watson et al., 1986, p. 788). Granted this request, his performance improved, but he continued to make some errors.

This patient had a number of unusual complaints. If he wanted to pick up an object, such as a cup of coffee, he would have to, he said, "tell my hand to pick it up" (Watson et al., 1986, p. 788). He had difficulty with his right hand not letting go of objects. For example, when starting his car, he would fail to release the key even after the engine was running. He had trouble performing habitual acts, such as those entailed in cooking meals. He noted a decreased ability to tap-dance and play the guitar, tasks at which he had previously been adept. He stated that occasionally his right hand did things of which he was unaware, reminiscent of the alien hand sign; however, he denied symptoms suggesting intermanual conflict. His neurologic exam showed no weakness or sensory loss.

This patient had a transcortical motor aphasia and an apraxia for transitive movements—that is, for movements normally made in relationship to an object or instrument, such as using a key or a hammer—that were more striking in the arms than in the legs, worse with the left limbs than the right, and most deficient when pantomiming to command, his performance usually improving with imitation and actual object use. He had no evidence of apraxia for intransitive movements—that is, movements not related to object use, such as saluting or waving goodbye—total-body movements, the orderly sequencing of ordinary movements, or mouth and face pantomimes. He had apraxia for bilateral hand movements, particularly those that required complex movements of each hand, such as playing the piano, whereas relatively simple movements, such as threading a needle, were done normally.

While attempting all motor tasks, the patient used verbal mediation, talking himself through the activities, which in fact exceeded in quantity all other kinds of spontaneous speech. For example, when told to demonstrate how he would blow out a match, he responded by saying, "Well, first I take the matches out, then I bring it up and blow" (Watson et al., 1986, p. 789). He had preserved insight and awareness of the apraxia and could discriminate well-performed from poorly performed pantomimes.

In conceptualizing their case, Watson and colleagues (1986) note that the SMA is located on the medial surface of the hemisphere anterior to the foot area of the primary motor cortex and dorsal to the cingulate sulcus (Penfield & Welch, 1951). Stimulation of the SMA produces complex limb movements, and blood flow to the SMA increases during the programming of complex limb movements (Orgogozo & Larsen, 1979). The SMA contains neurons that are active when movements are performed exclusively by the distal forelimb (Tanji & Kurata, 1982). However, the only lasting deficits of distal motor behavior reported in humans with SMA damage have been disturbances of alternating movement of the hands. SMA lesions have also been associated with a contralateral grasp reflex, a transient state of akinetic mutism, and a transient increase in the tone of proximal flexor muscles (Humphrey, 1979). In addition, SMA lesions can produce transcortical motor aphasia (Jonas, 1981).

Single-neuron recordings in monkeys have further suggested a role for the SMA in higher order motor control. Many SMA neurons begin discharging before learned complex movements are performed with either hand; a small percentage of neurons are active throughout the motor task while other neurons are active during preparation for movement but not during the movement itself (Brinkman & Porter, 1979). These neurons show instruction-specific changes in activity during a premovement preparatory period signaled by a light and preceding a somatosensory-triggered movement (Tanji et al., 1980).

According to Watson and colleagues (1986), bilateral ideomotor apraxia for transitive movements in their patient suggests that the SMA normally plays an important role in programming transitive movements of the limbs. They note that two of the most distinctive features of human development have been the acquisition of language and the use of tools, the latter necessarily requiring transitive movements. Aphasia is associated with left-hemisphere lesions, as is apraxia for transitive movements, whereas abnormalities of intransitive movements may occur after lesions of either hemisphere (Haaland & Flaherty, 1984).

Proper use of a tool requires both a centrally generated action command and sensory feedback from the activity so as to judge the efficacy of the action in producing the desired result. Since the SMA is relatively unresponsive to peripheral sensory stimulation, it has been suggested that the SMA is important for generating the central motor commands themselves. It has already been proposed that the left inferior parietal lobule contains the spatial and temporal representations of learned transitive movements (Heilman et al., 1982), and Watson and colleagues (1986) extend this hypothesis to suggest that the left SMA translates these representations into motor programs.

The Brain's Unconscious Initiation of Action

The conceptualization of the SMA as a sort of a "motor volition system" receives further support from a study by Libet and colleagues (1983), who focused their attention on a recordable EEG pattern, known as the *readiness potential* (RP), that precedes a freely voluntary, fully endogenous motor act. The investigators compared the onset of the RP with the reported time for appearance of the subjective experience of "wanting" or intending to act. They told their subjects, who were normal volunteers free of brain injury, to make a voluntary movement with their hand "whenever they wanted to." The only other thing they had to do was record the exact moment they made the "decision" to act (whether or not they actually carried it out) by noting the position of a slowly revolving dot on a circular clock-face-type of time recording apparatus.

It was found that the onset of brain activity clearly preceded, by at least several hundred milliseconds (thousandths of a second), the reported time of conscious intention to act; that is, the subjects became subjectively aware of their intention, or "wanting," to move only after the brain activity related to that movement had already begun. This relationship held even for subjects who reported that all of their self-initiated movements appeared "spontaneously." The investigators concluded that the cerebral initiation of a spontaneous, freely voluntary act can begin unconsciously, that is, before there is any (at least recallable) subjective awareness that a "decision" to act has been initiated by the brain. Note that just such an unconscious or *preconscious* process was hypothesized by Freud (1901) to underlie such parapraxes as misreadings and action slips.

These findings thus seem to indicate that the neuronal processes that precede a self-initiated voluntary action generally begin, as reflected in the readiness potential, substantially *prior* to the subjective awareness of conscious intention to perform that act, the time difference being several hundred milliseconds. It would thus appear that some neuronal activity associated with the eventual performance of the act has started well before any (recallable) conscious initiation or intervention could be possible.

> Put another way, the brain evidently "decides" to initiate or, at the least, prepare to initiate the act at a time before there is any reportable subjective awareness that such a decision has taken place. It is concluded that cerebral initiation even of a spontaneous voluntary act, of the kind studied here, can and usually does begin *unconsciously*. (Libet et al., 1983, p. 640)

The authors are quick to add that the term "unconscious" as used here refers simply to all processes that are not expressed as a conscious experience; this may include and does not distinguish among "preconscious," "subconscious," or other possible nonreportable nonconscious processes. Nevertheless, according to the authors, "these considerations would appear to introduce certain constraints on the potential of the individual for exerting conscious initiation and control over his voluntary acts" (Libet et al., 1983, p. 641).

In addition to concluding that spontaneous voluntary acts can be initiated unconsciously, the investigators acknowledge that there are at least two types of conditions in which conscious control *could* exert an influence on the process. First, there could be a "conscious veto" that aborts the performance of the type of "spontaneous" self-initiated acts under study here. This remains possible because reportable conscious intention, even though it appeared distinctly later than the onset of the RP, did appear a substantial period of time (about 150 to 200 milliseconds) before the beginning of the actual movement itself. Subjects reported that some recallable conscious urges to act were inhibited before any actual movement occurred; in such cases, the subject simply waited for another urge to appear, which, when consummated, constituted the actual event whose RP was recorded. Second, in those voluntary actions that are not "spontaneous" and quickly performed, that is, in those in which conscious deliberation (of whether to act or of what alternative choice of action to take) actually precedes the act, there could still occur conscious initiation and control. Everyone, after all, does some deliberating over many of the actions he/she may take. And, Libet and colleagues (1983) point out, the recorded RP probably represents neuronal activity in a limited portion of the brain, namely, the SMA.

The Supplementary Motor Area and the Neuropsychodynamics of Willed Actions

It would seem that regarding the SMA as an integral component in the neuropsychological "action–volition system" might help bridge the gap between apraxias and parapraxes. Goldberg (1985) has thoroughly reviewed the neuroanatomy, neurophysiology, and neuropsychology of the SMA, much of which we have already discussed in the context of the afore-mentioned case studies. In Goldberg's model, the SMA is a key element in a medial, bilaterally organized brain system that performs context-dependent selection, linkage, initiation, and anticipatory control of a set of "precompiled" motor subroutines, each of which corresponds to a particular component perceptuomotor strategy or schema of the complete action. Put more succinctly, the SMA organizes and executes specific sequences of motor actions that are directed toward a particular goal. It is not responsible for the actual motive behind that action sequence or for the goal it serves; nor does it directly control the actual muscle movements involved in carrying out the act. Rather, its role is that of an essential neurovolitional intermediary, ensuring that the motive is translated intact into the necessary motor elements that will secure the goal in question.

Action, says Goldberg (1985), is initiated through a developmental sequence in which increasing amounts of detail are specified the closer in time one approaches to the actual overt expression of that action. This microgenetic process of action-specification underlying the formation of a behavior recapitulates the evolutionary process of phylogenetic development of the relevant structures, with each participating structure manifesting its involvement through a component feature of the complete act—a statement, we may note, that could have been written by Jackson, and later Freud, a century ago. In this context, Goldberg views the SMA as a crucial link within a widely distributed, layered system of structures involved in the generation of action, rather than as a particular site from which voluntary movements are initiated.

Thus, in this model, the SMA is a zone of internal convergence within the premotor region of the medial frontal lobe, receiving projections from primary and secondary somatosensory areas, as well as from parietal association cortex. The SMA is linked reciprocally with the anterior cingulate part of limbic cortex and would appear to be a major cortical site through which limbic-mediated emotional and motivational outflow may influence cortical and subcortical motor structures.

Each SMA receives input from primary motor areas, as well as from other parts of premotor and prefrontal cortex, and then projects bilaterally back to primary motor areas (though more densely to the ipsilateral primary motor area), to the contralateral SMA, and to various subcortical structures. It sends projections bilaterally to the striatum and also projects strongly to the cerebellar cortex via the pontine nuclei, further steps in the subcortical loops involved in motor control. The SMA also sends direct projections to the spinal cord.

Through these multifarious connections, the SMA could potentially participate in the coordination of both axial (head and trunk) and distal (limb) musculature, ipsilaterally as well as contralaterally. Its pattern of inputs indicates that the SMA avails itself of sensory data conveying information about the external environment and about the body schema required for setting up and adapting motor programs. It is also the recipient of limbic-mediated inputs by way of its reciprocal connections with ventrally adjacent anterior cingulate cortex, conveying motivational-behavioral influences concerning internal needs and drives. Thus,

> the SMA would appear to be a major cortical site mediating the interaction between cortical limbic outflow via anterior cingulate cortex, the context-sensitive, goal-setting functions of the prefrontal cortex (whose outputs, along with those of many other associational areas of the cortex, are integrated and refocused onto the SMA via the basal ganglia reentrant circuit), the sensory analysis functions of the association cortex of the superior parietal lobule and the executive components of the motor system. (Goldberg, 1985, p. 577)

Laplane and colleagues (1977) proposed that the SMA acts to initiate and sustain spontaneous motor activity and that damage to the SMA thus produces more severe impairment of internally generated intentional action than environmentally contingent responsive action. Damasio and Van Hoesen (1980) came to similar conclusions in their report of three patients with SMA damage, which we considered earlier. Recall that these investigators hypothesized that the SMA provides the internal "drive for willed movement" but is not necessary for the eventual realization, or execution, of such movement, presumably because it was possible to demonstrate that simple movements could be performed in their SMA-damaged patients when the patients were prompted by external cues.

Goldberg and colleagues (1981) reported two cases, one of which was described earlier, in which left medial frontal cortex infarction involving the SMA caused organized goal-directed movements of the contralateral hand and arm to appear in apparently extravolitional fashion; that is, the movements arose in conflict with the verbalized internal context. This type of striking dissociative disorder has, as we have seen, been labeled the "alien hand sign." Although it has been thought that this disturbance results from a deterioration of interhemispheric communication, Goldberg and colleagues suggested that it might occur with damage to cortical structures like the SMA that lie in the medial wall of the contralateral frontal lobe.

The evidence thus suggests that the SMA normally functions to inhibit extravolitional goal-directed actions, that is, to ensure the intact connection between an action and the internally generated, emotionally, motivationally, and rationally driven "will" that impels it. Untethered from this inner volitional source by SMA damage, the action is captured by the cues of the external environment—situational prompts, commands from other people—and, indeed, in some cases, the affected person attempts to become this externalized environment himself by using language to talk himself through the behavior in question.

Gloor and colleagues (1982) refer to what they call *experiential immediacy*, the feeling that a particular percept or idea "means something." This normally requires the intact connection between neocortical sensory processing areas and limbic–emotional/motivational mechanisms. In some states, such as temporal lobe seizures, there may occur a disconnection between perception and emotion, leading to a flat, empty dissociative state where the world as a whole is experienced "without meaning." Based on this, Goldberg (1985) theorizes that there may be a similar requirement for limbic–emotional/motivational participation in order for an action to be regarded as volitional or self-referenced, in order for an individual to have a felt conviction that his/her action is coming from within, as opposed to being externally induced by hypnosis, suggestion, or direct command.

Thus, if the neural substrate mediating the coupling of limbic drive to the cortical executive motor areas is impaired, one might expect an impoverishment of volitional, inner-directed action and the appearance of relatively automatic behaviors occurring extravolitionally in response to a particular external context or cue. This would result from an abnormal imbalance favoring the initiation of environmentally contingent "automatic" actions, which are *responsive* in nature, rather than internally generated actions, which are *anticipatory*. The individual would become a passive reactor, rather than an active doer.

So it seems that an action owes its expression to a chain of neural mechanisms that first elaborates an intention, translates it into an organized, goal-directed act, and finally programs the sequence of precise neuromuscular events needed to carry it out, being guided all the while by internal and external feedback at each link in the chain. A disturbance in any of these links may be sufficient to deter an action from its ostensible purpose.

Hypothesizing the SMA as the nodal point for turning an intention into an act allows us to further speculate that the various neuropsychodynamic influences that account for an action slip—a "practic parapraxis," as it were—may operate preferentially on the SMA. This is similar to our earlier conception of SSII, the second somatosensory area, being the nodal point for the translation of neuropsychodynamic influences into hysterical conversion symptoms in the somatosensory sphere. Drawing, as Freud did, on the inevitable analogy between hysteria and parapraxes, we might attribute hysterical motor symptoms—immobilities, flailings, bizarre posturings, and so on—to neuropsychodynamic influences on the SMA that are more long-standing and stem from more "pathological" sources than those that characterize the origin of the more mundane action parapraxes of everyday life, following Freud's (1901) distinction, admittedly a fluid one, between neurotic symptoms and everyday slips.

Thus, SSII, SMA, and equivalent processing systems in the brain—some perhaps yet to be discovered—might be the crucial neuropsychodynamic links in our interpretation of inner and outer experience, as well as in the ability to exercise our will upon the world through our overt actions. These "second" and "supplementary" components of the brain's sensory and motor systems might be a good place to focus the efforts of an integrated neuropsychodynamic research program in quest of the connections between the ideogenic and the corporeal.

CHAPTER 16

The Neuropsychopathology of Everyday Life II: Language Slips

As this section of the book has tried to show, the genesis of the Freudian concept of the parapraxis may be found in Freud's early study of the aphasias. Indeed, as we have seen, the subject of language was one that intensely interested Freud throughout his life, and he wove it extensively into his theories of hysteria, dreams, humor, parapraxes, and psychoanalytic psychotherapy.

The Main Aphasic Syndromes: Phenomenology and Neuropsychology

The system of aphasiology that gradually evolved from the studies of Freud and his contemporaries and came to be consensually accepted among neurologists throughout the world has remained, in its broad strokes, essentially intact to this day. We now know that for most people the brain's language system is situated in the region surrounding the sylvian fissure of the left hemisphere. For purposes of context, a brief neurolinguistic précis is provided here.

The ability to produce spoken language in its usual fluid, grammatically correct form has been shown to rely on *Broca's area*, located at the foot of the third frontal convolution and named for Pierre Paul Broca (1861), who first described the syndrome of expressive speech disturbance. Damage to Broca's area produces an *expressive*, or *Broca's*, *aphasia* in which speech output is reduced, lacks fluency, is agrammatical, and may consist only of short explosive bursts of barely related utterances; the person seems generally unable to "put things into words." Damage to *Wernicke's area* (after Carl Wernicke, 1874), located in the posterior–superior temporal gyrus, results in a deficit in speech comprehension, that is, in *receptive*, or *Wernicke's*, *aphasia*. Speech may be fluent but semantically empty and jargony because the person has lost the ability to comprehend and thus monitor his own speech processes, as well as the speech of others. He is thus unable to understand what is said to him.

When the *arcuate fasciculus* connecting Broca's and Wernicke's areas is damaged, but the two eponymous regions themselves are spared, *conduction aphasia* results. Comprehension is essentially intact and speech output may seem fairly normal, although there is some *paraphasia*, or word confusion, as in using one word for another or mixing up the sounds of two different words (see the description in Chapter 13 of Freud's 1891 account). The most striking finding in conduction aphasia is the inability to repeat phrases spoken by another person, presumably because the connection between the comprehension system and the speech system has been interrupted.

In *transcortical aphasia*, Broca's and Wernicke's areas, as well as the arcuate fasciculus connecting them, are preserved, but the cortical areas surrounding the perisylvian speech zone have been damaged. This, in effect, deprives the speech zone of input from other association areas; the speech system itself is functional, but it has little to "talk about." Spontaneous speech may be reduced, comprehension may be impaired, but repetition is preserved—more than preserved, in many cases, since speech may have a compulsively imitative, echolalic, quality to it. In isolation from the rest of the brain, the language apparatus may operate as a sort of automatic, disembodied "speech-repeater."

Anomic aphasia, or just *anomia*, is the most common form of language disorder and typically has no specific localization. It may be seen in association with any of the other aphasias and is usually the first harbinger of a progressive neurological disorder affecting the language system and the last to clear up in a resolving neurological syndrome. Most language disorders in actual clinical practice are partial syndromes, combinations, or blends of the main aphasic classes. Disorders of reading and writing, *alexia* and *agraphia*, occur with damage to other areas of the brain that are connected with the central perisylvian language zone. Finally, *dysarthrias* and *dysphonias* involve the muscles of articulation and phonation and are not strictly disorders of language per se, although they frequently co-occur with them.

Paroxysmal Language Disorders

Although strokes, traumatic injuries, surgery, and other insults that damage the structure of the brain more or less permanently are the most frequent causes of organic aphasia, more transiently occurring and unusual forms of language disorder may result from other types of brain events. For example, transient inability to speak may be a symptom of an epileptic seizure (Rasmussen, 1974). Focal seizures arising from the motor cortex of either the dominant or nondominant cerebral hemisphere may cause speech arrest by interfering with the movement of the muscles of articulation—a dysarthria. When the seizure discharge involves the language areas around the sylvian fissure of the left hemisphere, there is transient epileptic aphasia. These phenomena are rarely the sole manifestations of an epileptic attack and are usually followed or accompanied by some kind of epileptic motor activity. Even less common is epileptic aphasia due to seizure activity in the supplementary motor area (SMA) of the dominant hemisphere, as in the following case, reported by Peled (1984).

A sixty-five-year-old right-handed man, a heavy smoker with chronic lung disease, mild diabetes, and hypertriglyceridemia, began over the course of two weeks to experience attacks of sudden inability to talk. These episodes lasted two to three minutes and recurred three to four times a day. He was admitted to the hospital and several times during his first two days there he suddenly became mute for about three minutes. During this period of speech arrest, he understood spoken commands, and there was no abnormal motor activity or paresis. He could repeat pantomimed motor tasks with both hands, but he could not write. EEG was normal between these attacks.

Because of the patient's history of diabetes, high triglycerides, and heavy smoking, his doctors at first suspected that the periods of speech arrest were short aphasic episodes due to transient ischemic attacks in the territory of the left carotid artery, the main source of blood supply to the brain. However, on one occasion, after being mute for about a minute, the patient suddenly raised his right hand and followed it with his gaze and a right head turn. This episode lasted about three minutes and subsided spontaneously, which suggested that the episodes were epileptic tonic adversive seizures.

This conclusion was reinforced by another such attack in which sudden rhythmic twitches on the right side of the face were followed by convulsions of the right extended arm and the right leg. The convulsions soon spread to the left side of the body and ended in a full-blown generalized tonic–clonic (grand mal) seizure with loss of consciousness and postictal confusion. CT scan demonstrated a suspicious small, round lesion in the upper posterior medial portion of the left frontal lobe, and a few days later, after left frontal craniotomy, a tumor was removed from the left SMA, just anterior to the motor leg region.

In conceptualizing the case, Peled (1984) cites Penfield and Roberts's (1959) earlier demonstration that electrical stimulation of the SMA in the superior parasagittal area of the frontal lobe could produce transient inability to speak. Electrical stimulation of either hemisphere might cause speech arrest by interrupting the motor mechanisms of vocalization whereas stimulation of the left SMA could cause an actual aphasic inability to speak by interfering with the language mechanism itself. According to Rasmussen (1974), aphasia can also occur, although rarely, as a manifestation of an epileptic seizure, resulting from paroxysmal neuronal discharge in the cortical language areas. Seizures arising in the left SMA may begin with a brief period of aphasic speech arrest, followed in most cases by a postural tonic seizure. We may thus consider that in nonepileptic cases, in the ordinary kind of verbal parapraxis where we "forget what we were saying" or have the experience where our "words die in our throats," we may be seeing disturbances in the same brain mechanisms produced by similar, if more subtle, paroxysmal events.

Just as seizure disorders can produce paroxysmal, parapraxis-like language phenomena, so, it appears, can migraine. Fleishman and colleagues (1983) report the case of a sixty-year-old right-handed woman who had enjoyed good general health, except for frequent headaches as an adolescent and young adult. These were severe and throbbing, often being centered behind the eyes or presenting as a tight band across the forehead. There was a strong family history of migraine. The episode of interest occurred while the patient was on vacation in the Caribbean, and she was able to provide an unusually detailed chronicle of the course of her attack.

> That day we were all on a picnic. We went in an open boat to a different beach, had lunch and snorkeled. I felt okay coming back on the boat, but later I felt headachy and nauseated. I was lying down, and picked up something to read, and realized that I could not comprehend the words that I was seeing. I think I could read individual letters, or at least some of them. I could recognize that [the letters] were individual. I knew what they were in a different sense than I knew words. I recognized that they were letters I knew, and I recognized they were words I knew, but I didn't know them. It was like seeing something in a different country. I really have trouble describing it.
>
> My usual thing is to be calm on the surface. I must have tried to read for five or ten minutes before I called my husband, because I couldn't understand . . . I couldn't believe it. I tried to read aloud to my husband. I remember saying "T . . . H . . ." and the word "THE," but then I had a really hard time. I would say a word and then say "That's not right," and then try again. He said that there were some words that I did not get right that I didn't pick up on, and some that I did. I felt like a kid trying to sound it out. My vision was fine, I saw the letters clearly . . . I think I could have traced the letters. I was not aware of any other impairment. My husband said it lasted about half an hour. After a while, I said "I can't do this anymore," and I went to sleep. (Fleishman et al., 1983, p. 115)

In conceptualizing their case, Fleishman and colleagues (1983) note that from the time of Dejerine's (1891, 1892) classic case reports, two distinct types of alexia have been recognized (also see Benson, 1979). *Alexia with agraphia* is associated with damage to the angular gyrus of the left hemisphere, and involvement of surrounding tissue may result in accompanying right hemiparesis, right hemisensory impairment, or a right visual field loss. The syndrome of *alexia without agraphia*, or *pure alexia*, is less common and is associated with damage to the dominant occipital lobe and splenium, or rear section, of the corpus callosum. The patient experiences a right homonymous hemianopia, a preserved ability to write, but impaired ability to read—even to read what he/she has just written. With varying degrees of severity, this may be accompained by difficulty in naming colors and objects. Greenblatt (1976) described a closely related syndrome of "subangular alexia" in which a lesion deep in the white matter of the left parietal lobe undercuts the angular gyrus; patients with such well-localized lesions have alexia without agraphia or hemianopia.

Fleishman and colleagues (1983) further point out that the pattern and nature of migrainous attacks often change during mid-life. In fact, migrainous accompaniments—the "migraine equivalents" we discussed in a previous chapter—may first appear after age forty in the absence of a prior history of migraine in what has been described as a "flurry" of mid-life migraine activity (Fisher, 1971, 1980). In Fleishman and colleagues' case, the personal and family history of migraine argues strongly for migraine-induced vasospasm as the mechanism responsible for their patient's alexic episode.

Apparently, migraine-induced transient language disturbance is not so rare an occurrence. Bigley and Sharp (1983) report the case of a thirty-five-year-old physician who had experienced two attacks, spaced three years apart, of right homonymous hemianopia followed by bifrontal throbbing headaches lasting twelve to twenty-four hours; the last episode was also followed by five minutes of numbness and decreased coordination in his right hand. Two years later, while waiting for a train to take him home after a sleepless thirty-six-hour shift on call, the doctor experienced a right homonymous hemianopia. Forty-five minutes later his vision returned to normal, but he developed a dull, throbbing bifrontal headache.

It was then that he attempted to read his ticket stub and discovered that although he could see individual letters and words on the stub, he could not understand what they meant. He tried to sound out the syllables, but the content of the words remained incomprehensible. When asked for directions by another train passenger, the doctor was able to give an appropriate reply, and his own speech sounded normal to him. He then heard and understood several announcements over the railway station loudspeaker and responded properly to the conductor's request for his ticket.

During the course of this episode the doctor made notations on his ticket stub of the time of onset and duration of his symptoms, and his handwriting appeared intact. About thirty minutes later he regained his ability to comprehend the words on his ticket stub, as well as sentences from a book he was carrying. He then noted numbness in his right hand that lasted for five minutes; this was followed by a throbbing bifrontal headache that persisted for twenty-four hours.

In conceptualizing their case, Bigley and Sharp (1983) note that alexia without agraphia is typically caused by lesions that interrupt both right and left visual cortex outflow to the dominant angular gyrus (Benson, 1979; Geschwind, 1965). Dejerine's (1892) original case and most subsequent cases have resulted from infarction of the left posterior cerebral artery, but many other causes have been described. In Bigley and Sharp's migraine-induced case, ischemia of the inferior occipital lobe, which is supplied by the lateral occipital branch of the posterior cerebral artery, could have caused the doctor's transient alexia without agraphia. The intact full visual fields indicate that the calcarine branch of the medial occipital artery was supplying adequate flow to the visual cortex. Finally, the transient right-hand numbness could have resulted from vasoconstriction of the proximal thalamogeniculate branches of the posterior cerebral artery that supply the ventral posterior thalamus, a thalamic nucleus important in somatosensory processing.

Permanent Language Disorders: Generality versus Specificity

Clinicians tend to assume that organic language disorders will be rather global in their effects, while psychogenic, or functional, language disorders may be more selective, depending on the specific symbolic significance of the content. Syndromes like alexia without agraphia, either permanent or transient, show us that functions we commonly regard as indissoluble wholes during states of health may be functionally dissected by neurologic disease—or by the neuropsychodynamic alterations that occur "in everyday life." But what about instances where this neuropsychodynamic selectivity seems to affect not the process but the very content of what is impaired and what is spared?

Consider the case, reported by Hart and colleagues (1985), of a thirty-four-year-old right-handed college graduate and systems analyst for a large U.S. government agency who suffered a left-hemisphere stroke, resulting at first in a global aphasia and right hemiparesis. Within a month this had resolved to a mild expressive aphasia with mild hemiparesis. The patient subsequently experienced several transient ischemic attacks, and a left internal carotid artery occlusion was diagnosed. CT scan obtained at one month postonset revealed an infarction of the left frontal lobe and basal ganglia.

More than two years later, the patient was still experiencing considerable difficulty naming certain objects. Anomia is a common residual poststroke language disorder; the remarkable feature of this case, however, was that the naming disorder was confined exclusively to the semantic category of fruits and vegetables. The patient showed a strikingly circumscribed inability to name such common items as a peach or orange from his visual inspection of them or pictures of them, while being able to easily name less common objects, such as an abacus and sphinx. He could categorize items correctly as fruits or vegetables when their names were presented auditorily, suggesting that this was not a conceptual confusion but a bona fide disorder of naming restricted to items seen visually or pictorially. This conclusion was supported by his ability to categorize correctly all the *written* names of the same fruits and vegetables whose pictures he had found difficult to classify.

Hart and colleagues (1985) point out three important implications of this case for the ultimate development of what they believe would be a unified theory of language. First, the selective impairment of information in specific superordinate categories suggests that the brain's organization of the semantic system—the system of "meanings"—in some sense honors those categorical distinctions. That is, if disorders of naming can occur only with respect to fruits and vegetables, then fruits and vegetables, as well as other equally narrow categories, may be organized—in some people's brains at least—as self-contained units of knowledge.

Second, the dissociation in categorization ability between performance with lexical, or written, instances (which is intact) and with pictorial instances (which is impaired) suggests that lexical categorization can be accomplished on the basis of strictly lexical, as opposed to semantic, information. That is, how the material is presented—in writing versus as a picture or the thing itself—may be more important to the brain's filing systems than what that material actually consists of (fruits, vegetables, or whatever).

Third, although a general dissociation between name recognition and name retrieval has been supported previously by results from aphasic patients, the category-specific dissociation found in this case indicates that the output lexicon is addressed by semantically categorized information that can be disrupted highly selectively. In other words, particular classes of input can affect the retrieval of names from the memory store in a highly selective way.

But what is the nature of the memory process itself?

CHAPTER 17

The Neuropsychopathology of Everyday Life III: Memory Slips

The subject of memory is important to virtually every aspect of psychoanalytic theory. Without memory, after all, how could unconscious material exist in the psyche? And what determines the kinds of things we remember, what we forget, and what, stored deeply within the inner precincts of the mind, stubbornly resists our will to recall it?

The Memory Systems: Phenomenology and Neuropsychology

Many neuropsychologists like to think of memory in terms of four main stages or categories: input, consolidation, storage, and retrieval. *Input* refers to the initial reception of stimuli by the brain, and disturbances may result from sensory processing deficits or difficulty shifting, focusing, or maintaining attention; obviously, you cannot remember something if it did not "get in" in the first place. *Consolidation* involves a sort of "stamping in" and cross-indexing of the incoming data with other material already stored in the brain. If this process is interrupted, the material may be forgotten after only a short time, since it has had little time to "peg" itself onto other, related, kinds of material. The more unfamiliar the material is, the less of this neural cross-referencing can occur and therefore the more easily it is forgotten.

Where consolidation ends and *storage* begins may be somewhat difficult to pin down precisely, but the latter term is generally used to describe a more stable, long-lasting incorporation and integration of material as it becomes multiply represented throughout the brain. Information stored

210

in memory, especially if it is recalled, referenced, and used repeatedly, is usually quite refractory to loss through organic brain damage, although exceptions do occur, as we will soon see. Finally, all the consolidation and storage in the world does little good if one cannot access that information when one needs it, that is, if one cannot exercise the function of *retrieval*. Of course, intact storage with faulty retrieval is basic to the definition of *repression*, which is so important a concept in psychoanalysis.

Once again generalizing for the purposes of discussion, there appear to be two main types or classes of memory impairment syndrome that neuropsychologists typically encounter, each associated with damage to different combinations of the types of memory processes just considered, and each involving separate components of the brain's memory system. In *hippocampal*, or *temporal lobe*, *amnesia* there is usually no significant problem in the initial input stage or in retrieving information from the long-term memory store, but the ability to consolidate and store new information is disrupted. Events that the person has experienced over and over again since the injury, people he has met, things he has done, simply fail to "register"; the patient lives in a world dominated by what he has learned and experienced up to the time of the injury.

The most striking cases of this syndrome occur after bilateral anterior temporal lobe surgery for the control of intractable epilepsy, an operation that removes the anterior temporal lobes and the hippocampi that lie within them, which are important for memory consolidation; this is what happened to "H. M." (Milner et al., 1968), probably the single most famous case in modern clinical neuropsychology. Other, less common, causes include bilateral posterior cerebral artery strokes and herpes simplex encephalitis. More transient forms of this syndrome occur after electroconvulsive therapy, a grand mal seizure, a blow to the head producing unconsciousness, or other events that temporarily interfere with memory consolidation.

A different kind of memory syndrome results when the damage is relatively restricted to the vicinity of the dorsomedial nucleus of the thalamus and the mammillary bodies of the hypothalamus, which lie in the subcortical diencephalon of the brain. In this accordingly named *diencephalic amnesia*, the main deficits are in initial input of information and especially in the retrieval of what may have been otherwise adequately consolidated and stored. The patient fails to recall information when needed, even though specialized testing, cuing, and prompting may demonstrate that the material is "in there" in some form or another.

The rich reciprocal connections of this diencephalic memory system with the frontal lobes accounts for why context-appropriate retrieval deficits occur commonly in the frontal lobe syndrome discussed in earlier chapters. The most prominent type of diencephalic memory disorder is seen in patients with Korsakoff's syndrome (whose dreams so impressed Freud, remember), in which the pathological process affects specifically those diencephalic structures around the third ventricle that are involved in memory, namely the dorsomedial thalamus and the mammillary bodies. But in organic memory disorders, as with other neuropsychological phenomena, transient syndromes may occur, which we consider next.

Amnesias: Global and Partial, Transient and Permanent

The syndrome of isolated confusion with amnesia was originally described by Bender (1956) and later designated *transient global amnesia* (TGA) by Fisher and Adams (1958, 1964). Transient global amnesia is described as a temporary, albeit relatively prolonged, episode of memory impairment, to be distinguished from transient amnesia associated with obvious temporal lobe epilepsy, cerebral ischemia, or brain tumors compressing the neuroanatomical structures important for memory. Transient global amnesia occurs mainly in persons older than fifty, usually presents without other neurological symptoms, and commonly lasts between four and eight hours, durations beyond twenty-four hours being rare.

Consciousness and a knowledge of one's own identity are usually preserved. Immediate recall may be intact, but there is usually an inability to acquire new information of any length or complexity, a relative loss of memory for recent events—including those of the attack itself—and a variable retrograde amnesia that may extend backward in time for days to years. During the attack the patient is typically perplexed, anxious, and aware of his memory difficulties. Rarely are other neurological deficits present, and the performance of common, routine, everyday tasks is largely unimpaired. In some cases, simple behavior may appear quite normal until the person is required to do something demanding or out of the ordinary.

The cerebral conditions responsible for the syndrome are unclear, but transient ischemic attacks (Heathfield et al., 1973; Jensen & Olivarius, 1981), epileptic discharges (Fisher & Adams, 1964), and migrainous disturbances (Caplan et al., 1981; Olivarius & Jensen, 1979) have all been considered. Although most authorities regard the etiology as vascular, Fisher (1982; Fisher & Adams, 1964) believes that a seizure-like electrophysiological disturbance typically underlies the disorder.

Fisher (1982) reported a series of cases in which attacks of transient global amnesia were precipitated by a variety of stressful circumstances. These cases are especially relevant to our present discussion because of the similarity to descriptions in the psychodynamic literature of traumatic events producing psychogenic or hysterical losses of memory. Note also the striking similarity to the quintessentially "Freudian" types of parapraxes described in *The Psychopathology of Everyday Life*. Indeed, without any inkling of their organic etiology, these cases could easily be attributed to purely psychogenic causes. Instead, perhaps we can view them as prime examples of how organicity determines the process while psychology shapes the content—one of the key precepts of the neuropsychodynamic model. Some typical cases follow.

A man was handcuffed and robbed in his drugstore by two thieves. When the police arrived, he was able to recount the robbery to them— just before losing all memory for the event.

A woman's husband died suddenly before her eyes, whereupon she became amnesic for the next eighteen hours.

A woman whose daughter had been receiving obscene phone calls for five years was persuaded by the police to participate in a plan to trap the perpetrator. The mother was to wait for the offending caller to make contact and then immediately set off a series of electronic signals. The call came but no signals were activated; the woman was subsequently found in an amnesic state that lasted for four hours. She later recalled hearing the obscene caller's voice, but her next memory was of being in the emergency room two hours later.

A proud man had been forced to resign from his longtime position, an action that hurt him deeply. On his last day of work he got up in the morning and asked bewilderedly, "What was I supposed to do today?" His memory returned in about six hours.

While dejectedly walking to a bank to sign a document authorizing the state to confiscate his family business, a man became amnesic and forgot to keep the appointment.

A woman was having a bitter argument with her husband concerning another woman whom they blamed for their son's suicide when she suddenly asked, "Where did I get this dress?" Upon looking around, she noticed that the apartment in which the couple had lived for the last nine years now appeared foreign to her.

A man was tearfully participating in a church service dedicating a pipe organ presented in memory of his late wife when he began to read the same sentences in his prayer book over and over again.

In conceptualizing these cases, Fisher (1982) notes that a common precipitating factor was some kind of emotionally charged event. Inasmuch as memory and emotion involve closely related brain systems, that is, the hippocampus and limbic system, it is not surprising that abnormally intense neurophysiological events in one might trigger disturbances in the other, although the precise mechanism by which this occurs remains to be clarified. Certainly, however, such events are the exception rather than the rule, and Fisher speculates that in some cases the effects of aging might predispose certain people to a neurophysiological instability in this brain system. Also of note in many of these transient amnesic attacks is a certain blunting of emotion itself, which presents clinically as a notable contrast between the severity of the situation, that is, having a serious memory lapse, and the mildness of the patient's reaction—compare *la belle indifférence* of hysteria.

The most prominent feature during spells of transient global amnesia in these cases was the constant repetition of questions or comments. The questions were always repeated in approximately the same order, using almost identical sentences and words. It was as if a fragment of behavior had become "trapped" and a neural program was being played over and over like a needle stuck in a record groove. Fisher (1982) speculates that when the proper functioning of the hippocampal–limbic system is interrupted, the rest of the brain may become a sort of stereotyped "query machine." That is, most behavior we typically engage in is goal-directed, and if the object or purpose of that goal is disturbed by interference with the memory system, the interrogative activity of the brain perseverates aimlessly in a sort of disembodied state. The fact that the central nervous system becomes repetitious when memory fails suggests that this hippocampal–limbic system plays an essential role in the onward progressive flow of neural activity from moment to moment, as one experience or thought succeeds another.

But is transient global amnesia always *global*? The aforementioned cases were notable for the fact that during the attacks the patients existed in a kind of fugue state of fluctuating awareness. Even if the instigating circumstances had a psychodynamic flavor to them, the extent of the disturbance of normal waking consciousness was far greater than what we would expect to see in the context of a typical Freudian parapraxis. Do organic analogues exist of the more usual cases where some aspects of memory are disturbed but mental intactness is otherwise largely preserved?

Such appears to be the case in the following report by Damasio and colleagues (1983). A fifty-four-year-old right-handed woman with an advanced degree in physics and a successful career as a science editor had suffered from motion sickness as a child and began having simple migraine headaches at about age forty-five. About nine months previously, the character of the headaches changed to classic migraine with visual half-field disturbances. On one occasion the patient had difficulty with language, especially writing, and another time she experienced what she described as a "strange event." Like the migrainous woman in the last chapter who assiduously chronicled her language difficulties during her attack, the present patient kept a detailed running account of the course of her episode:

Looking at my work. Don't recognize the page of the manuscript I am editing! Flip back and forth, but can't make up my mind what exactly I was doing. (Am clear about the main purpose, not the page I'm on or what I was doing to it.)

Looking at my calendar to enter note of this "event," find names of people I dealt with in last ten days disturb me: I am not sure who they are. Most entries, though, are clear to me.

I read back what I wrote at beginning of the first page: I don't recognize the wording I used! I remember starting to write this, but I'm interested that the beginning of it seems strange.

Every time I read back some of what I have written, I find statements that puzzle me because I don't remember putting them down. Trivial wordings, but still they puzzle me because I don't recognize them. (Note: all along I have been sure of what, who, where I am and what I am doing here.)

When I first looked at my calendar to write down the note about this episode, I found I was puzzled by a couple of names I could see.

Got to lunch all right. Felt unsure of identity of old friends in the hall. But conversed OK. Got to the lunch line and had moment of panic about how to sign in, then remembered. However, glanced at what person before me wrote on the card to be sure. Started my Social Security number and had slight panic before finishing it, I assume correctly. (Damasio et al., 1983, p. 656)

The symptoms had largely cleared by the end of the day, and were gone by the next morning. When the patient was seen by the doctors, her neuropsychological testing was normal but EEG showed electrophysiological abnormalities from the region of the left temporal lobe.

In conceptualizing their case, Damasio and colleagues (1983) note that the history and findings in this patient are compatible with a diagnosis of classic migraine. They cite Caplan and colleagues' (1981) review to support the idea that in many cases such episodes as described here are the result of migraine-induced transient ischemia in the memory-related structures of the temporal lobe limbic system. This patient also had abnormal electophysiological activity in the left anterior temporal region, which may have been independent of migraine or part of the syndrome itself (cf. Lennox & Lennox's [1960] concept of "migralepsy" discussed in Chapter 5).

When told by the doctors about the diagnosis of transient global amnesia, the patient replied that there had been nothing "global" about her memory loss at all, and that she herself would prefer to call her amnesia "partial." Typical of transient amnesias, her episode occurred suddenly, lasted about five hours, and terminated without residual deficit. At no point during the attack did the patient lose her personal orientation or become agitated, although she was moderately anxious and understandably concerned with her bizarre condition. Nevertheless, she retained the ability to reflect on and chronicle her experiences and actions and was able to "remember that she could not remember" during the episode— what Freud would regard as the sine qua non of a memory parapraxis.

Damasio and colleagues (1983) speculate that this patient's preserved spatial orientation and nonverbal memory for the episode were due to sparing of the structures in the right temporal lobe during the attack while structures in the left temporal lobe were affected. The preserved right-sided structures could have maintained normal function and permitted proper nonverbal evocation related to the encoding of the events that were taking place.

A case with yet a different presentation—a truly global and long-lasting amnesia (or "nontransient partial amnesia"?)—appeared not in the professional literature but as a human-interest story in a daily newspaper (Palm Beach Post, 1985). On February 24, 1971, forty-nine-year-old James McDonnell of Larchmont, New York, fell down the back stairs of his home. The next day he lost control of his car during a violent sneezing fit and crashed. The day after that, while at work, he complained of dizziness and a headache and fell down another flight of stairs. On March 11 he had yet another car accident, which resulted in a brief loss of consciousness and a mild concussion. On March 29, 1971, he decided to walk home from an errand instead of taking a bus because he had a headache and thought some fresh air would do him good. That was the last his family saw of him. "The next thing I knew I was in Philadelphia," the newspaper article quotes him as saying. "I don't know how I got there."

As the years passed with no sign of her husband's return, McDonnell's wife, Anne, had him declared legally dead in 1976 but claims she kept hoping that someday he would return. She continued to live at the couple's house in Larchmont and retained the telephone listing under his name. On Christmas morning, 1985, Mrs. McDonnell had returned from church and was preparing breakfast when the doorbell rang and her now sixty-four-year-old husband appeared and said, "Hello, Anne."

Mr. McDonnell related to his wife that he had spent the last fifteen years in Philadelphia as Jim Peters, a short-order cook, bartender, and seasonal Santa Claus for children at an orphanage. He apparently remembered that his first name was Jim, but he took the surname Peters from a storefront. He lived in Philadephia in a house that he bought, and he occasionally played poker with his new friends. On Christmas Eve, he claimed, he bumped his head in the cellar of the luncheonette where he worked. The lost memories of his past life flooded back, and he rushed home to Larchmont on the next train. His main problems to date have been getting himself restored to legal living status, looking for a job, and settling insurance matters.

One is tempted to dismiss such a case as factitious, since it seems less in the nature of an organic memory disorder than something along the lines of the Hollywood bonk-on-the-head: "where-am-I?" version of amnesia. But consider the following description of nine well-studied cases reported by Haas and Ross (1986). In each of these patients, aged eleven to twenty-eight, a mild head injury triggered an amnesic attack grossly out of proportion to the degree of trauma. During these attacks patients were unable to form new memories for two to twenty-four hours, had extensive retrograde amnesia, voiced repetitive queries, were disoriented for time, but were otherwise neurologically intact.

One case from this series involves a twenty-four-year-old woman who was arguing with her husband when she accidently stepped on a shoe, lost her balance, and fell backward, striking her head on a wooden night table. She immediately rose from the floor, sobbing and holding her head in pain. Her husband dutifully applied an ice pack to her bleeding scalp and then drove her to the hospital. During the trip the woman began to ask repeatedly what had happened to her and who was taking care of the children. Despite her husband's responses to these questions, she kept asking over and over again all during the journey to the hospital—recall Fisher's (1982) description of the memory-disconnected brain as a "query machine."

In the emergency room the woman was able to recognize her husband, knew where she was, and recalled her home address and the names of her three young children. However, she did not know the month or the year, had no memory of the doctors attending her, and could not recall having had her scalp shaved and sutured. Later that evening she complained of a mild headache. Up until the time her husband left her hospital bedside, she continued to ask the same questions she had asked during the ride to the hospital.

On the morning of the second hospital day the patient's overall condition was unchanged and the repetitive inquiries continued unabated. At this point, the extent of her recent and remote memory problem was becoming clear. She had no recollection of her sister having had a baby two days before the fall or of herself holding the infant the morning of the accident. She could not recall the Thanksgiving holiday celebration at her house five days earlier and was unable to remember a recent local election. However, by evening she was able to remember most of what was said to her, and her retrograde amnesia was less severe. Recent and remote memory remained partially impaired for several days. The woman has remained permanently and totally amnesic for the accident itself and for the subsequent twenty-four hours.

In conceptualizing their cases, Haas and Ross (1986) note that all the patients, including the woman just described, were alert and articulate after their "mild" head injuries, although they appeared slightly bewildered about what had happened. Although disoriented for time and unable to form new, lasting memories—thus being left with permanent amnesia for the period surrounding the accidents—immediate recall seemed to be preserved. Apart from the amnesia and disorientation, intellectual functions were largely intact. All of these features, together with the retrograde amnesia and repetitive queries and comments, are exactly like those said to characterize transient global amnesia (Bender, 1956, 1960; Fisher, 1982). If so, the authors suggest, head trauma—even apparently minor head trauma, by the usual clinical criteria—can be added to the list of other hypothesized TGA precipitants, such as electrophysiological dysfunction and cerebral ischemia.

Haas and Ross (1986) propose that these kinds of posttraumatic amnesic attacks constitute a previously unrecognized variant of posttraumatic migraine. Other types of temporary neurological disturbance have been reported after mild head injuries, mainly in children and young adults. These include confusion, hemiparesis, blindness, amnesia, or varying combinations of these symptoms. Headache and vomiting are typically part of the clinical picture, and these attacks usually last from hours to about a day or so. In general, the literature suggests that these episodes are manifestations of migrainous cerebral disturbances triggered by mild blows to the head (Haas & Lourie, 1984). According to Haas and Ross (1986), the amnesic cases in their present series have much in common with traumatic migraine. Both are disturbances of cerebral function grossly disproportionate to the degree of head trauma, both are self-limited episodes with durations generally in the range of a few hours to a day, and both occur primarily in children and young adults and may affect a person more than once.

Amnesia: Organic or Psychogenic?

Like the specific language deficits (as for fruits and vegetables) discussed in the last chapter, impairment that involves a dissociation between narrowly specific classes of memory content is often viewed as a sure sign of functional memory disturbance. When the impairment is mild, the dissociation is dismissed as a parapraxis; when it is severe, it is regarded more seriously as an hysterical memory loss. *Retrograde amnesia* refers to impairment in the ability to remember events and facts perceived and encoded prior to a critical precipitating brain event and is distinguished from *anterograde amnesia*, which is failure to consolidate and retain new information learned after the critical event. In cases of *organic* retrograde amnesia, the precipitating incident usually takes the form of brain disease, head trauma, or electroconvulsive shock treatment (Angelergues, 1969; Butters, 1979; Hirst, 1982; Kopelman, 1987; Squire, 1982, 1986).

But retrograde amnesia may also occur in the complete absence of detectable brain pathology; it may then be regarded as a consequence of severe *psychological* trauma and termed *functional retrograde amnesia.* The onset of this functional retrograde amnesia is often dramatic: patients suddenly cannot remember their name, where they live, or anything about their personal past. The inconsistency between the profound nature of the retrograde memory loss and the often otherwise intact neurological and neuropsychological profile is what typically raises the suspicion that the memory problem is psychogenic.

Schacter and colleagues (1982) directly addressed the issue of functional versus organic amnesia in their quantitative description of memory performance by a patient suffering from functional retrograde amnesia. Their study also tested the hypothesis that functional retrograde amnesia entails a differential impairment of episodic versus semantic memory. As originally described by Tulving (1972), *episodic memory* is concerned with information about personal experiences that are tied to a particular temporal and spatial context, for example, what a good time you had when you spent the summer of 1976 at your Uncle Fred's bungalow in Maine. In contrast, *semantic memory* is concerned with general knowledge of facts, rules, and concepts, knowledge that is not linked to specific autobiographical events, for example, that the boiling point of water is two hundred twelve degrees Fahrenheit or that George Bush is the current U.S. president in 1991. The episodic—semantic distinction has proved useful in studies of organic amnesia, where the two types of memory are sometimes found to be dissociated by different forms of brain damage.

Schacter and colleagues' presumably psychogenic case concerned a twenty-one-year-old Canadian man with a tenth-grade education. He had approached a policeman on the street in downtown Toronto complaining of excruciating back pains and was immediately taken to a local hospital. He carried no identification, and when he was questioned in the emergency room about who he was and where he was from, it became clear that he could not remember his name, address, or almost any other information about himself or his past. However, the patient did give a nickname, "Lumberjack," and reported working for a courier service during the year prior to his hospitalization. When contacted, the courier service confirmed the patient's employment and also mentioned that he had been given the nickname "Lumberjack" by his fellow workers. The patient knew what city he was in and was able to name many of the major downtown streets, as well as the name of the local baseball and hockey teams. He also knew the name of the prime minister of Canada and possessed some information about recent political events.

The patient's photo was published in a newspaper; a cousin saw it and came to the hospital the next day. She identified the patient, but he did not recognize her. The cousin reported that the patient's grandfather had died the previous week and that the patient had been closer to his grandfather than to any other person. However, the patient himself did not recall going to the funeral and could not remember anything about his grandfather.

His amnesia cleared the next evening while he was watching an elaborate cremation and funeral sequence in the concluding episode of the television miniseries *Shogun*. He later reported that as he watched the funeral scene, an image of his grandfather began to take shape in his mind. He then remembered his grandfather's death, as well as the recent funeral. During the next few hours the large sections of his personal past that had been inaccessible for the previous four days also returned. After emerging from the amnesic episode, the patient was able to recall what had happened to him during the twelve hours prior to the time he first became aware that he did not know who he was. The last thing he remembered was walking at night on a downtown street after his grandfather's funeral in a state of shock and depression.

The patient was given a general medical and neurological workup, as well as a neuropsychological assessment. His medical history included a motor vehicle accident at the age of four in which he sustained some damage to the right temporal region. A CT scan revealed evidence of previous right-sided temporal damage, and there was an area of decreased density that probably represented gliosis. No other abnormalities were observed.

For the purposes of this study, semantic memory was investigated with the Famous Faces Test from the Boston Retrograde Amnesia Battery. This test includes forty-eight faces of people who became famous during each of the six decades from the 1920s to the 1970s. Episodic memory was assessed with an autobiographical cuing procedure. In this task, subjects are presented with a common English word and asked to retrieve a specific personal memory related to it; they are also required to date the retrieved event.

The patient's performance on the Famous Faces Test, tapping semantic memory, was nearly identical across two test sessions while his performance on the autobiographical cuing procedure, tapping episodic memory, substantially changed from session to session. Cuing procedures revealed that in spite of the patient's restricted access to episodic memory during the amnestic period, a relatively intact "island" of episodic memories could be uncovered.

In conceptualizing their case, Schacter and colleagues (1982) point out that one of the most consistently reported observations of organic retrograde amnesia is that it is temporally organized; that is, there is a gradient of impairment from more recent to more remote memories. Early clinical investigators claimed that retrieval of recently acquired memories is more severely impaired than retrieval of older memories (Ribot, 1882; Russell & Nathan, 1932); recent experimental studies have tended to confirm this observation, at least in some patient groups (Albert et al., 1979; Squire & Cohen, 1982). Unlike the case in typical organic amnesias, then, in the present patient's functional amnesia, recent memories did not seem to be less accessible than remote memories. He was able to retrieve scattered episodic memories from a number of different times in his life and to retrieve many memories from the "island" that included events of about one year prior to testing.

Schacter and colleagues (1982) suggest that a clue to the nature of the organization of functional retrograde amnesia may come from considering one aspect of the memories that constituted this patient's "island"; these memories were characterized by the presence of considerable positive emotion. During the amnesic period "Lumberjack" described his job at the courier service in the pleasantest of terms, noting that "I really liked that job" and "I enjoyed working there—it was a lot of fun." After the amnesia cleared, he described his time at the courier service as one of the happiest periods in his life whereas most of his other experiences were described in either neutral or negative terms. These observations suggest to Schacter and colleagues that functional retrograde amnesia may be primarily organized along *affective* lines, rather than according to the temporal dimension found in organic amnesia.

It would in fact be easy to argue that this functional retrograde amnesia case was not so "functional" after all. There was a history of head injury, as well as positive, or at least suggestive, CT findings. But perhaps cases like these best illustrate, again, the neuropsychodynamic principle that organicity may determine the mechanism of a symptom or parapraxis but the content depends on a complex constellation of individual predisposition, life history, and precipitating circumstances.

Parapraxic Misidentification

Staton and colleagues (1982) report the case of a twenty-three-year old man with no past neurologic or psychiatric history who was found unconscious after a car accident. At the hospital, X rays revealed no skull fracture but EEG showed right temporal slowing. The patient recovered from the acute effects of the injury, but eight years after the accident he was, at age thirty-one, unmarried and unemployed. He said he felt desperate and described living in a world that seemed to be a fantasy. Friends and relatives, including his parents and siblings, were not "real" but were slightly altered "look-alikes," or doubles. This was also true of places, including the family farm and the city where he was hospitalized. He even denied that he was the true version of himself, because several aspects of his present appearance, including a lost tooth and a foot callus, were different from what he remembered. "If I were really me, I'd have a place of my own—I'd be working," he asserted.

He described several elaborate delusions or confabulations that seemed to ease the desperation of his "unreal" life. He believed that the entire eight-year period of disability and "unreality" lived since the accident had really occurred some time previously and had culminated in complete recovery. He expected his current reliving of past life experiences, although entirely unreal, to have the same optimistic outcome—that is, he would recover. It was in this context that all current experiences seemed to be false duplications of similar previous experiences. He also believed that the present could not be October 1978, arguing that it must be "approximately 1975" because his physician had told him that he could be "nearly back to normal," married, and working by the time he was thirty (which would be in 1977) and also because his old girlfriend, who had recently married someone else, would still be single if it were 1975. Consistent with this disorientation to time, he denied the reality of recent world events.

A CT scan produced several positive findings: (1) atrophy in the region of the posterior right hippocampus and adjacent temporal lobe; (2) a discrete area of moderate atrophy deep in the posterior–superior temporal lobe at the temporoparietal junction, in a region traversed by occipitotemporal fibers; (3) mild atrophy at the right parieto-occipital junction; (4) mild perisylvian atrophy of the right posterior frontal operculum; and (5) mild, diffuse frontal lobe atrophy.

Neuropsychological testing was carried out. The overall results were consistent with right-hemisphere dysfunction, primarily of the posterior association cortex. The patient demonstrated difficulties with nonverbal auditory discrimination and a perceptual disorder associated with posterior right temporal lobe dysfunction, but he did not show amusia (loss of musical appreciation), which is related to more anterior temporal lobe lesions. Thus, the deficits observed in this patient were primarily related to the right temporal lobe; minor right parietal and frontal lobe involvement was also suggested.

In conceptualizing their case, Staton and colleagues (1982) note that on clinical evaluation this patient's most evident problem was his inability to integrate recent observations with premorbid experience. The investigators suggest that a disconnection of prior memory stores from new memory registration is the essential impairment underlying reduplicative paramnesia (and perhaps Korsakoff's syndrome as well). Such a defect of memory association would involve disconnection of the hippocampus from certain sites of past memory stores. If present, frontal lobe indifference, or lack of regard for the environment, might facilitate a continuing misinterpretation of reality.

The investigators note that the most common prominent clinical feature of reduplicative paramnesia is inaccurate time orientation. Normally, the ability to place events correctly in time is a complex process requiring integration of a multiplicity of present cues with past experiences. This patient's duplications were duplications into the past, that is, to a previous time or to a previously occupied location, or were based on the previous appearance of a person or object (recall our earlier discussion of screen memories and also Anna O's curious spell of living in the past). The present patient thus could not integrate present cues in a manner permitting accurate orientation to present time and place. The basis for his current orientation was therefore essentially a recollection from the past. Such orientation from past memory suggests that brain sites responsible for orientation are closer, anatomically or functionally, to stores of past experiences than to stores of recent memory. Storage of past memory at sites distant from the hippocampi could be responsible for the anatomical disconnection postulated here.

The CT scan results, combined with the neuropsychological impairment of visuospatial memory, suggest that the deep right temporo-parieto-occipital (TPO) junction is one location where a memory system disconnection producing disorientation could occur. Disruption of the occipital–hippocampal connections might disconnect past from present visual memories, producing disorientation and a primary amnesia of the Korsakoff type, such as reduplicative paramnesia. Perhaps the greater the extent of the TPO injury, the more likely that reduplicative paramnesia will involve inaccurate orientation in multiple spheres, including time. The right TPO junction may thus be the primary association area responsible for orientation.

Finally, the investigators suggest that reversible disconnections may explain the transient duplications associated with cerebral edema, metabolic encephalopathy, seizure activity, and functional psychosis. Persisting reduplicative paramnesia, however, probably requires brain atrophy or irreversible disconnection, that is, some form or relatively permanent organic impairment.

The study of such phenomena as reduplicative paramnesia is important for another reason, as well. These phenomena illustrate the close neuropsychodynamic relationships among hysteria, dreams, and parapraxes, in all of which these kinds of reduplications—and other phenomena—are frequently seen. Thus, the grand synthesis of clinical and everyday mental functioning that Freud began to develop within his early brain schema, and which he was to later pursue in the realm of the psyche, may indeed now be explicitly possible by means of the neuropsychodynamic model. We will now delineate the parameters of that model as it relates to the core of the Freudian metapsychology.

PART FIVE

Integration

All our provisional ideas in psychology will presumably some day be based on an organic substructure.

—SIGMUND FREUD,
On Narcissism: An Introduction

No one is fitted to begin the materialistic study of the brain unless he has a good knowledge of psychology.

—JOHN HUGHLINGS JACKSON,
Selected Writings

CHAPTER 18

Neuropsychology and Metapsychology: Toward a Neuropsychodynamic Synthesis

In this chapter we take a look at how various theorists have used the facts and findings of neuropsychology to construct their own models of psychoanalytic metapsychology. Then, building on the data and principles of the previous chapters, we attempt to synthesize a neuropsychodynamic framework that can serve to guide further clinical and empirical work in the brain and behavioral sciences (see also Miller, 1986a, 1990, 1991).

The Freudian Metapsychology

The present description focuses on the main features of the Freudian metapsychology and, in attempting to trace its evolution, adopts a sort of "time capsule" approach; that is, it will concentrate on the seminal works of Freud that first laid out the specifics of his mental model at different stages in his thinking.

As we saw in Chapter 9 of the present book, the first fully articulated Freudian metapsychology appeared in 1900 with the famous Chapter 7 of *The Interpretation of Dreams*. Here, Freud delineated the two principles of mental functioning that would inform his conceptualization of consciousness and personality throughout his subsequent writings. For Freud, the *primary process* represents the basic, instinctual, "primitive" or "irrational" drive state of the individual, the psychical system that is present from birth and retains its infantile desire for immediate tension discharge and lack of access to rational, verbal mediation. The *secondary process*, by

227

contrast, develops later to deal with the real world in a practical manner, to enable to the individual to achieve some measure of instinctual need-gratification by effecting a compromise with reality.

The essence of this model was carried over into Freud's 1915 essay *The Unconscious*. Freud begins by reemphasizing the relationship between symptoms, slips, and dreams—that their existence points to the presence in all of us of a realm of mental functioning that eludes our conscious apperception.

> Anyone who is ignorant of pathological facts, who regards the parapraxes of normal people as accidental, and who is content with the old saw that dreams are froth, has only to ignore a few more problems of the psychology of consciousness in order to spare himself any need to assume an unconscious mental activity. (Freud, 1915, p. 168)

An intriguing feature of this essay is Freud's apparent need to point out to his readers the ultimate neuropsychological primacy of his evolving metapsychology, while in virtually the same breath pointedly deferring his theorizing from the concrete structure of the nervous system to the more abstract functionings of the mind:

> Research has given irrefutable proof that mental activity is bound up with the function of the brain as it is with no other organ. We are taken a step further—we do not know how much—by the discovery of unequal importance of the different parts of the brain and their special relations to particular parts of the body and to particular mental activities. But every attempt to go on from there to discover a localization of mental processes, every endeavor to think of ideas as stored up in nerve cells and of excitations as travelling along nerve-fibres, has miscarried completely. The same fate would await any theory which attempted to recognize, let us say, the anatomical position of the system Cs.—conscious mental activity—as being in the cortex, and to localize the unconscious processes in the subcortical parts of the brain. There is a hiatus here which at present cannot be filled, nor is one of the tasks of psychology to fill it. Our psychical topography has *for the present* nothing to do with anatomy; it has reference not to anatomical localities, but to regions in the mental apparatus, wherever thay may be situated in the body. (Freud, 1915, pp. 174–175)

By 1915 the division into primary and secondary processes, although retained conceptually, had been supplemented by a new terminology. The *unconscious*, or *Ucs.*, was now the repository of primitive, infantile, instinctual drives and wishes, was guided by the primary process, and possessed several special cognitive characteristics, such as exemption from mutual contradiction, timelessness, and replacement of external reality by its psychical representation. The *conscious* system, or Cs., retained control over voluntary motility, withstood the "onslaught of neurosis," and only broke down in psychotic states; however, the control of the Cs. over emotions was less complete. Conflicts between the two systems were inevitable, and not just in mental disorders.

> Even within the limits of normal life we can recognize that a constant struggle for primacy over affectivity goes on between the two systems Cs. and Ucs., that certain spheres of influence are marked off from one another, and that admixtures between the operative forces occur. (Freud, 1915, p. 179)

Interposed between the Cs. and Ucs., therefore, is a third system, the *preconscious*, or *Pcs.*, whose task it is to facilitate communication between the other two entities, to give them an order in time, to set up a series of "censorships" to insulate the Cs. from the Ucs.'s raw drives and wishes, and to titrate manageable doses of instinctual material to enter consciousness for assimilation with the demands of reality. Accordingly, the Pcs. is involved in "reality testing," and is the fundamental basis for conscious memory.

In this metapsychological system, a key role is played by language. One of the prime differences between a conscious and an unconscious presentation, says Freud, is that a conscious presentation comprises the mental image of the thing plus the word for the thing while an unconscious presentation includes the mental image of the thing only. The system Pcs. only comes about, in fact, by the *thing-presentation*, as Freud termed it, being linked with the corresponding *word-presentation*. This, in turn, brings about a higher form of psychological organization that makes it possible for the primary process of the Ucs. to be succeeded by the secondary process, which is dominant in the Pcs. Consciousness and an apprehension of reality, then, depend on the adequate development and operation of the faculty of language.

> Now, too, we are in a position to state precisely what it is that repression denies to the rejected presentation in the transference neuroses; what it denies to the presentation is translation into words which shall remain attached to the object. A presentation which is not put into words, or a psychical act which is not hypercathected, remains thereafter in the Ucs., in a state of repression. (Freud, 1915, p. 202)

Lest there be any doubt, Freud makes the connection between language and consciousness even more explicit, contrasting it with the predominantly imagistic cognition of unconscious thought, a point he had first articulated fifteen years earlier.

In the last few pages of *The Interpretation of Dreams*, which was published in 1900, the view was developed that thought-processes, i.e. those acts of cathexis which are comparatively remote from perception, are in themselves without quality and unconscious, and that they attain their capacity to become conscious only through being linked with the residues of perceptions of *words*. But word-presentations, for their part, too, are derived from sense-perceptions, in the same way as thing-presentations of objects cannot become conscious through the medium of their *own* perceptual residues. Probably, however, thought proceeds in systems so far remote from the original perceptual residues that they have no longer retained anything of the qualities of those residues, and, in order to become conscious, need to be reinforced by new qualities. Moreover, by being linked with words, cathexes can be provided with quality even when they represent only *relations* between presentations of objects and are thus unable to derive any quality from perceptions. Such relations, which become comprehensible only through words, form a major part of our thought-processes. As we can see, being linked with word-presentations is not yet the same thing as becoming conscious, but only makes it possible to become so; it is therefore characteristic of the system Pcs. and of that system alone. (Freud, 1915, pp. 202–203)

By 1923, in *The Ego and the Id*, many of the functions served by the Cs. and Pcs. had been assumed by the *ego*, a term that, since Freud's earliest writings, had been used descriptively and somewhat unsystematically but now becomes reified into a formal metapsychological construct:

We have formed the idea that in each individual there is a coherent organization of mental processes; and we call this his *ego*. It is to this ego that consciousness is attached; the ego controls the approaches to motility—that is, to the discharge of excitations into the external world; it is the mental agency which supervises all its own constituent processes, and which goes to sleep at night, though even then it exercises the censorship on dreams. From this ego proceed the repressions, too, by means of which it is sought to exclude certain trends in the mind not merely from consciousness but also from other forms of effectiveness and activity. In analysis these trends which have been shut out stand in opposition to the ego, and the analysis is faced with the task of removing the resistances which the ego displays against itself with the repressed. (Freud, 1923, p. 7)

And the ego achieves many of its aims, it appears, through the medium of language:

The question, "how does a thing become conscious?" would thus be more advantageously stated: "How does a thing become preconscious?"

And the answer would be: "Through becoming connected with the word-presentations corresponding to it." (Freud, 1923, p. 10)

Freud goes on to explain that these word-presentations are the residues of memories, having begun as conscious, if unverbalizable, perceptual impressions, and are capable of becoming conscious again through their subsequent linking with mature language. Not that it is impossible for memories to emerge into consciousness in largely imagistic form; Freud recognized that for many people nonverbal mnemic imagery is the preferred form of reminiscence. But as, for example, the study of dreams teaches us, what becomes conscious in visual thinking is typically only the concrete subject matter of the thought, while the more complex cognitive inter-relationships among the elements of that subject matter—what we ordinarily call *thinking*—cannot be given full expression in strictly visual form.

Thinking in pictures is, therefore, only a very incomplete form of becoming conscious. In some way, too, it stands nearer to unconscious processes than does thinking in words, and it is unquestionably older than the latter both ontogenetically and phylogenetically. (Freud, 1923, p. 11)

Again, Freud cannot resist drawing analogies between psychological and neurological functioning. He may be using nervous system terminology in a metaphorical sense, as some writers have contested, but the metaphor he chooses to use is nevertheless that of the brain.

We might add, perhaps, that the ego wears a "cap of hearing" [editorial footnote in the original: "Horkappe," i.e. the auditory lobe]—on one side only, as we learn from cerebral anatomy. It might be said to wear it awry. . . . The ego is first and foremost a bodily ego; it is not merely a surface entity, but is itself the projection of a surface. If we wish to find an anatomical analogy for it we can best identify it with the "cortical homunculus" of the anatomists, which stands on its head in the cortex, sticks up its heels, faces backward and, as we know, has its speech-area on the left-hand side. (Freud, 1923, p. 15)

By this time, the Freudian metapsychology had become inextricably linked with Freudian instinct theory, which we will not deal with in detail here (see Holt, 1985, 1989; Pine, 1990). Suffice it to say that the *id* now becomes the repository of primitive instinctual drives, largely unconscious, and that the ego is seen as the system that the id exploits to carry out the latter's wishes in accordance with the demands of the real world.

The ego seeks to bring the influence of the external world to bear upon the id and its tendencies, and endeavors to substitute the reality principle for the pleasure principle which reigns unrestrictedly in the id. For the ego, perception plays the part which in the id falls to instinct. The ego represents what may be called reason and common sense, in contrast to the id, which contains the passions. (Freud, 1923, p. 15)

A third mental system in this revised metapsychology, the *superego*, is even more tied to developmental instinct theory, emerging, as it supposedly does, out of the early psychosexual confusions of the Oedipus complex and serving as a repressive force upon the instinct-driven id, even as it derives its energy from it.

Thus, the super-ego is always close to the id and can act as its representative vis-a-vis the ego. It reaches deep down into the id and for that reason is farther from consciousness than the ego. (Freud, 1923, pp. 38–39)

And then, in a footnote, Freud intriguingly adds:

It may be said that the psycho-analytic or metapsychological ego stands on its head no less than the anatomical ego—the "cortical homunculus." (Freud, 1923, p. 39)

Viewing the now fairly complete metapsychology from a therapeutic standpoint, Freud proclaims, "Psychoanalysis is an instrument to enable the ego to achieve a progressive conquest of the id" (1923, p. 46).

For many years, as we know, a purely mentalistic metapsychology informed psychoanalysis as a psychotherapeutic and social science discipline. But before long, breakthroughs in the neurosciences forced psychoanalytic clinicians and researchers to take a closer look at the psychodynamic theories underlying their practices.

Neuropsychology and Metapsychology I: Cerebral Localization

Neuropsychology, like other scientific disciplines, has had its fads and fashions. As we will see, earlier writers spoke of lobes and levels of the brain, reflecting the sharp increase in knowledge of cerebral localization of function that occurred in the two decades following the Second World War. By the late 1960s and early 1970s, attention had turned to the role of the two cerebral hemispheres as the arbiters of consciousness and personality, an emphasis that continues to this day. Accordingly, neuropsychological conceptualizations of psychoanalytic principles have all reflected the prevailing zeitgeist.

A number of writers have chosen to emphasize the role of the brain's frontal and temporal lobes in mediating important metapsychological processes. The frontal lobes, especially, have always received great attention from neuropsychologists, having the unique, if dubious, distinction among neuroanatomic structures of being seen at one time or another as a "riddle" (Teuber, 1964) or a "problem" (Nauta, 1971).

From a modern perspective, conceptions of the role of the frontal lobes in human cognition have generally emphasized their controlling or modulating influence on mental processes. Whereas other brain regions subserve the basic operative conditions for the performance of intellectual activities such as language, memory, and perception, the frontal lobes, especially the more anterior so-called *prefrontal* regions, serve to organize these intellectual activities as a whole, including the planning, carrying out, and evaluating of these activities (Damasio, 1979; Luria, 1980; Teuber, 1964).

The frontal lobes synthesize exteroceptively received information about the outside world and information about internal drive states of the body, thus providing the means by which the behavior of the organism is regulated according to the effects produced by its actions. The frontal lobes judge and regulate ongoing external perception and calculate appropriate responses to what is being perceived, for the purpose of preserving the individual's overall mental and physical equilibrium. The frontal lobes provide for temporal contiguity of experience and behavior, which enables the individual to carry out complex series of goal-directed actions, utilizing internal and external feedback about the effects of those actions in both fulfilling inner needs and satisfying the demands of reality (Damasio, 1979; Fuster, 1985; Luria, 1980; Nauta, 1971; Teuber, 1964).

Many of these insights about frontal lobe functioning were understood at least since the time of Goldstein's (1936, 1942) work, so it is not surprising that a number of psychoanalytically oriented writers drew parallels between psychodynamic phenomena and those observed in patients with focal brain injury. For example, Frank (1950) studied the thought, affect, and behavior of chronic schizophrenics who had undergone prefrontal lobotomy; he concluded that the operation caused a quantitative shift of instinctual impulsivity and a change in the balance of psychic representation.

In psychoanalytic psychotherapy, observed Frank (1950), the lobotomized patients could not free-associate meaningfully, nor could they enter into a transference relationship in the usual sense. The ego seemed to have become rigidified, to have lost the quality of "autoplasticity." The lobotomized patients were unable to do creative work or to have religious or artistic experiences. All those functions that involve internalization and symbolic elaboration—what we would call preconscious functions— were severely impaired. The frequency of both dreams and daydreams in these patients was much reduced after lobotomy, and what manifest dream content did occur was greatly simplified. In fact, the dream content had the character of direct wish fulfillment, much like the dreams of children, albeit with adult-type wishes. Thus, the lobotomized patients dreamed of consuming tasty delicacies, of becoming fabulously wealthy, or of satisfying their sexual desires with gleeful sybaritic excess.

On the basis of these observations, Frank (1950) theorized that prefrontal lobotomy produces an "emotional asymbolia." In this conceptualization, the forebrain, including the intact frontal lobes, is an important instrument for the integrity of the preconscious system. Lobotomy, by resulting in a defensive hypercathexis and constriction of ego boundaries, enables the psychic apparatus to ward off flooding by id derivatives. Being thus isolated from internal need states, instead of being able to deal with them adaptively, these postlobotomy patients have great difficulty in handling life outside the structured milieu of the hospital.

Kubie (1953) was one of the first writers to attempt a formal brain model of Freudian metapsychology, focusing not so much on the frontal regions of the brain as on the temporal lobes and their subcortical connections. Prior research by neurosurgeon Wilder Penfield and his colleagues had shown that the cortex of the temporal lobes is a veritable storehouse of past experiences. These memories—many of them "forgotten"— could be accessed during brain surgery by direct stimulation of the temporal lobe, especially the right lobe. The implications of these findings for the recovery of repressed memories were not lost on writers seeking a link between brain and psyche.

Kubie (1953) first directed his attention to the limbic system, much of which lies within the brain's temporal lobes and which he regarded as a kind of neuroanatomical junction between the cortex above and hypothalamus below. The limbic system would thus correspond to a psychological association pathway for both internal and external perceptions from such structures as the eye, ear, body wall, body apertures, genitals, and viscera. Information from these systems could reach the temporal lobe by way of the thalamus (except for smell, which has a more direct route to the limbic system).

> Here then, within the temporal lobe and its connections, is the crossroads where the "I" and the "non-I" pole of the symbol meet. It is impossible to overestimate the importance of this fact that the temporal lobe complex constitutes the mechanism for integrating the past and the present, the phylogenetically and ontogenetically old and new, and at the same time the external and internal environments of the central nervous system. It is through the temporal lobe and its connections that the "gut" component of memory enters into our psychological processes and the symbol acquires its dual poles of reference. (Kubie, 1953, p. 31)

Thus, says Kubie, it is through the temporal lobes and their limbic connections that the data that link us to the inner and outer worlds of experience are coordinated and integrated. It is this temporal lobe system that allows us to both project and introject. The temporal–limbic complex mediates the translation into somatic disturbance of those tensions that are generated on the level of psychological experience; Kubie goes so far as to characterize this temporal lobe–limbic system complex as the "psychosomatic organ."

Turning to memory, Kubie (1953) interprets the contemporary neurological data to suggest that the raw material of remembering is stored in the central nervous system in more than one way and that these varied hiding places are not equally accessible. What does make memories accessible, Kubie says, is the connection to language. Verbally accessible memories tend to consist of nonspecific generalizations from many discrete experiences, with a predominantly intellectual, cortical, and relatively nonemotional content, and are linked predominantly to auditory and visual imagery. However, these same experiences are contemporaneously stored in the form of exteroceptive and interoceptive "gut" memories of discrete experiences, in which vivid sensory images constitute the essence of the memory process, often without words. Such memories are far more difficult to access.

> In this sense the verbal or neopallial recovery of the past, on which psychoanalytic technique depends, is itself a screening device. To a far greater extent than we have realized, words serve as screens to cover sensory or "gut" memories, with the inevitable consequence that every verbal memory serves to screen a deeper memory. It would seem that the conception of screen memories should be understood broadly in relation to the function of language, and should no longer be restricted to the special case to which the term has been limited in the past, but should be given a more general and inclusive usage, specifically to include the screening which is done by all verbal devices. (Kubie, 1953, p. 48)

One year later Ostow's (1954, 1955) two-part theoretical integration of neurology and psychoanalysis appeared. Like Frank (1950), Ostow (1954) was impressed by the results of prefrontal lobotomy on the thought, affect, and behavior of its recipients. Citing the contemporary psychosurgical literature, Ostow noted that the operation almost invariably produces a lack of depth in the personality. Postlobotomy patients are cheerful, complacent, and largely indifferent to the opinions and feelings of others. Quite open and objective about their faults, they nevertheless seldom express contrition and seem devoid of the usual defense mechanisms of normal adults. As is true of children, immediate aims and impulses, rather than long-term goals, dominate their behavior. While their ability to recall the past is intact, their personal histories have diminished interpretive value for them; they seem no more interested in their own past emotional crises and personal challenges than if these had happened to someone else.

On the basis of these observations, Ostow (1954) suggested that the main effects of prefrontal lobotomy are a loss of the ability to maintain a fully affective consciousness of self and a loss of the ability to fantasize. In order to achieve fantasy, Ostow points out, the normal individual must block out the environmental interruptions and proceed by means of concentration to envisage a large number of variables. He must construct in his imagination a set of circumstances with himself as the central figure while at the same time remaining at an overall "objective" vantage point, surveying the results and watching his own progress through the maze of individual scenes and activities. Only by means of fantasy, Ostow says, can works of art, music, literature, architecture, mechanical design, and so on be accomplished, and this is the area that has been obliterated in the patient with prefrontal lobotomy (see Miller, 1988b, for a fuller discussion of the neuropsychodynamics of creativity).

From this, Ostow (1954) surmises that at least one of the tasks of the frontal lobes is the creation of derivatives of instinctual drives, which is essential for the adaptive satisfaction of basic needs. For humans, in whom the development of the frontal lobes reaches its phylogenetic apex, such derivative creation, Ostow argues, liberates us from the stereotypical quality of instinctual gratification seen in animals and results in the creative activities characteristic of the human species.

Ostow (1954) further speculates that the anatomical proximity of the premotor frontal region to motor cortex and to the motor speech area permits the execution, the "acting out," of the derivatives of unconscious fantasies formulated by some mechanism in the prefrontal region and called into action at the appropriate time by another mechanism in that same or related region. Ostow points out that prior to the phylogenetic appearance of the premotor region, the dorsomedial nucleus of the thalamus projects to the striatum (basal ganglia), a phylogenetically older motor system. However, in higher mammals, especially man, instead of activating a motor system with a limited number of stereotyped responses, the dorsomedial nucleus—which Ostow assumes is in some way connected with instinctual gratification—now activates a system, namely, the premotor region, that can create drive derivatives; that system, in turn, has access to a more flexible and adaptive new motor system.

> I attempt to explain the apparent strength of motivation as a function of the ability to construct derivatives of instinctual drives and unconscious

fantasies and to transfer psychic energy from these to their conscious derivatives. Impairment of consistency of motivation I explain as a consequence of impairment of function of the device that regulates the orderly procession of fantasies so as to maintain continuity of motivation without rigidity. It therefore seems reasonable to me to assign to the premotor frontal region the functions of devising and energizing derivatives of instinctual drives and unconscious fantasies and of regulating the rate and sequence in which unconscious fantasies determine day-to-day behavior. If one accepts the formulation that neurosis or psychosis is caused by incomplete or unsuccessful repression, then one can understand that damage to the frontal lobe can relieve an individual of neurotic symptoms by depriving him of the power to form symptoms and—what is the same thing—the power to create, express, and enjoy himself as a human being. (Ostow, 1954, pp. 337–338)

In the second part of his thesis, Ostow (1955) turns his attention to the brain's temporal lobes. Within these structures, Ostow says, lie systems that have the function of matching percepts with preconscious memories and thereby with unconscious repressed memories and fantasies. The matching of a current percept with a preconscious memory is typically accompanied by a feeling of recognition, a frequent component of temporal lobe seizures, often referred to as *déjà vu*. The result of the assessment of the instinctual value of current percepts is expressed in terms of subjective feeling, of affect that is consistent with the person's knowledge of himself. In other words, the temporal lobe mechanism is needed not to answer the question, How do I like this experience? but How *would* I like this experience?—that is, What is typical for me as a person?

Ostow (1955) theorizes that the production of an unconscious wish fantasy, along with its drive derivatives, begins in the frontal lobes. These derivatives are then presented to the temporal lobes, perhaps specifically to the hippocampus, in order to form the basis for evaluation of incoming and ongoing environmental stimuli. The information descriptive of the presenting environmental situation, elaborated in terms of each separate modality—vision, hearing, touch—in various perceptual processing areas of the cortex, converges on the temporal lobes to form an integrated picture and thence projects to the hippocampus where the evaluation-matching process takes place. Ostow (1955) concludes:

In summary, it has been suggested in this paper that the procession of unconscious wish fantasies and the formulation of their derivatives takes place in the frontal lobes. The temporal lobe has the function of matching the external environmental situation with preconscious memories, perhaps with especial concern for implications of danger.

A derivative of an unconscious wish fantasy or memory that concep-
tualizes the dominant instinctual drive is selected and the affect appropriate to the unconscious wish fantasy becomes conscious. Then,
if the affect is not a negative one, the derivative fantasy is re-created.
The results of the matching and comparison, including the affect
generated, are conveyed to the frontal lobe by way of the efferent
tracts of the temporal lobe, especially the fornix, so as to provide the
frontal lobe with information required by it in guiding the procession
of unconscious fantasies. In this way the individual is equipped to
pursue a given set of instinctual goals, consistently but not rigidly,
making the most out of every situation, with a minimum of waste
motion. (pp. 419–420)

More recently, Epstein (1987) has proposed a metapsychological
conceptualization that attempts to capitalize on the insights of modern
neuropsychology. Epstein begins by pointing out that the prefrontal areas
have widespread connections not only with subcortical areas but with the
rest of the cortex, thereby being influenced by and exerting influence
upon wide and diverse regions of the brain. Epstein cites Stuss and Benson's
(1986) idea of frontal lobe functioning as carrying out "executive" control
over other brain activities and thus over complex behavior. This includes
not only control but also anticipation, goal selection, preplanning, and
monitoring. Frontal lesions disrupt long-range planning, conceptualization
of inner and outer worlds, inhibition of emotional display, and drive
initiation and control. Thus, the prefrontal system appears to exert a
general regulatory–organizing effect on all higher sensorimotor and
ideational–affective processes. In this view, self-awareness is one of the
highest attributes of frontal lobe functioning, and self-awareness requires
that the ego take regard of the total personal constellation.

> These postulated functions of the prefrontal areas and the phenomenology
> of their lesioning are virtually synonymous with the ego functions and
> deficits postulated in psychoanalytic thought. Indeed, at this high level
> of integration, dichotomy between cerebral and mental phenomena
> becomes increasingly irrelevant. (Epstein, 1987, p. 164)

Such ego capacities as curiosity and cognitive striving, Epstein goes
on to say, derive their power from hedonic sources—which, neuropsychologically speaking, means from the integration of subcortical, nonfrontal
cortical, and frontal cortical regions. The same applies, says Epstein (1987),
to such affect-endowed symbol systems as love of country and religion.

> The most intense causes of anxiety in the human are those related to
> dissolution of the self and/or loss of ego control over outer and inner
> worlds. The development of the human frontal lobes would, then,

seem to give survival primacy to a subjective sense of hedonically equilibrated self cohesion and of ego control. The former would be challenged, for example, by environmental situations of phobic quality. (p. 165)

Neuropsychology and Metapsychology II: Hemispheric Asymmetry

Surgical section of the corpus callosum and the other major commissures connecting the two halves of the brain has been shown to result in the so-called *disconnection syndrome*, in which information received and processed in one hemisphere cannot be directly utilized by the other, especially when interhemispheric access of information is artifically constrained, as in the experimental neuropsychology lab (Gazzaniga, 1970, 1985; Geschwind, 1965; Sperry, 1968, 1974). Frequently, a curious interhemispheric "competition" is manifested, where a spontaneous habitual gesture or emotional reaction generated by the right hemisphere will be reported as ego-alien—that is, not part of the person's "self"—by the verbally communicative left hemisphere. By and large, however, these "split-brain" patients function relatively normally by learning to use various compensatory self-cuing strategies to keep the two hemispheric entities in touch with each other. Cases of congenital callosal agenesis do occur, but these appear to result in a lesser degree of disconnection symptomatology than surgical commissurotomy (Saurwein & Lassonde, 1983). Studies with commissurotomy patients, along with patients having unilateral brain damage, have provided neuropsychologists with insight into the roles each hemisphere plays in consciousness and information processing.

While varying in the particulars, a consensual summary description of the respective roles of the two human cerebral hemispheres in higher mental processes would probably run as follows. The *"dominant"* (*"major"*) *hemisphere*—in most people the *left*—is specialized for linguistic processing and logical descriptive analysis, although it seems to play a role in some aspects of positive emotionality; it is especially good at perceptual and conceptual analysis of details and operates most effectively within a consecutive temporal framework; it plays a special role in the perceiving of differences and in the interpretation of the literal, syntactic, and semantic qualities of spoken communication. The *"nondominant"* (*"minor"*) *hemisphere*—in most people the *right*—is specialized for spatial processing and the coding of images; it is especially good at the gestaltic synthesis of forms and is more intuitive and inferential; it seems to operate most effectively in perceiving similarities based on broad qualitative features; and it seems to play a special role in facial recognition, in emotional experience and expression, especially negative emotionality, and in the interpretation of the inflective and prosodic qualities of spoken communication (Gazzaniga, 1985; Hecaen & Albert, 1978; Ley & Bryden, 1979; Ross & Rush, 1981; Ross et al., 1981; Sackeim & Gur, 1978; Sackeim et al., 1982; Springer & Deutsch, 1985; Tucker, 1981; Walsh, 1978).

Picking up on this modern neuropsychological revival of interest in the two cerebral hemispheres—the functional differences between the left and right hemispheres were known clinically since the nineteenth century (Harrington, 1985) and were clearly recognized by Freud in his neurological writings—a number of writers have recently attempted to integrate this knowledge base with psychoanalytic metapsychology. For example, Galin (1974) regards certain aspects of right-hemisphere functioning as congruent with primary process cognition:

> The right hemisphere reasons by a nonlinear mode of association, rather than by syllogistic logic; its solutions are based on multiple converging determinants, rather than a simple causal chain. It is much superior to the left hemisphere in part-whole relationships, e.g. grasping the concept of the whole from just the part. (p. 574)

Conversely, what we refer to as secondary process thought, or "rational" thinking, is seen by Tucker (1981) to be associated with the type of logical, verbal–analytic cognitive representation that requires the left hemisphere's linear and sequential operations. The study of split-brain patients suggests to Galin (1974) that the isolated right hemisphere can sustain emotional responses and goals divergent from those of the left. Hoppe (1977) goes even further, postulating that surgical disconnection produces an interruption of the preconscious stream of thought between the two hemispheres, resulting in a separation of Freud's (1915) "word-presentations" from "thing-presentations." In addition, says Hoppe, the surgery results in a predominance of feedback-free primary process activity in the right hemisphere, since access to secondary process linguistic–analytic cognition is interrupted.

Extrapolating in the other direction, Hoppe (1977) theorizes that some psychoanalytic patients may suffer from what he calls a *functional commissurotomy*. This state does not necessarily involve brain damage in the usual sense but may develop by some as yet undetermined type of cross-callosal inhibition—a sort of functional *forme fruste* of the surgical disconnection syndrome. Primary process-type mental events would then be free to develop a life of their own and thus form the basis for what is observed clinically as repression. Functionally disconnected from the right, the verbal left hemisphere cannot articulate to the self the nonrational, imagistic, and emotionally charged content of the right hemisphere's mental activity. This activity, then, remains for all intents and purposes "unconscious."

The cerebral commissures do not reach full physiological and functional maturation until adolescence. Galin (1974) provides an example of how the insufficiently developed interhemispheric communication in young children might constitute the developmental basis for the repression of conflict. Suppose a mother presents her child with a positive verbal message ("What a good boy!") but at the same time delivers a negative nonverbal one (she says it with a scowl or with a sarcastic intonation). If the interhemispheric communication system is dysfunctional or inadequately developed, each hemisphere will perceive and interpret the separate aspects of the mother's message. Since the left hemisphere constitutes the self-articulatory system, the verbally identified self or ego will react and behave in accordance with the verbal message. At the same time, however, the emotional reactions elicited by the nonverbal aspects of the message will continue to operate "below the surface." This is because the right hemisphere has processed the information in its own way but is barred from communicating with the left. This leaves the mental content devoid of conscious–verbal consolidation. In future situations where female or parent-like authority figures provide a certain type of communication, the person will experience a negative emotional reaction. But because inadequate interhemispheric transfer and consolidation took place at the early stage of development, the basis for this confusion has remained unanalyzed, unarticulated, non-ego-integrated, and therefore "repressed." In such situations, the person may experience confusion or discomfort without any consciously recognized cause and will thus undergo "conflict."

Viewing this type of interhemispheric consciousness-structuring mechanism from the standpoint of its therapeutic implications, Stone (1977) comments:

> What has in the past been spoken of metapsychologically as the task of "making the unconscious conscious," may involve the kind of dominant hemisphere processing of visual, unverbalized constructs fed into it from the minor hemisphere. For optimal adaptation, we are most likely dependent upon continuous exchange of information and continuous shift of "dominance" between the two hemispheres. The more we can allow each mode of communication to shed light upon the other, the greater may be the degree of mastery whether in the interpersonal or environmental realm. (p. 281)

To take this yet a step further, the very *process* of psychoanalytic psychotherapy might depend on the optimal combination of hemispheric processing modalities. Freud (1912), for all his emphasis on language as a facilitator of consciousness and insight, pointed out the frequent necessity of the analyst's using a different kind of cognitive processing mode in apprehending the messages behind a patient's free associations:

> The technique is a very simple one. . . . It consists of not directing one's notice to anything in particular and in maintaining the same "evenly suspended attention" (as I have called it) in the face of all that one hears. . . . It will be seen that the rule of giving equal notice to everything is the necessary counterpart to the demand made on the patient that he should communicate everything that occurs to him without criticism or selection. . . . To put it in a formula: [the analyst] must turn his own unconscious like a receptive organ toward the transmitting unconscious of the patient. (pp. 111–112, 115)

Joseph (1982) has applied an explicitly neurodevelopmental approach to the social origins of thought and language. He notes that the motor areas of the cortex mature before the sensory areas and that the left hemisphere develops before the right. This, he argues, gives the left hemisphere a competitive advantage in the acquisition of motor representation whereas the later-maturing right hemisphere has an advantage in the establishment of sensory–affective representation, including limbic mediation of emotion and motivation. Joseph views thinking as a left-hemisphere internalization of language that corresponds to the increased maturation of intracortical and subcortical structures and fiber pathways and the myelination of the callosal connections that subserve information transfer between the hemispheres. He argues that verbal–logical thought is a means of organizing, interpreting, and explaining impulses that arise in the nonlinguistic portions of the nervous system so that the language-dependent regions may achieve understanding.

Joseph (1982) emphasizes both the motivational and sociodevelopmental aspects of speech–thought development. The earliest forms of communication, and thus social speech, are embedded in limbic activity, since limbic speech provides a context within which associations may be formed and schemas developed. Language slowly develops from the construction and association of these schemas and vocalization–experience pairings. Thinking proper, however, does not appear until much later in development; moreover, although it is a semi-independent motor function, it remains influenced by social–limbic language throughout life.

Because early in development interhemispheric communication is incomplete, the left hemisphere utilizes language to explain to itself the behavior in which it observes the self to be engaged. As the commissures mature and intrahemispheric and interhemispheric information flow increases, the left hemisphere also acts to organize linguistically the individual's internal experiences. As development proceeds, interhemispheric information exchange continues to grow and the left-hemisphere language substrate increasingly acts to organize, as well as inhibit, sensory–limbic right-hemispheric transmissions and initiated behaviors. Rather than passively observe the self's sensory–limbic actions as they occur in the environment, the left hemisphere now actively engages in the formulation of behavior, achieving understanding prior to the occurrence of the behavior. At some point in normal development, the crucial stage is reached where the interpretation or evaluation of a behavior precedes its execution. Behavior no longer has to be emitted and its effect on the environment overtly observed in order for self-modulation to occur; this represents the maturation of the left-hemisphere mechanisms responsible for direct self-articulation and verbal self-control.

Like Galin (1974), Joseph (1982) theorizes about the implications of intercerebral maturation for the development of self-insight versus conflict:

> In that the emerging human organism is asymmetrically arranged, with apparently little interaction and informational exchange between the cerebral hemispheres, the effects of early "socializing" experiences could have potentially profound effects, indeed. As a good deal of this early experience is likely to have its unpleasant, if not traumatic moments, it is fascinating to consider the latter ramifications of the early emotional learning occurring in the right hemisphere unbeknownst to the left; learning and associated emotional responding may later be completely unaccessible to the language centers of the brain, even when extensive interhemispheric transfer is possible. In this regard, the curious asymmetrical arrangement of function and maturation may well predispose the developing organism to later come upon situations in which it finds itself responding emotionally, nervously, anxiously, or "neurotically" without linguistic knowledge, or without even the possibility of linguistic understanding as to the cause, purpose, eliciting stimulus or origin of its behavior. Instead, like the egocentric child, the individual may be faced with behavior that he may explain only after it occurs: "I don't know what came over me." (p. 24)

Tinnin (1989) proposes the existence of what he calls a *governing mental system*, or GMS, in the verbally dominant left hemisphere. The GMS is hypothesized to maintain the unity of the mental functions of both hemispheres; to govern volition and to "own" behavior; to regulate information input, storage, and output by verbal symbolization, thereby being limited in its access to mental contents not amenable to verbal symbolization; and to be responsible for the faculty of subjective consciousness.

It appears, then, that the brain agency responsible for mental unity, volition, and consciousness may be represented by the labels "GMS" or "ego," and that these two may be one and the same. I contend the brain substrate for the ego is Wernicke's area and that the ego, then, is intimately involved in the brain dynamics of divergent laterality, convergent cerebral dominance, and obligatory mental unity. (Tinnin, 1989, p. 407)

Tinnin (1989) goes on to delineate six psychological functions of the GMS that he believes are synonymous with the autonomous functions of the ego postulated by Hartmann (1939). These six functions are the following: (1) *identity*, or subjective mental unity; (2) *volition*, a willing and owning of behavior; (3) *symbolization*, the basic mechanism of information processing; (4) *time*, the major axis for the sequential ordering of elements in consciousness; (5) *reality perception*, the distinguishing of objects from the self, required for object representation in consciousness; and (6) *body image*, the distinguishing of self as unique and separate from objects, required for self-representation in consciousness.

Back to the Future: Freud's Brain and the Neuropsychodynamic Model

Luria's (1980) now-classic studies of patients with orbitobasal frontal lobe lesions found these individuals to show a state of overall reduced activity and to be easily distracted by irrelevant stimuli. As with frontal patients generally, it was usually impossible for them to organize their attention and to keep it focused on a definite plan. Luria was particularly struck by the serious disturbances in self-regulating nonspecific activation processes (as measured, for example, by the electroencephalographic orienting response) by means of language. Whereas in normal subjects presentation of a problem to solve by means of verbal instruction produced a stable orienting reflex, in frontal lobe patients verbal instruction did not restore an extinguished response and an instruction that should have increased the patient's electrophysiologic or plethysmographic activity produced no change.

Luria (1980) took this as evidence that the mediobasal zones of the frontal lobes are mainly concerned with higher forms of regulation of short- and long-term processes of nonspecific activation, all taking place with the aid of language, or the "speech system," as he called it. According to this conception, the human mediobasal frontal lobes participate in the activation induced by a spoken instruction and are part of the brain system directly involved in the processes associated with the higher forms of active attention.

In normal subjects there occurs a lasting increment in amplitude of the evoked potential under the influence of a spoken instruction, signifying a mobilization of voluntary attention. Luria (1980) points out that this response is ill-defined in the child, develops progressively in early adolescence, and appears in stable form only at about age twelve to fifteen— at a time when frontal cortex is beginning to play a more intimate part in complex and stable forms of higher voluntary attention. The role of the frontal lobes in directing and modulating the task- or situation-appropriateness of behavior appears to require this component of sociodevelopmentally fostered verbal mediation. For Luria, then, voluntary attention, unlike the elementary orienting reactions, is not biologically fixed in its origin but develops as a social act and depends crucially upon the function of language.

One conclusion, therefore, is that the role of the frontal lobes in social interaction relates to their role in attentional scanning and affective evaluation. The socially adroit individual is sensitive to internal and external social cues. Many of these have an inborn phylogenetic basis: for example, the nuances of interaction that species-specifically guide behavior within social hierarchies or interactions between the sexes. But for humans, a linguistic or verbal component is suffused throughout virtually everything we do. Accordingly, one effect of frontal damage may be to disrupt what is normally the intimate relationship between verbal behavior and socially relevant aspects of attention.

Thus, according to our present neuropsychodynamic model, language from the beginning guides and motivates the ontogenetically progressive internalization of certain standards, certain regularities, on the basis of which our behavior achieves a certain measure of both intrapersonal specificity/predictability and adaptiveness to a wide range of situations— healthy "ego functions," in the parlance of psychoanalysis. Through language, we build up the stability-in-time (Nauta, 1971) that allows us to judge behavior in relation to both the environment and ourselves. The left-hemisphere autoarticulatory guiding function of speech becomes accessed by this frontal mechanism, and the processes of attention, self-regulation, and social behavior become progressively internalized over the course of the individual's development.

If frontal lobe activity underlies the recursive evaluation and planning of behavior and if the left-hemisphere language system provides a means of autoarticulating thoughts, feelings, and goals, then how might these two functional systems collaborate in the processes of identity formation and personality integrity, that is, in the generation of consciousness and a stable ego?

Markus (1983) makes the point that self-knowledge that can be abstracted, symbolized, and articulated is particularly significant self-knowledge, because it can be communicated to others and thus represents those aspects of self that are likely to have the most impact on social behavior:

> More generally, in selecting certain arenas in which to monitor and regulate one's behavior, one is constructing an identity in a very real sense. And perhaps, the more self-schemas an individual develops, the more articulated the cognitive self becomes and the more willful control is exerted over behavior. The more self-knowledge is amassed and the more possible selves delineated, the more situations will be selected or framed so as to be commensurate with one's personality. (p. 562)

Thus, the construction of a personal identity involves the elaboration of self-generated and recursively evaluated self-schemas and the integration of these schemas into a cohesive personality framework. In our present neuropsychodynamic formulation, the left-hemisphere verbal autoarticulatory capacity operates, with frontal lobe guidance, both to guide behavior and to appraise feedback from that behavior's impact on the physical and social worlds. In this way is self-knowledge progressively developed and an identity hewn from the emotion–perception–activity mélange of successive daily experiences. The increasingly volitional control of the verbal articulatory capacity also enables the growing person to explicitly communicate to others, with progressive degrees of refinement, facets of this identity—feelings, desires, perspectives—even as self-communication evolves correspondingly. This process facilitates the development of the appreciation of self as actor, that is, of self-consciousness in the adaptive sense, and thus imbues behavior with the volition requisite for truly ego-autonomous action.

In this regard, hysterical symptoms, dreams, and parapraxes share the common feature of occurring—phenomenologically, psychodynamically, or both—*outside* the realm of normal volitional consciousness. And common to all three is some perturbation of the self-articulatory role of language in interpreting and guiding an individual's thoughts, feelings, and actions. This book has presented numerous case histories documenting the brain damage-produced dissociation of such neurocognitive functions as language, memory, perception, and movement from active, conscious, volitional control. The argument has been made that these severe, frankly "organic," cases are merely the boldly instantiated exemplars of more common everyday neuropsychodynamic events that continually determine and shape our fears and wishes, goals and aspirations, personalities and pathologies.

From the neuropathological to the psychopathological and finally to the domain of the normal—this is the legacy of Freud's brain that can, in our day, with our new tools, begin to be reapplied to the syndromes that afflict our patients and, indeed, to the problems that plague our world.

In a retrospective moment, Freud (1925) wrote:

Looking back, then, over the patchwork of my life's labors, I can say that I have made many beginnings and thrown out many suggestions. Something will come of them in the future, though I cannot myself tell whether it will be much or little. I can, however, express a hope that I have opened up a pathway for an important advance in our knowledge. (p. 120)

Similarly, the ideas of the present book are presented not as the last word, but as a requisite first step. If we can turn our clinical acumen, our productive research efforts, and our modern biotechnologies to the task of exploring the as yet sketchily charted terrain of the neuropsychodynamic model, we may revivify and extend the original vision of Freud's brain in ways its creator could scarcely have imagined.

References

Adamec, R. (1975). Behavioral and epileptic determinants of predatory attack behavior in the cat. *Canadian Journal of Neurological Science, 2*, 457–456.

Adams, R. D., & Victor, M. (1977). *Principles of Neurology*. New York: McGraw-Hill.

Adler, A. (1911). Beitrag zur Lehre vom Widerstand. *Zentralblatt für Psychoanalyse, 1*, 214.

Albert, M. L., & Obler, L. K. (1975, October). *Mixed polyglot aphasia*. Paper presented at the Academy of Aphasia, Victoria, BC, Canada.

Albert, M. S., Butters, N., & Levin, J. (1979). Temporal gradients in retrograde amnesia of patients with alcoholic Korsakoff's disease. *Archives of Neurology, 36*, 211–216.

Alexander, M. P., Stuss, D. T., & Benson, D. F. (1979). Capgras syndrome: A reduplicative phenomenon. *Neurology, 29*, 334–339.

Amacher, P. (1965). Freud's neurological education and its influence on psychoanalytic theory. *Psychological Issues, 4*(Monograph 16), 1–95.

Angelergues, R. (1969). Memory disorders in neurological disease. In P. J. Vinken & G. W. Bruyn (Eds.), *Handbook of Clinical Neurology: Vol. 3. Disorders of Higher Nervous Activity* (pp. 268–292). Amsterdam: North-Holland.

Angus, J. W. S., & Simpson, G. M. (1970). Hysteria and drug-induced dystonia. *Acta Psychiatrica Scandinavica, 52*, 76–86.

Arseni, C., Botez, M. I., & Maretsis, M. (1966). Paroxysmal disorders of the body image. *Psychiatry and Neurology, 151*, 1–14.

As, A. (1963). The recovery of forgotten language knowledge through hypnotic age regression: A case report. *American Journal of Clinical Hypnosis, 5*, 24–29.

Aston-Jones, G., Foote, F. L., & Bloom, F. E. (1984). Anatomy and physiology of locus coeruleus neurons: Functional implications. In M. G. Ziegler & C. R. Lake (Eds.), *Norepinephrine: Clinical Aspects*. Baltimore: Williams & Wilkins.

Bakan, P. (1977–1978). Dreaming, REM sleep and the right hemisphere: A theoretical integration. *Journal of Altered States of Consciousness, 3*, 285–307.

249

Balint, R. (1909). Seelenahmung des "Schauens," optische Ataxie, raumliche Storung der Aufmerksamkeit. *Monatsschriffte für Psychiatrie und Neurologie, 25,* 51–81.

Bastian, H. C. (1869). Disorders of speech. *British Foreign Medical-Chirurgical Review, 43,* 69, 209, 470.

Bendefeldt, F., Miller, L. L., & Ludwig, A. M. (1976). Cognitive performance in conversion hysteria. *Archives of General Psychiatry, 33,* 1250–1254.

Bender, L., & Schilder, P. (1933). Encephalopathia alcoholica: Polioencephalitis haemorrhagia superior of Wernicke. *Archives of Neurology and Psychiatry, 29,* 990–1053.

Bender, M. B. (1956). Syndrome of isolated episodes of confusion with amnesia. *Journal of the Hillside Hospital, 5,* 212–215.

Bender, M. B. (1960). Single episode of confusion with amnesia. *Bulletin of the New York Academy of Medicine, 36,* 197–207.

Bender, M. B., Rudolph, S. H., & Stacy, C. B. (1971). The neurology of the visual and oculomotor systems. In A. B. Baker & L. H. Baker (Eds.), *Clinical Neurology* (Vol. 1, pp. 270–280). Philadelphia: Harper & Row.

Benson, D. F. (1979). *Aphasia, Alexia and Agraphia.* New York: Churchill Livingstone.

Benson, D. F., Gardner, H., & Meadows, J. C. (1976). Reduplicative paramnesia. *Neurology, 26,* 147–151.

Benton, A. L. (1980). The neuropsychology of facial recognition. *American Psychologist, 35,* 176–186.

Benton, A. L., & Van Allen, M. W. (1972). Prosopagnosia and facial discrimination. *Journal of Neurological Science, 15,* 167–172.

Bernfeld, S. (1944). Freud's earliest theories and the school of Helmholtz. *Psychoanalytic Quarterly, 13,* 341–362.

Berson, R. J. (1983). Capgras' syndrome. *American Journal of Psychiatry, 140,* 969–978.

Bertini, M. (1973). REM sleep as a psychological "agency" of memory. In W. P. Koella & P. Levin (Eds.), *Sleep: Physiology, Biochemistry, Psychology, Pharmacology, Clinical Implications* (pp. 61–62). Basel: Karger.

Betlheim, S., & Hartmann, H. (1924). Uber Fehlreaktionen des Gedachtnisses bei Korsakoffschen Psychose. *Archiv für Psychiatrie und Nervenkrankheiten, 72,* 278.

Bickford, R. G., Whalen, J. L., & Klass, D. W. (1956). Reading epilepsy: Clinical and electrographic studies of a new syndrome. *Transactions of the American Neurological Association, 81,* 100–102.

Bigley, G. K., & Sharp, F. R. (1983). Reversible alexia without agraphia due to migraine. *Archives of Neurology, 40,* 114–115.

Binz, C. (1878). *Uber den Traum.* Bonn.

Bogen, J. E. (1979). The callosal syndrome. In K. M. Heilman & E. Valenstein (Eds.), *Clinical Neuropsychology* (pp. 308–359). New York: Oxford University Press.

Botez, M. I., Olivier, M., Vezina, J. L., Botez, T., & Kaufman, B. (1985). Defective revisualization: Dissociation between cognitive and imagistic thought. Case report and short review of the literature. *Cortex, 21,* 375–389.

Bouckoms, A., Martuza, R., & Henderson, M. (1986). Capgras syndrome with subarachnoid hemorrhage. *Journal of Nervous and Mental Disease, 174,* 484–488.

Bower, G. H. (1981). Mood and memory. *American Psychologist, 36,* 129–148.

Breuer, J., & Freud, S. (1895/1982). *Studies on Hysteria.* New York: Harper Colophon/Basic Books.

Brinkman, C., & Porter, R. (1979). Supplementary motor area in the monkey: Activity of neurones during the performance of a learned motor task. *Journal of Neurophysiology, 42,* 681–709.

Brion, S., & Jedynak, C.-P. (1972). Trouble du transfert interhémisphérique à propos de trois observations de tumeurs du corps calleux: Le signe de la main étrangère. *Revue Neurologique, 126,* 257–266.

Broca, P. (1861). Remarques sur le siège de la faculté du langage articulé suivies d'une observation d'aphémie. *Bulletin de la Société Anatomique, Paris, 6,* 330.

Brodal, A. (1969). *Neurological Anatomy in Relation to Clinical Medicine* (2nd ed.). New York: Oxford University Press.

Butters, N. (1979). Amnesic disorders. In K. M. Heilman & E. Valenstein (Eds.), *Clinical Neuropsychology* (pp. 439–474). New York: Oxford University Press.

Buxbaum, E. (1949). The role of a second language in the formation of ego and superego. *Psychoanalytic Quarterly, 18,* 279–289.

Capgras, J., & Reboul-Lachaux, J. (1923). L'illusion des "sosies" dans un délire systematisé chronique. *Bulletin de la Société Clinique de Médecine Mentale, 11,* 6–16.

Caplan, L., Chedru, F., Lhermitte, F., & Mayman, C. (1981). Transient global amnesia and migraine. *Neurology, 31,* 1167–1170.

Carlson, R. J. (1979). The mother tongue in psychotherapy. *Canadian Journal of Psychiatry, 24,* 542–545.

Carpenter, M. B. (1976). *Human Neuroanatomy* (7th ed.). Baltimore: William & Wilkins.

Charcot, J. M. (1889). *Lectures on the Diseases of the Nervous System, Delivered at La Saltpêtrière, 1872.* London: New Sydenham Society.

Cloninger, C. R., Reich, T., & Guze, S. (1975). The multifactorial model of disease transmission: III. Familial relationship between sociopathy and hysteria (Briquet's syndrome). *British Journal of Psychiatry, 127,* 23–32.

Crick, F., & Mitchison, G. (1983). The function of dream sleep. *Nature, 304,* 111–114.

Cripe, L. I. (1988, June 13–17). *The clinical use of the MMPI with neurologic patients: A new perspective.* Paper presented at the Army Medical Department Psychology Conference, Seattle, WA.

Critchley, M. (1953). *The Parietal Lobes.* New York: Hafner.

Cubelli, R., Caselli, M., & Neri, M. (1984). Pain endurance in unilateral cerebral lesions. *Cortex, 20,* 369–375.

Currie, S., Heathfield, K. W. G., Henson, R. A., & Scott, D. F. (1971). The clinical course and prognosis of temporal lobe epilepsy: A survey of 666 patients. *Brain, 34,* 173–180.

Damasio, A. R. (1979). The frontal lobes. In K. M. Heilman & E. Valenstein

(Eds.), *Clinical Neuropsychology* (pp. 360–412). New York: Oxford University Press.

Damasio, A. R., Damasio, H., & Van Hoesen, G. W. (1982). Prosopagnosia: Anatomical basis and behavioral mechanisms. *Neurology, 32,* 331–341.

Damasio, A. R., Graff-Radford, N. R., & Damasio, H. (1983). Transient partial amnesia. *Archives of Neurology, 40,* 656–657.

Damasio, A. R., & Van Hoesen, G. W. (1980). Structure and function of the supplementary motor area. *Neurology, 30,* 359.

Darwin, C. (1872). *The Expression of the Emotions in Man and Animals.* London: John Murray.

David, A. S., & Bone, I. (1985). Hysterical paralysis following status epilepticus: Case report and review of the concept. *Journal of Nervous and Mental Disease, 173,* 437–440.

Dejerine, J. (1891). Sur un cas de cécité verbale avec agraphie, suivi d'autopsie. *Mémoires de la Société de Biologie, 3,* 197–201.

Dejerine, J. (1892). Contribution à l'étude anatomopathologique et clinique des différentes variétés de cécité verbale. *Mémoires de la Société de Biologie, 4,* 61–90.

de Zulueta, F. I. S. (1984). The implications of bilingualism in the study and treatment of psychiatric disorders: A review. *Psychological Medicine, 14,* 541–557.

Dimond, S. J. (1980). *Neuropsychology: A Textbook of Systems and Psychological Functions of the Human Brain.* London: Butterworths.

Drake, M. E., & Coffey, C. E. (1983). Complex partial status epilepticus simulating psychogenic unresponsiveness. *American Journal of Psychiatry, 140,* 800–801.

Eccles, J. C. (1973). *The Understanding of the Brain.* New York: McGraw-Hill.

Ellenberger, H. F. (1970). *The Discovery of the Unconscious: The History and Evolution of Dynamic Psychiatry.* New York: Basic Books.

Ellenberger, H. F. (1972). The story of Anna O.: A critical review with new data. *History of the Behavioral Sciences, 8,* 267–279.

Engel, G. L. (1970). Conversion symptoms. In C. M. MacBryde & R. S. Blacklow (Eds.), *Signs and Symptoms* (pp. 650–668). London: Pitman Medical.

Epstein, A. W. (1964). Recurrent dreams: Their relationship to temporal lobe seizures. *Archives of General Psychiatry, 10,* 25–30.

Epstein, A. W. (1967). Body image alterations during seizures and dreams of epileptics. *Archives of Neurology, 16,* 613–619.

Epstein, A. W. (1987). The phylogenesis of the "ego," with remarks on the frontal lobes. *American Journal of Psychoanalysis, 47,* 161–166.

Epstein, A. W., & Simmons, N. N. (1983). Aphasia with reported loss of dreaming. *American Journal of Psychiatry, 140,* 108–109.

Fancher, R. E. (1973). *Psychoanalytic Psychology: The Development of Freud's Thought.* New York: Norton.

Feinberg, T. E., Haber, L. D., & Leeds, N. E. (1990). Verbal asomatagnosia. *Neurology, 40,* 1391–1394.

Fenton, G. W. (1986). Epilepsy and hysteria. *British Journal of Psychiatry, 149,* 28–37.

Ferenczi, S. (1926). *Further Contributions to the Theory and Technique of Psychoanalysis.* London: Hogarth Press.

Ferro, J. M., & Kertesz, A. (1984). Posterior internal capsule infarction associated with neglect. *Archives of Neurology, 41,* 422–424.

Finkelnburg, R. (1870). Vortrag in der Nierdernheim Gessellschaft der Aerzte, Bonn, Berlin. *Klinische Wochenschrift, 7,* 449.

Fischman, L. G. (1983). Dreams, hallucinogenic drug states and schizophrenia: A psychological and biological comparison. *Schizophrenia Bulletin, 9,* 73–94.

Fisher, C. M. (1971). Cerebral ischemia: Less familiar types. *Clinical Neurosurgery, 18,* 267–336.

Fisher, C. M. (1980). Late-life migraine accompaniments as a cause of unexplained transient ischemic attacks. *Canadian Journal of Neurological Science, 7,* 9–17.

Fisher, C. M. (1982). Transient global amnesia: Precipitating activities and other observations. *Archives of Neurology, 39,* 605–608.

Fisher, C. M., & Adams, R. D. (1958). Transient global amnesia. *Transactions of the American Neurological Association, 83,* 143–146.

Fisher, C. M., & Adams, R. D. (1964). Transient global amnesia. *Acta Neurologica Scandinavica, 40*(Suppl. 9), 1–83.

Fleishman, J. A., Segall, J. D., & Judge, F. P. (1983). Isolated transient alexia: A migrainous accompaniment. *Archives of Neurology, 40,* 115–116.

Flor-Henry, P. (1978). Gender, hemispheric specialization and psychopathology. *Social Science and Medicine, 12B,* 155–162.

Flor-Henry, P. (1979). On certain aspects of the localization of the cerebral systems regulating and determining emotion. *Biological Psychiatry, 15,* 677–698.

Flor-Henry, P. (1985). Psychiatric aspects of cerebral lateralization. *Psychiatric Annals, 15,* 429–434.

Flor-Henry, P., Fromm-Auch, D., Tapper, M., & Shopflocher, M. (1981). A neuropsychological study of the stable syndrome of hysteria. *Biological Psychiatry, 16,* 601–626.

Foulkes, D. (1978). *A Grammar of Dreams.* New York: Basic Books.

Frank, J. (1950). Some aspects of lobotomy (prefrontal leucotomy) under psychoanalytic scrutiny. *Psychiatry, 13,* 35–42.

Frankel, M., & Cummings, J. L. (1984). Neuro-ophthalmic abnormalities in Tourette's syndrome: Functional and anatomic implications. *Neurology, 34,* 359–361.

French, J. D., Hernandez-Peon, R., & Livingston, R. G. (1955). Projections from cortex to cephalic brainstem (reticular formation) in monkey. *Journal of Neurophysiology, 18,* 74–94.

Freud, S. (1891/1953). *On Aphasia: A Critical Study.* New York: International Universities Press.

Freud, S. (1893/1966). Some points for a comparative study of organic and hysterical motor paralyses. *Standard Edition, 1,* 157–172.

Freud, S. (1895/1966). Project for a scientific psychology. *Standard Edition, 1,* 283–391.

Freud, S. (1900/1965). *The Interpretation of Dreams.* New York: Norton.

Freud, S. (1901/1971). *The Psychopathology of Everyday Life.* New York: Norton.

Freud, S. (1912/1958). Recommendations to physicians practicing psychoanalysis. *Standard Edition, 12,* 110–120.

Freud, S. (1914/1957). On narcissism: An introduction. *Standard Edition, 14,* 60–102.

Freud, S. (1915/1957). The unconscious. *Standard Edition, 12,* 161–215.

Freud, S. (1923/1960). *The Ego and the Id.* New York: Norton.

Freud, S. (1925/1963). *An Autobiographical Study.* New York: Norton.

Freud, S., & Rie, O. (1891). *Klinische Studie uber die halbseitige Cerebellahmung der Kinder.* Vienna: Deuticke.

Fromm, E. (1970). Age regression with unexpected reappearance of a repressed childhood language. *International Journal of Clinical and Experimental Hypnosis, 18,* 79–88.

Funk, C. (1911). On the clinical nature of the substance which cures polyneuritis in birds induced by a diet of polished rice. *Journal of Physiology, 43,* 395–400.

Fuster, J. M. (1985). The frontal lobes, mediator of cross-temporal contingencies. *Human Neurobiology, 4,* 169–179.

Galin, D. (1974). Implications for psychiatry of left and right cerebral specialization: A neurophysiological context for unconscious processes. *Archives of General Psychiatry, 31,* 572–583.

Galin, D., Diamond, R., & Braff, D. (1977). Lateralization of conversion symptoms: More frequent on the left. *American Journal of Psychiatry, 134,* 578–580.

Gastaut, H., & Zifkin, B. G. (1984). Ictal visual hallucinations of numerals. *Neurology, 34,* 950–953.

Gazzaniga, M. S. (1970). *The Bisected Brain.* New York: Appleton-Century-Crofts.

Gazzaniga, M. S. (1985). *The Social Brain: Discovering the Networks of the Mind.* New York: Basic Books.

Gelineau, J. (1880). De la narcolepsie. *Gazette de l'Hôpital, 53,* 626–628.

Geschwind, N. (1965). Disconnection syndromes in animals and man. *Brain, 88,* 237–294.

Gilles de la Tourette, G. (1885). Étude sur une affection nerveuse caracterisée par l'incoordination motrice accompagnée d'echolalie et de copralalie. *Archives of Neurology, 9,* 19–42.

Gloning, I., Gloning, K., & Hoff, H. (1968). *Neuropsychological Symptoms and Syndromes in Lesions of the Occipital Lobe and the Adjacent Areas.* Paris: Gauthier-Villars.

Gloor, P., Oliver, A., Quesney, L. F., Andermann, F., & Horowitz, S. (1982). The role of the limbic system in experiental phenomena of temporal lobe epilepsy. *Annals of Neurology, 12,* 129–144.

Goddard, G. V., McIntyre, D. C., & Leetch, C. K. (1969). A permanent change in brain functioning resulting from daily electrical stimulation. *Experimental Neurology, 25,* 295–330.

Gogol, D. (1874). *Aphasie, Apraxie, Agnosie.* Berlin: Springer.

Goldberg, E. (1985). Akinesia, tardive dysmentia and frontal lobe disorder in schizophrenia. *Schizophrenia Bulletin, 11,* 255–263.

Goldberg, G. (1985). Supplementary motor area structure and function: Review and hypotheses. *Behavioral and Brain Sciences, 8,* 567–616.

Goldberg, G., Mayer, N. H., & Toglia, J. U. (1981). Medial frontal cortex infarction and the alien hand sign. *Archives of Neurology, 38,* 683–686.

Goldstein, G. (1978). Cognitive and perceptual differences between schirophrenics and organics. *Schizophrenia Bulletin, 4,* 255–263.

Goldstein, K. (1936). The modification of behavior consequent to cerebral lesions. *Psychiatric Quarterly, 10,* 586–596.

Goldstein, K. (1942). *Aftereffects of Brain Injuries in War.* New York: Grune & Stratton.

Gowers, W.R. (1892). *A Manual of Diseases of the Nervous System.* London: Churchill.

Gowers, W. R. (1907). *The Borderland of Epilepsy: Faints, Vagal Attacks, Vertigo, Migraine, Sleep Symptoms and Their Treatment.* Philadelphia: Blackiston.

Greenblatt, S. H. (1976). Subangular alexia without agraphia or hemianopsia. *Brain and Language, 3,* 229–245.

Greenson, R. (1950). The mother tongue and the mother. *International Journal of Psychoanalysis, 31,* 18–23.

Greenwood, P., Wilson, D. H., & Gazzaniga, M. S. (1977). Dream report following commissurotomy. *Cortex, 13,* 311–316.

Grossman, S. P. (1967). *A Textbook of Physiological Psychology.* New York: Wiley.

Guiloff, R. J., & Fruns, M. (1988). Limb pain in migraine and cluster headache. *Journal of Neurology, Neurosurgery and Psychiatry, 51,* 1022–1031.

Gur, R. E., & Gur, R. C. (1975). Defense mechanisms, psychosomatic symptomatology and conjugate lateral eye movements. *Journal of Consulting and Clinical Psychology, 43,* 416–420.

Gur, R. E., & Gur, R. C. (1977). Correlates of conjugate lateral eye movements in man. In S. Harnad, R. W. Doty, & L. Goldstein (Eds.), *Lateralization in the Nervous System.* New York: Academic Press.

Guze, S., Woodruff, R., & Clayton, P. (1971). Hysteria and antisocial behavior: Further evidence of an association. *American Journal of Psychiatry, 127,* 957–960.

Haaland, K. Y., & Flaherty, D. (1984). The different types of limb apraxia errors made by patients with left vs. right hemisphere damage. *Brain and Cognition, 3,* 370–384.

Haas, D. C., & Lourie, H. (1984). Delayed deterioration of consciousness after trivial head injury in childhood. *British Medical Journal, 289,* 1625.

Haas, D. C., & Ross, G. S. (1986). Transient global amnesia triggered by mild head trauma. *Brain, 109,* 251–257.

Harrington, A. (1985). Nineteenth-century ideas on hemisphere differences and "duality of mind." *Behavioral and Brain Sciences, 8,* 617–660.

Harrison, M. J. G. (1981). Dysphasia during sleep due to an unusual vascular lesion. *Journal of Neurology, Neurosurgery and Psychiatry, 44,* 739–740.

Hart, J., Berndt, R. S., & Caramazza, A. (1985). Category-specific naming deficit following cerebral infarction. *Nature, 316,* 439–440.

Hartmann, H. (1939/1958). *Ego Psychology and the Problem of Adaptation.* New York: International Universities Press.

Hayman, M. A., & Abrams, R. (1977). Capgras syndrome and cerebral dysfunction. *British Journal of Psychiatry, 130*, 68–71.

Head, H. (1922). An address on the diagnosis of hysteria. *British Medical Journal, i*, 827.

Heathfield, K. W. G., Croft, P. B., & Swash, M. (1973). The syndrome of transient global amnesia. *Brain, 96*, 729–736.

Hecaen, H., & Albert, M. L. (1978). *Human Neuropsychology*. New York: Wiley.

Hecaen, H., & Angelergues, R. (1962). Agnosia for faces (prosopagnosia). *Archives of Neurology, 7*, 92–100.

Hecaen, H., & de Ajuriaguerra, J. (1954). Balint's syndrome (psychic paralysis of vision) and its minor forms. *Brain, 77*, 373–400.

Hecaen, H., de Ajuriaguerra, J., David, M., Rouques, M. B., & Dell, R. (1950). Paralysie psychique du regard de Balint au cours de l'évolution d'une leuco-encéphalite type Balo. *Revue Neurologique, 83*, 81–104.

Heilman, K. M. (1979). Neglect and related disorders. In K. M. Heilman & E. Valenstein (Eds.), *Clinical Neuropsychology* (pp. 268–307). New York: Oxford University Press.

Heilman, K. M., Rothi, L. J., & Valenstein, E. (1982). Two forms of ideomotor apraxia. *Neurology, 32*, 342–346.

Heilman, K. M., Schwartz, H., & Watson, R. T. (1978). Hypoarousal in patients with neglect syndrome and emotional indifference. *Neurology, 28*, 229–232.

Heilman, K. M., & Valenstein, E. (1979). Mechanisms underlying hemispatial neglect. *Annals of Neurology, 5*, 166–170.

Hendricks, J. C., Morrison, A. R., & Mann, G. L. (1982). Different behaviors during paradoxical sleep without atonia depend on pontine lesion site. *Brain Research, 239*, 81–105.

Hernandez-Peon, R., Chavez-Iberra, G., & Aguilar-Figueroa, E. (1963). Somatic evoked potentials in one case of hysterical anesthesia. *Electroencephalography and Clinical Neurophysiology, 15*, 889–896.

Hernandez-Peon, R., Scherrer, H., & Jouvet, M. (1956). Modification of electrical activity in cochlear nucleus during "attention" in unanesthetized cats. *Science, 123*, 331.

Hirst, W. (1982). The amnesic syndrome: Descriptions and explanations. *Psychological Bulletin, 91*, 435–460.

Hoboda, D. (1986). Paradoxical sleep facilitation by interictal activity of right temporal origin. *Biological Psychiatry, 21*, 1267–1278.

Hobson, J. A. (1988). *The Dreaming Brain*. New York: Basic Books.

Hobson, J. A., & McCarley, R. W. (1977). The brain as a dream state generator: An activation–synthesis hypothesis of the dream process. *American Journal of Psychiatry, 134*, 1335–1338.

Holt, R. R. (1965). A review of some of Freud's biological assumptions and their influence on his theories. In N. S. Greenfield & W. C. Lewis (Eds.), *Psychoanalysis and Current Biological Thought* (pp. 93–124). Madison: University of Wisconsin Press.

Holt, R. R. (1985). The current status of psychoanalytic theory. *Psychoanalytic Psychology, 2*, 289–315.

Holt, R. R. (1989). *Freud Reappraised: A Fresh Look at Psychoanalytic Theory.* New York: The Guilford Press.

Hooshmand, H., Sepdham, T., & Vries, J. K. (1974). Klüver–Bucy syndrome: Successful treatment with carbamazepine. *Journal of the American Medical Association, 229,* 1782.

Hoppe, K. D. (1977). Split brains and psychoanalysis. *Psychoanalytic Quarterly, 46,* 220–244.

Humphrey, D. R. (1979). On the cortical control of visually directed reaching: Contributions by non-precentral motor areas. In R. E. Talbott & D. R. Humphrey (Eds.), *Posture and Movement* (pp. 51–112). New York: Raven Press.

Humphrey, M. E., & Zangwill, O. L. (1951). Cessation of dreaming after brain injury. *Journal of Neurology, Neurosurgery and Psychiatry, 14,* 322–325.

Itard, J. M. G. (1825). Mémoire sur quelques fonctions involontaires des appareils de la locomotion, de la préhension et de la voix. *Archives of General Medicine, 8,* 385–407.

Jackson, J. H. (1864). Clinical remarks on cases of defects of expression (by words, writing, signs, etc.) in diseases of the nervous system. *Lancet, i,* 604–605.

Jackson, J. H. (1932). *Selected Writings of John Hughlings Jackson* (J. Taylor, Ed.). London: Hodder & Stoughton.

Jacobs, L., Feldman, M., & Diamond, S. P. (1973). Palinacousis: Persistent or recurring auditory sensations. *Cortex, 9,* 275–282.

Janet, P. (1894). *État Mental des Hystériques.* Paris.

Jeliffe, S. E. (1906). Aphasia, hemiparesis and hemianesthesia in migraine. *New York Medical Journal, 83,* 33–36.

Jensen, T. S., & Olivarius, B. de F. (1981). Transient global amnesia: Its clinical and pathophysiological basis and prognosis. *Acta Neurologica Scandinavica, 63,* 220–230.

Jonas, S. (1981). The supplementary motor region and speech emission. *Journal of Communicative Disorders, 14,* 349–373.

Jones, E. (1953). *The Life and Work of Sigmund Freud.* New York: Basic Books.

Jones, E. G., & Powell, T. P. S. (1969a). Connections of the somatosensory cortex of the rhesus monkey: I. Ipsilateral cortical connections. *Brain, 92,* 477–502.

Jones, E. G., & Powell, T. P. S. (1969b). Connections of the somatosensory cortex in the rhesus monkey: II. Contralateral cortical connections. *Brain, 92,* 717–730.

Joseph, R. (1982). The neuropsychology of development: Hemispheric laterality, limbic language and the origin of thought. *Journal of Clinical Psychology, 38,* 4–33.

Jouvet, M. (1962). Recherches sur les structures nerveuses et les mécanismes responsables des différentes phases du sommeil physiologique. *Archives of Italian Biology, 100,* 125–206.

Jouvet, M., & Delorme, F. (1965). Locus coeruleus et sommeil paradoxal. *Comptes Rendus des Séances de la Société de Biologie, 159,* 895–899.

Juergens, S. M., Fredrickson, P. A., & Pfeiffer, F. E. (1986). Balint's syndrome mistaken for visual conversion reaction. *Psychosomatics, 27,* 597–599.

Jus, A., Jus, K., Villeneuve, A., Pires, A., Lachance, R., Fortier, J., & Villeneuve, R. (1973). Studies on dream recall in chronic schizophrenic patients after prefrontal lobotomy. *Biological Psychiatry, 6,* 275–293.

Kaitin, K. I. (1986). Sleep disturbance produced by electrical stimulation of the locus coeruleus in a human subject. *Biological Psychiatry, 21,* 710–716.

Kay, M. C., & Levin, H. S. (1982). Prosopagnosia. *American Journal of Ophthalmology, 94,* 75–80.

Kenshalo, D. R., & Isensee, O. (1980). Response of primate SI cortical neurons to noxious stimuli. *Neuroscience Abstracts, 6,* 245.

Kerr, N. H., & Foulkes, D. (1981). Right hemisphere mediation of dream visualization: A case study. *Cortex, 17,* 603–610.

Klein, G. S. (1954). Need and regulation. In M. R. Jones (Ed.), *Nebraska Symposium on Motivation* (pp. 224–274). Lincoln: University of Nebraska Press.

Kleitman, N. (1963). *Sleep and Wakefulness.* Chicago: University of Chicago Press.

Klüver, H., & Bucy, P. C. (1939). Preliminary analysis of functions of the temporal lobes in monkeys. *Archives of Neurology and Psychiatry, 42,* 979–1000.

Konorski, J., & Lawicka, W. (1964). Analysis of errors by prefrontal animals in the delayed reponse test. In J. M. Warren & K. Akert (Eds.), *The Frontal Granular Cortex and Behavior.* New York: McGraw-Hill.

Kopelman, M. D. (1987). Amnesia: Organic and psychogenic. *British Journal of Psychiatry, 150,* 428–442.

Korsakoff, S. S. (1887). Disturbance of psychic function in alcoholic paralysis and its relation to the disturbance of the psychic sphere in multiple neuritis of non-alcoholic origin. *Vestnik Psichiatrii,* Vol. IV, Fascicle 2.

Koukkou, M., & Lehman, D. (1983). Dreaming: The functional state-shift hypothesis. A neurophysiological model. *British Journal of Psychiatry, 142,* 221–231.

Kretschmer, E. (1926). *Hysteria.* New York: Basic Books.

Krishnan, R. R., Volow, M. R., Cavenar, J. O., & Miller, P. P. (1984). Dreams of flying in narcoleptic patients. *Psychosomatics, 25,* 423–425.

Kubie, L. S. (1953). Some implications for psychoanalysis of modern concepts of the organization of the brain. *Psychoanalytic Quarterly, 22,* 21–52.

Lader, M. (1973). The psychophysiology of hysterics. *Journal of Psychosomatic Research, 17,* 255–269.

Lader, M., & Sartorius, N. (1968). Anxiety in patients with conversion symptoms. *Journal of Neurology, Neurosurgery and Psychiatry, 31,* 490–495.

Lang, A. E., & Marsden, C. D. (1983). Spasmodic dysphonia in Gilles de la Tourette's disease. *Archives of Neurology, 40,* 51–52.

Laplane, D., Talairach, J., & Meininger, V. (1977). Clinical consequences of corticectomies involving the supplementary motor area in man. *Journal of Neurological Science, 34,* 301–314.

Larkin, K. T. (1984). The neurobiology of the narcoleptic syndrome. *International Journal of Neuroscience, 26,* 1–17.

Lauritzen, M. (1987). Cerebral blood flow in migraine and cortical spreading depression. *Acta Neurologica Scandinavica, 76*(Suppl. 113), 1–35.

Lennox, W. G., & Lennox, M. A. (1960). *Epilepsy and Related Disorders*. Boston: Little, Brown.

Lesser, R. P., Lueders, H., Conomy, J. P., Furlan, A. J., & Dinner, D. S. (1983). Sensory seizure mimicking a psychogenic seizure. *Neurology, 33,* 800–802.

Leuret, F. (1834). *Fragments Psychologiques sur la Folie*. Paris.

Levy, D. E. (1988). Transient CNS deficits: A common, benign syndrome in young adults. *Neurology, 38,* 831–836.

Levy, J., & Trevarthen, C. (1976). Metacontrol of hemispheric function in human split brain patients. *Journal of Experimental Psychology: Human Perception and Performance, 2,* 299–312.

Levy, R., & Behrman, J. (1970). Cortical evoked responses in hysterical hemianesthesia. *Electroencephalography and Clinical Neurophysiology, 29,* 400–404.

Levy, R., & Mushin, J. (1973). Somatosensory evoked responses in patients with hysterical anesthesia. *Journal of Psychosomatic Research, 17,* 81–84.

Ley, R. G., & Bryden, M. P. (1979). Hemispheric differences in recognizing faces and emotions. *Brain and Language, 7,* 127–138.

Libet, B., Gleason, C. A., Wright, E. W., & Pearl, D. K. (1983). Time of conscious intention to act in relation to onset of cerebral activity (readiness potential): The unconscious initiation of a freely voluntary act. *Brain, 106,* 623–642.

Liepmann, H. (1900). Das krankheitshild der Apraxie (motorischen Asymbolie). *Monatsschriffte für Psychiatrie, 8,* 15–44, 102–132, 182–197.

Lishman, W. A. (1978). *Organic Psychiatry: The Psychological Consequences of Cerebral Disorder*. London: Blackwell.

Liveing, E. (1873). *On Megrim: Sick-Headache and Some Allied Disorders: A Contribution to the Pathology of Nerve Storms*. London: Churchill.

Ludwig, A. M. (1972). Hysteria: A neurobiological theory. *Archives of General Psychiatry, 20,* 771–777.

Ludwig, A. M. (1980). *Principles of Clinical Psychiatry*. New York: The Free Press.

Lugaresi, E., Medori, R., Montagna, P., Baruzzi, A., Cortelli, P., Lugaresi, A., Tinuper, P., Zucconi, M., & Gambetti, P. (1986). Fatal familial insomnia and dysautonomia with selective degeneration of thalamic nuclei. *New England Journal of Medicine, 315,* 997–1003.

Luria, A. R. (1960). *The origin and cerebral organization of man's conscious action*. Lecture to the XIX International Congress of Psychology, London. Moscow: Moscow University Press.

Luria, A. R. (1980). *Higher Cortical Functions in Man* (2nd ed.). New York: Basic Books.

MacLean, P. D. (1949). Psychosomatic disease and the "visceral brain." *Psychosomatic Medicine, 11,* 338–353.

Maeder, A. (1908). Nouvelles contributions à la psychopathologie de la vie quotidienne. *Archives de Psychologie, 7,* 283.

Maeder, A. (1912). Uber die Funktion des Traumes. *Jahrbuch für Psychoanalyse und Psychopathologie Forschung, 4,* 692.

Magaro, P. A., Smith, P., & Ashbrook, R. M. (1983). Personality style differences in visual search performance. *Psychiatry Research, 10,* 131–138.

Malone, D. R., Morris, H. H., Kay, M. C., & Levin, H. S. (1982). Prosopagnosia: A double dissociation between the recognition of familiar and unfamiliar faces. *Journal of Neurology, Neurosurgery and Psychiatry, 45,* 820–822.

Malone, G. L., & Leiman, H. I. (1983). Differential diagnosis of palinacousis in a psychiatric patient. *American Journal of Psychiatry, 140,* 1067–1068.

Marin, R. S., & Tucker, G. J. (1981). Psychopathology and hemisphere dysfunction: A review. *Journal of Nervous and Mental Disease, 169,* 546–555.

Markus, H. (1983). Self-knowledge: An expanded view. *Journal of Personality, 51,* 543–565.

Marsden, C. D. (1986). Hysteria: A neurologist's view. *Psychological Medicine, 16,* 277–288.

Masson, J. M. (Ed.). (1985). *The Complete Letters of Sigmund Freud to Wilhelm Fliess, 1887–1904.* Cambridge, MA: Harvard University Press.

Meadows, J. C. (1974). The anatomical basis of prosopagnosia. *Journal of Neurology, Neurosurgery and Psychiatry, 37,* 489–501.

Meares, R., & Horvath, T. (1972). "Acute" and "chronic" hysteria. *British Journal of Psychiatry, 121,* 653–657.

Merrin, E. L. (1981). Schizophrenia and brain asymmetry: An evaluation of evidence of dominant lobe dysfunction. *Journal of Nervous and Mental Disease, 169,* 405–413.

Merrin, E. L., & Silberfarb, P. M. (1976). The Capgras phenomenon. *Archives of General Psychiatry, 33,* 965–968.

Merskey, H. (1978). Hysterical phenomena. *British Journal of Hospital Medicine, 19,* 305–309.

Merskey, H. (1986). The importance of hysteria. *British Journal of Psychiatry, 149,* 23–28.

Merskey, H., & Buhrich, N. A. (1975). Hysteria and organic brain disease. *British Journal of Medical Psychology, 48,* 359–366.

Merskey, H., & Trimble, K. (1979). Personality, sexual adjustment and brain lesions in patients with conversion symptoms. *American Journal of Psychiatry, 136,* 179–182.

Merskey, H., & Watson, G. D. (1979). The lateralization of pain. *Pain, 7,* 271–280.

Miller, L. (1984a). Neuropsychological concepts of somatoform disorders. *International Journal of Psychiatry in Medicine, 14,* 31–46.

Miller, L. (1984b). Hemispheric asymmetry of cognitive processing in schizophrenics. *Psychological Reports, 55,* 932–934.

Miller, L. (1986a). Some comments on cerebral hemispheric models of consciousness. *Psychoanalytic Review, 73,* 129–144.

Miller, L. (1986b). "Narrow localizationism" in psychiatric neuropsychology. *Psychological Medicine, 16,* 729–734.

Miller, L. (1986c). The subcortex, frontal lobes and psychosis. *Schizophrenia Bulletin, 12,* 340–341.

Miller, L. (1986–1987). Is alexithymia a disconnection syndrome? A neuropsychological perspective. *International Journal of Psychiatry in Medicine, 16,* 199–209.

Miller, L. (1987). Neuropsychology of the aggressive psychopath: An integrative review. *Aggressive Behavior, 13,* 119–140.

Miller, L. (1988a). Neuropsychological perspectives on delinquency. *Behavioral Sciences and the Law*, 6, 409–428.

Miller, L. (1988b). Ego autonomy, creativity and cognitive style: A neuropsychodynamic approach. *Psychiatric Clinics of North America*, 11, 383–397.

Miller, L. (1989). On the neuropsychology of dreams. *Psychoanalytic Review*, 76, 375–401.

Miller, L. (1990). *Inner Natures: Brain, Self and Personality*. New York: St. Martin's Press.

Miller, L. (1991). Brain and self: Toward a neuropsychodynamic model of ego autonomy and personality. *Journal of the American Academy of Psychoanalysis*, 19, 213–234.

Milner, B. (1963). Effects of different brain lesions on card sorting. *Archives of Neurology*, 9, 90–100.

Milner, B., Corkin, S., & Teuber, H.-L. (1968). Further analysis of the hippocampal amnesic syndrome: 14-year followup study of H.M. *Neuropsychologia*, 6, 215–234.

Mitchell, S. W. (1872). *Injuries of Nerves and their Consequences*. Philadelphia: Lippincott.

Morrison, A. R. (1979). Brainstem regulation of behavior during sleep and wakefulness. In J. M. Sprague & A. N. Epstein (Eds.), *Progress in Psychobiology and Physiological Psychology* (Vol. 8, pp. 91–131). New York: Academic Press.

Morrison, R. L., & Tarter, R. E. (1984). Neuropsychological findings relating to Capgras syndrome. *Biological Psychiatry*, 19, 1119–1128.

Mountcastle, V. B. (1974). Neural mechanisms in somesthesia. In V. B. Mountcastle (Ed.), *Medical Physiology* (13th ed., pp. 307–347). St. Louis: Mosby.

Mountcastle, V. B., Lynch, J. C., & Georgopoulos, A. (1975). Posterior parietal association cortex of the monkey: Command functions for operations within extrapersonal space. *Journal of Neurophysiology*, 38, 875–908.

Mountcastle, V. B., & Powell, T. P. S. (1959). Neural mechanisms subserving cutaneous sensibility with special reference to the role of afferent inhibition in sensory perception and discrimination. *Bulletin of the Johns Hopkins Hospital*, 105, 201–232.

Muller, H. F. (1985). Prefrontal cortex dysfunction as a common factor in psychosis. *Acta Psychiatrica Scandinavica*, 71, 431–440.

Murri, L., Arena, R., Siciliano, G., Mazzotta, R., & Muratorio, A. (1984). Dream recall in patients with focal cerebral lesions. *Archives of Neurology*, 41, 183–185.

Murri, L., Massatani, G., Siciliano, L., & Arena, R. (1985). Dream recall after sleep interruption in brain-injured patients. *Sleep*, 8, 356–362.

Nakada, T., Lee, H., Kwee, I. L., & Lerner, A. M. (1984). Epileptic Klüver–Bucy syndrome: Case report. *Journal of Clinical Psychiatry*, 45, 87–88.

Nauta, W. J. (1971). The problem of the frontal lobe: A reinterpretation. *Journal of Psychiatric Research*, 8, 167–187.

Nightingale, S. (1982). Somatoparaphrenia: A case report. *Cortex*, 18, 463–467.

Obler, L. K., Albert, M. L., & Gordon, H. (1975, October). *Asymmetrical cerebral dominance for language in fluent bilinguals.* Paper presented at the Academy of Aphasia, Victoria, BC, Canada.

Ochs, S. (1965). *Elements of Neurophysiology.* New York: Wiley.

Olesen, J., Larsen, B., & Lauritzen, M. (1981). Focal hyperemia followed by spreading oligemia and impaired activation of rCBF in classical migraine. *Annals of Neurology, 9,* 344–352.

Olivarius, B. de F., & Jensen, T. S. (1979). Transient global amnesia in migraine. *Headache, 19,* 335–338.

Orgogozo, J. M., & Larsen, B. (1979). Activation of the supplementary motor area during voluntary movement in man suggests it works as a supramotor area. *Science, 206,* 847–850.

Ostow, M. (1954). A psychoanalytic contribution to the study of brain function: I. The frontal lobes. *Psychoanalytic Quarterly, 23,* 317–338.

Ostow, M. (1955). A psychoanalytic contribution to the study of brain function: II. The temporal lobes. III. Synthesis. *Psychoanalytic Quarterly, 24,* 383–423.

Palliard, J., Michel, F., & Stelmach, G. (1983). Localization without content: A tactile analogue of "blind sight." *Archives of Neurology, 40,* 548–551.

Palm Beach Post. (1985, December 28). Fifteen years of amnesia ends with reunion for couple. p. A2.

Peled, R. (1984). Speech arrest and supplementary motor area seizures. *Neurology, 34,* 110–111.

Pena-Casanova, J., Roig-Rovira, T., Bermudez, A., & Tolosa-Saro, E. (1985). Optic aphasia, optic apraxia and loss of dreaming. *Brain and Language, 26,* 63–71.

Penfield, W. E. (1952). Memory mechanisms. *Archives of Neurology and Psychiatry, 67,* 178–198.

Penfield, W. E., & Erickson, T. C. (1941). *Epilepsy and Cerebral Localization.* Springfield, IL: Thomas.

Penfield, W. E., & Faulk, M. E. (1955). The insula: Further observations on its function. *Brain, 78,* 445–470.

Penfield, W. E., & Jasper, H. (1954). *Epilepsy and the Functional Anatomy of the Human Brain.* Boston: Little, Brown.

Penfield, W. E., & Roberts, L. (1959). *Speech and Brain Mechanisms.* Princeton, NJ: Princeton University Press.

Penfield, W. E., & Welch, K. (1951). The supplementary motor area of the cerebral cortex. *Archives of Neurology and Psychiatry, 66,* 289–317.

Perley, M. G., & Guze, S. (1962). Hysteria: The stability and usefulness of clinical criteria. *New England Journal of Medicine, 266,* 421–426.

Pick, A. (1903). Clinical studies: III. On reduplicative paramnesia. *Brain, 26,* 260–267.

Pine, F. (1990). *Drive, Ego, Object, and Self: A Synthesis for Clinical Work.* New York: Basic Books.

Pitres, A. (1895). Étude sur l'aphasie chez les polyglottes. *Revue de Médecine, 15,* 873–899.

Poppel, E., Held, R., & Frost, D. (1973). Residual visual function after brain wound involving the central visual pathway in man. *Nature, 243,* 295–296.

Post, R. M. (1980). Intermittent versus continuous stimulation: Effect of time interval on the development of sensitization or tolerance. *Life Sciences, 26,* 1275–1282.

Post, R. M. (1981). Lidocaine-kindled limbic seizures: Behavioral implications. In J. A. Wada (Ed.), *Kindling 2.* New York: Raven Press.

Post, R. M., & Kopanda, R. T. (1976). Cocaine, kindling and psychosis. *American Journal of Psychiatry, 133,* 627–634.

Post, R. M., Rubinow, D. R., & Ballenger, J. C. (1984). Conditioning, sensitization and kindling implications for the course of affective illness. In R. M. Post & J. C. Ballenger (Eds.), *Neurobiology of Mood Disorders.* Baltimore: Williams & Wilkins.

Post, R. M., Rubinow, D. R., & Ballenger, J. C. (1986). Conditioning and sensitization in the longitudinal course of affective illness. *British Journal of Psychiatry, 149,* 191–201.

Post, R. M., Uhde, T. W., Putnam, F. W., Ballenger, J. C., & Berrettini, W. H. (1982). Kindling and carbamazepine in affective illness. *Journal of Nervous and Mental Disease, 170,* 717–731.

Racine, R. (1978). Kindling: The first decade. *Neurosurgery, 3,* 234–252.

Ramani, S. V. (1983). Primary reading epilepsy. *Archives of Neurology, 40,* 39–41.

Ramani, S. V., Quesney, L. F., Olsen, D., & Gumnit, R. J. (1980). Diagnosis of hysterical seizures in epileptic patients. *American Journal of Psychiatry, 137,* 705–709.

Rasmussen, T. (1974). Seizures with local onset. In P. J. Vinken & G. W. Bruyn (Eds.), *Handbook of Clinical Neurology* (pp. 80–81). Amsterdam: North-Holland.

Regestein, Q. R., Reich, P., & Mufson, M. J. (1983). Narcolepsy: An initial clinical approach. *Journal of Clinical Psychiatry, 44,* 166–172.

Reynolds, J. R. (1869). Remarks on paralysis and other disorders of motion and sensation, dependent on idea. *British Medical Journal, ii,* 483–485.

Ribot, T. (1882). *Diseases of Memory.* New York: Appleton.

Ribot, T. (1883). *Les Maladies de la Mémoire.* Paris: Alcan.

Ribstein, M. (1974). Hypnagogic hallucinations. In M. H. Chase, W. C. Stern, & P. L. Walter (Eds.), *Sleep Research* (pp. 145–160). Los Angeles: Brain Information Service.

Robert, W. (1886). *Der Traum als Naturnotwendigkeit erklart.* Hamburg.

Rosen, S. R. (1951). Vasomotor responses in hysteria. *Journal of the Mount Sinai Hospital, 18,* 179–190.

Ross, E. D., Harney, J. H., deLacoste-Utamsing, C., & Purdy, P. D. (1981). How the brain integrates affective and propositional language into a unified behavioral function: Hypothesis based on clinicoanatomic evidence. *Archives of Neurology, 38,* 745–748.

Ross, E. D., & Rush, A. J. (1981). Diagnosis and neuroanatomical correlates of depression in brain-damaged patients: Implications for a neurology of depression. *Archives of General Psychiatry, 38,* 1344–1354.

Roth, B., & Bruhova, S. (1969). Dreams in narcolepsy, hypersomnia and dissociated sleep disorders. *Experimental Medicine and Surgery, 27,* 187–209.

Roy, A. (1980). Hysteria. *Journal of Psychosomatic Research, 24,* 53–56.

Ruiz, E. J. (1976). Influence of bilingualism on communication in groups. *International Journal of Group Psychotherapy, 25,* 391–395.

Russell, W. R., & Nathan, P. W. (1932). Traumatic amnesia. *Brain,* 69, 280–300.

Sackeim, H. A., Greenberg, M. S., Weiman, A. L., Ruben, C. G., Hungerbuhler, J. P., & Geschwind, N. (1982). Hemispheric asymmetry in the expression of positive and negative emotions. *Archives of Neurology, 39,* 210–218.

Sackeim, H. A., & Gur, R. C. (1978). Lateral asymmetry in intensity of emotional expression. *Neuropsychologia, 16,* 473–482.

Sacks, O. (1985). *Migraine: Understanding a Common Disorder.* Los Angeles: University of California Press.

Salamy, A. (1978). Commissural transmission: Maturational changes in humans. *Science, 200,* 1409–1411.

Saurwein, H., & Lassonde, M. C. (1983). Intra- and interhemispheric processing of visual information in callosal agenesis. *Neuropsychologia, 21,* 167–171.

Schacter, D. L., Wang, P. L., Tulving, E., & Freedman, M. (1982). Functional retrograde amnesia: A quantitative case study. *Neuropsychologia, 20,* 523–532.

Schanfald, D., Pearlman, C., & Greenberg, R. (1985). The capacity of stroke patients to report dreams. *Cortex, 21,* 237–247.

Schenck, C. H., Bundlie, S. R., Ettinger, M. G., & Mahowald, M. W. (1986). Chronic behavioral disorders of human REM sleep: A new category of parasomnia. *Sleep, 9,* 293–308.

Scherner, K. A. (1861). *Das Leben des Traumes.* Berlin.

Seidman, L. J. (1983). Schizophrenia and brain dysfunction: An integration of recent neurodiagnostic findings. *Psychological Bulletin, 93,* 195–338.

Shapiro, A. K., & Shapiro, E. (1977). Subcategorizing Gilles de la Tourette's syndrome. *American Journal of Psychiatry, 134,* 818–819.

Shapiro, D. (1965). *Neurotic Styles.* New York: Basic Books.

Slater, E. (1965). Diagnosis of hysteria. *British Medical Journal, i,* 1395–1399.

Slater, E., & Glithero, E. (1965). A followup of patients diagnosed as suffering from "hysteria." *Journal of Psychosomatic Research, 9,* 9–13.

Smokler, I. A., & Shevrin, H. (1979). Cerebral lateralization and personality style. *Archives of General Psychiatry, 36,* 949–954.

Sours, J. A. (1963). Narcolepsy and other disturbances in the sleep–waking rhythm: A study of 115 cases with review of the literature. *Journal of Nervous and Mental Disease, 137,* 525–542.

Spencer, S. S., Spencer, D. D., Williamson, P. D., & Mattson, R. H. (1983). Sexual automatisms in complex partial seizures. *Neurology, 33,* 527–533.

Sperry, R. W. (1968). Mental unity following surgical disconnection of the cerebral hemispheres. *Harvey Lectures, 62,* 293–323.

Sperry, R. W. (1974). Lateral specialization in the surgically separated hemispheres. In F. O. Schmitt & F. G. Worden (Eds.), *The Neurosciences: Third Study Program* (pp. 5–19). Cambridge, MA: MIT Press.

Springer, S. P., & Deutsch, G. (1985). *Left Brain, Right Brain* (rev. ed.). New York: Freeman.

Squire, L. R. (1982). The neuropsychology of human memory. *Annual Review of Neuroscience, 5,* 241–273.

Squire, L. R. (1986). The neuropsychology of memory dysfunction and its assessment. In I. Grant & K. M. Adams (Eds.), *Neuropsychological Assessment of Neuropsychiatric Disorders* (pp. 268–299). New York: Oxford University Press.

Squire, L. R., & Cohen, N. J. (1982). Remote memory, retrograde amnesia and the neuropsychology of memory. In L. S. Cermak (Ed.), *Human Memory and Amnesia*. Hillsdale, NJ: Erlbaum.

Standage, K. P., & Fenton, G. W. (1975, June). *Organic factors in the etiology of hysterical disorders: A controlled study of pseudoseizure cases.* Paper presented at the annual scientific meeting of the Society of Biological Psychiatry, New York.

Staton, R. D., Brumback, R. A., & Wilson, H. (1982). Reduplicative paramnesia: A disconnection syndrome of memory. *Cortex, 18,* 23–36.

Stern, D. B. (1977). Handedness and the lateral distribution of conversion reactions. *Journal of Nervous and Mental Disease, 164,* 122–128.

Stern, M. M. (1988). *Repetition and Trauma: Toward a Teleonomic Theory of Psychoanalysis.* Hillsdale, NJ: The Analytic Press.

Stern, T. A., & Murray, G. B. (1984). Complex partial seizures presenting as a psychiatric illness. *Journal of Nervous and Mental Disease, 172,* 625–627.

Stone, M. H. (1977). Dreams, free association, and the nondominant hemisphere: An integration of psychoanalytical, neurophysiological, and historical data. *Journal of the American Academy of Psychoanalysis, 5,* 255–284.

Strub, R. L., & Black, F. W. (1981). *Organic Brain Syndromes: An Introduction to Neurobehavioral Disorders.* Philadelphia: Davis.

Stuss, D. T., & Benson, D. F. (1984). Neuropsychological studies of the frontal lobes. *Psychological Bulletin, 95,* 3–28.

Stuss, D. T., & Benson, D. F. (1986). *The Frontal Lobes.* New York: Raven Press.

Sulloway, F. J. (1979). *Freud, Biologist of the Mind: Beyond the Psychoanalytic Legend.* New York: Basic Books.

Sully, J. (1893). The dream as a revelation. *Fortnightly Review, 53,* 354.

Talairach, J., Bancaud, J., & Geier, S. (1973). The cingulate gyrus and human behavior. *Electroencephalography and Clinical Neurophysiology, 34,* 45–52.

Tanji, J., & Kurata, K. (1982). Comparison of movement-related neurons in two cortical motor areas of primates. *Journal of Neurophysiology, 400,* 633–653.

Tanji, J., Taniguchi, K., & Saga, T. (1980). Supplementary motor area: Neuronal response to motor instructions. *Journal of Neurophysiology, 43,* 60–68.

Terzian, H., & Ore, G. D. (1955). Syndrome of Klüver and Bucy: Reproduced in man by bilateral removal of the temporal lobes. *Neurology, 5,* 373.

Teuber, H.-L. (1964). The riddle of frontal lobe function in man. In J.M. Warren & K. Akert (Eds.), *The Frontal Granular Cortex and Behavior* (pp. 410–477). New York: McGraw-Hill.

Thompson, R. F. (1975). *Introduction to Physiological Psychology.* New York: Harper & Row.

Tinnin, L. (1989). The anatomy of the ego. *Psychiatry, 52,* 404–409.

Triarhou, L. C., & del Cerro, M. (1985). Freud's contribution to neuroanatomy. *Archives of Neurology, 42,* 282–287.

Tucker, D. M. (1981). Lateral brain function, emotion, and conceptualization. *Psychological Bulletin, 89*, 19–43.

Tulving, E. (1972). Episodic and semantic memory. In E.Tulving & W. Donaldson (Eds.), *Organization of Memory*. New York: Academic Press.

Van den Hoed, J., Lucas, E. A., & Dement, W. C. (1979). Hallucinatory experiences during cataplexy in patients with narcolepsy. *American Journal of Psychiatry, 136*, 1210–1211.

Van Lacker, D. R., Cummings, J. L., Kreiman, J., & Dobkin, B. H. (1988). Phonagnosia: A dissociation between familiar and unfamiliar voices. *Cortex, 24*, 195–209.

Vertes, R. P. (1984). Brainstem control of the events of REM sleep. *Progress in Neurobiology, 22*, 241–288.

Victor, M., Adams, R. D., & Collins, G. H. (1971). *The Wernicke–Korsakoff Syndrome: A Clinical and Pathological Study of 245 Patients, 82 with Post-Mortem Examinations*. Philadelphia: Davis.

Vygotsky, L. S. (1962). *Thought and Language*. Cambridge, MA: MIT Press.

Walsh, K. W. (1978). *Neuropsychology: A Clinical Approach*. New York: Churchill Livingstone.

Watson, R. T., Fleet, W. S., Gonzalez-Rothi, L., & Heilman, K. M. (1986). Apraxia and the supplementary motor area. *Archives of Neurology, 43*, 787–792.

Weintraub, M. I. (1978). *A Clinician's Manual of Hysterical Conversion Reactions*. New York: Interdisciplinary Communications Media.

Weiskrantz, L., Warrington, E. K., & Sanders, M. D. (1974). Visual capacity in the hemianopic field following a restricted occipital ablation. *Brain, 97*, 719–728.

Wernicke, C. (1874). *Der aphasische symptomenkomplex*. Breslau, Poland: Cohn & Weigert.

Wernicke, C. (1881). *Lehrbuch der Gehirnkrankheiten für Aerztz und Studirende* (Vol. 2, pp. 229–242). Kassel, Germany: Theodor Fischer.

West, E. D. (1984). Right hemisphere function in schizophrenia. *Lancet, i*, 344.

Whitely, A. M., & Warrington, E. K. (1977). Prosopagnosia: A clinical, psychological and anatomical study of three patients. *Journal of Neurology, Neurosurgery and Psychiatry, 40*, 395–403.

Whitlock, F. A. (1967). The aetiology of hysteria. *Acta Psychiatrica Scandinavica, 43*, 144–162.

Whitsel, B. L., Petrucelli, L. M., & Werner, G. (1969). Symmetry and connectivity in the map of the body surface in somatosensory area II of primates. *Journal of Neurophysiology, 32*, 170–183.

Whitty, C. W. M. (1967). Migraine without headache. *Lancet, ii*, 283–285.

Wilcox, J., & Waziri, R. (1983). The Capgras symptom and nondominant cerebral dysfunction. *Journal of Clinical Psychiatry, 44*, 70–72.

Williamson, P. D., Spencer, D. D., Spencer, S. S., Novelly, R. A., & Mattson, R. H. (1985). Complex partial seizures of frontal lobe origin. *Neurology, 18*, 497–504.

Winson, J. (1985). *Brain and Psyche: The Biology of the Unconscious*. New York: Anchor/Doubleday.

Woodruff, R. A., Clayton, P. I., & Guze, S. B. (1971). Hysteria: Studies of diagnosis, outcome and prevalence. *Journal of the American Medical Association, 215,* 425–428.

Woolsey, C. N., Erickson, T. C., & Gilson, W. E. (1979). Localization in somatic sensory and motor areas of human cerebral cortex as determined by direct recording of evoked potentials and electrical stimulation. *Journal of Neurosurgery, 51,* 476–506.

Wundt, G. (1900). *Volkerpsychologie.* Leipzig.

Wundt, W. (1874). *Grundzuge der physiologischen Psychologie.* Leipzig.

Young, G. B., & Blume, W. T. (1983). Painful epileptic seizures. *Brain, 106,* 537–554.

Ziegler, J. J., Imboden, J. B., & Meyer, E. (1960). Contemporary conversion reactions: A clinical study. *American Journal of Psychiatry, 116,* 901–910.

Ziegler, J. J., Imboden, J. B., & Rodgers, D. A. (1963). Contemporary conversion reactions: III. Diagnostic considerations. *Journal of the American Medical Association, 186,* 307–311.

Zihl, J., & Von Cramon, D. (1979). Collicular function in human vision. *Experimental Brain Research, 35,* 419–429.

Index